FANTASTIC!
A Celebration of Fans Discovering Doctor Who

FANTASTIC!
A Celebration of Fans Discovering Doctor Who

Edited by Nicholas Seidler

Wauwatosa, Wisconsin

Fantastic!: A Celebration of Fans Discovering Doctor Who is Copyright © 2025 Zepo Publishing LLC

All rights reserved. This book or parts thereof may not be reproduced in any form, stored in any retrieval system, or transmitted in any form by any means – electronic, mechanical, photocopy, recording, or otherwise – without prior written permission of the publisher, except as provided by United States of America copyright law and fair use. For permission requests or correspondence, write to the publisher "Attention: Fantastic Permissions Coordinator," at the address below.

ISBN: 979-8-89257-007-7 (Paperback)
ISBN: 979-8-89257-008-4 (Hardcover)
ISBN: 979-8-89257-009-1 (E-Book)

Library of Congress Control Number: 2025947130

Edited by Nicholas Seidler
Cover Painted and Designed by Elijah Kraling
Book layout and design by Nicholas Seidler
Typeset in the Alternate Gothic Extra Cond ATF, Arial, **OTPIFormula-One**, and Times New Roman fonts.

Printed in the United States of America.

First print edition: 18 October 2025

Zepo Publishing LLC
PO Box 26062
Wauwatosa, Wisconsin
53226
United States of America

zepopublishing@gmail.com

www.zepopublishing.com

Check the back of this book to see how to give the citation for the book if you are using it for homework or a reference.

The term Suncoast Motion Picture Company is a registered United States trademark of 2428392 Inc of Ascaster, Ontario, Canada. The term Novotel is a registered United States trademark of Issy-les-Moulineaux, France. The term A&E is a registered United States trademark of A&E Television Networks LLC of New York, New York, USA. The term Livejournal is a registered United States trademark of Advertising Agency "Index 20" LLC of Moscow, Russian Federation. The term Australian Broadcasting Corporation is a registered United States trademark of Australian Broadcasting Corporation, Ultimo, NSW, Australia. The term Blakes 7 is a registered United States trademark of B& Enterprises Limited of London, United Kingdom. The term Waldenbooks is a registered United States trademark of Barnes & Noble Inc of New York, New York, USA. The term Class is a registered United States trademark of BBC Studios of London, United Kingdom. The term Big Finish is a registered United States trademark of Big Finish Productions Limited of Maidenhead, United Kingdom. The term The Joy of Painting is a registered United States trademark of Bob Ross Inc of Chantilly, Virginia, USA. The term To Be Or Not To Be is a registered United States trademark of Brooksfilm Ltd of Encino, California, USA. The term Buck Rogers is a registered United States trademark of Buck Rogers Company of Bryn Mawr, Pennsylvania, USA. The term Build-A-Bear Workshop is a registered United States trademark of Build-A-Bear Workshop of St. Louis, Missouri, USA. The term Jammie Dodger is a registered United States trademark of Burton's Foods Limited of Hertordshire, United Kingdom. The term Candy Jar Books is a registered United States trademark of Candy Jar Limited of Cardiff, United Kingdom. The terms Spock, Star Trek, and Star Trek The Next Generation are registered trademarks of CBS Studios Inc. of New York, New York, USA. The term Dapol is a registered United States trademark of Dapol Limited of Wrexham, United Kingdom. The terms Captain Carrot and Wonder Woman are registered United States trademarks of DC Comics of Burbank, California, USA. The term Britbox is a registered United States trademark of Denipurna Limited of London, United Kingdom. The term DePaul University is a registered United States trademark of DePaul University of Chicago, Illinois, USA. The term Lilo & Stitch is a registered United States trademark of Disney Enterprises Inc. of Burbank, California, USA. The term Museum of Pop Culture is a registered United States trademark of Experience Learning Community of Seattle, Washington, USA. The term TV Guide is a registered United States trademark of Fandom Inc. of San Francisco, California, USA. The term Starlog is a registered United States trademark of Fangoria Holdings LLC of Atlanta, Georgia, USA. The term Forbidden Planet is a registered United States trademark of Forbidden Planet IP Holdings LLC of New York, New York, USA. The term Gen Con is a registered United States trademark of Gen Con LLC of Seattle, Washington, USA. The term Pot Noodle is a registered United States trademark of Golden Wonder Limited of Broxburn, West Lothian, United Kingdom. The term YouTube is a registered United States trademark of Google LLC of Mountain View, California, USA. The term Guinness World Records is a registered United States trademark of Guinness World Records Limited of London, United Kingdom. The term Wild, Wild World of Animals is a registered United States trademark of HBO of New York, New York, USA. The term Hot Topic is a registered United States trademark of Hot Topic Merchandising Inc of City of Industry, California, USA. The term Hulu is a registered United States trademark of Hulu LLC of Santa Monica, California, USA. The term Radio Times is a registered United States trademark of Immediate Media Limited of London, United Kingdom. The terms Space 1999 is a registered United States trademark of ITC Entertainment Group Limited of London, United Kingdom. The term The Prisoner is a registered United States trademark of ITC Entertainment Holdings Ltd of London, United Kingdom. The term İthaki is a registered United States trademark of İthaki Yayin Grubu of Istanbul, Turkiye. The term The Avengers is a registered United States trademark of ITV Rights limited of London, United Kingdom. The term Sainsbury's is a registered United States trademark of J Sainsbury plc of London, United Kingdom. The term Hagstrom is a registered United States trademark of Kappa Map Group LLC of Fort Washington, Pennsylvania, USA. The term ExCeL Exhibition Centre is a registered United States trademark of London International Exhibition Centre plc of London, United Kingdom. The terms Han Solo, Star Wars, and The Empire Strikes Back are registered United States trademarks of Lucasfilm Entertainment Company LTC LLC of San Francisco, California, USA. The term Starburst is a registered United States trademark of Malibu Comic Entertainment Inc. of West Lake Village, California, USA. The term Barbie is a registered United States trademark of Mattel Inc. of El Segundo, California, USA. The terms Logan's Run and Masque of the Red Death are registered United States trademarks of Metro-Goldwin-Meyer of Culver City, California, USA. The term Milwaukee Area Technical College is a registered United States trademark of Milwaukee Area Technical College of Milwaukee, Wisconsin, USA. The terms Saturday Night Live and Sliders are registered United States trademark of NBC Universal Media LLC of New York, New York, USA. The term Netflix is a registered United States trademark of Netflix Inc of Los Gatos, California, USA. The term New Jersey Network is a registered United States trademark of New Jersey Network Public Broadcasting Authority of Toronto, Canada. The term TVOntario is a registered United States trademark of Ontario Educational Communications Authority of Toronto, Canada. The term Panini is a registered United States trademark of Panini Societa Per Azioni of Modena, Italy. The term Virgin Books is a registered United States trademark of Penguin

Random House of New York, New York, USA. The term Countdown is a registered United States trademark of Polystyle Publications of London, United Kingdom. The term Postkolik is a registered United States trademark of Postkolik Tekstil ve Bilgisayar Sanayi Ticaret Limited Şirketi of Istanbul, Turkiye. The term PBS is a registered United States trademark of Public Broadcasting Service of Arlignton, Virginia, USA. The term Metra is a registered United States trademark of Regional Transportation Authority of Chicago, Illinois, USA. The term Napster is a registered United States trademark of Rhapsody International Inc of Nashville, Tennessee, USA. The term Press Gang is a registered United States trademark of Richmond Films & Television of London, United Kingdom. The term Comic-Con is a registered United States trademark of San Diego Comic Convention of San Diego, California, USA. The term Writing Magazine is a registered United States trademark of Scholastic Inc of New York, New York, USA. The terms 3-2-1 Contact, Sesame Street, and The Electric Company are registered United States trademarks of Sesame Workshop of New York, New York, USA. The term Beta is a registered United States trademark of Sony Corporation of Tokyo, Japan. The term Quark is a registered United States trademark of Sony Pictures Television of Culver City, California, USA. The term Simplicity is a registered United States trademark of Stitch Acquisition Corp of Berwick, Pennsylvania, USA. The terms BBC, Blackadder, Blue Peter, Cybermen, Daleks, Doctor Who, Doctor Who Adventures. I, Claudius, Saturday Superstore, TARDIS, The Multi-Coloured Swap Shop, Whoniverse, and Words and Pictures are registered United States trademarks of the British Broadcasting Corporation.of London, United Kingdom. The term Farscape is a registered United States trademark of The Jim Henson Company Inc of Los Angeles, California, USA. The term The Lawrence Welk Show is a registered United States trademark of The Welk Group Inc of Los Angeles, California, USA. The term Mr Bean is a registered United States trademark of Tiger Aspect Kids & Family Limited of London, United Kingdom. The term TikTok is a registered United States trademark of TikTok Ltd of Grand Cayman, Cayman Islands. The term Dreamwatch is a registered United States trademark of Titan magazines of London, United Kingdom. The term Bassett's Jelly Babies is a registered United States trademark of Trebor Bassett Limited of London, United Kingdom. The term Tumblr is a registered United States trademark of Tumblr Inc of New York, New York, USA. The term Buffy the Vampire Slayer, The A-Team, and The Rocky Horror Picture Show is a registered United States trademark of Twentieth Century Fox Film Corporation of Los Angeles, California, USA. The term UK Gold is a registered United States trademark of UK Gold Television Limited of London, United Kingdom. The terms Battlestar Galactica, Emergency, Frankenstein, Knight Rider, Syfy, The Bionic Woman, The Mummy, The Six Million Dollar Man, and Voyagers! are registered United States trademarks of Universal City Studios LLC of Universal City, California, USA. The term Sci-Fi Channel is a registered United States trademark of USA Networks of New York, New York. The terms Babylon 5 and Supernatural are registered United States trademarks of Warner Bros. Entertainment Inc of Burbank, California, USA. The term Weetabix is a registered United States trademark of Weetabix Limited of Northamptonshire, United Kingdom. The term WinMX is a registered United States trademark of WinMX LLC of Windsor, Ontario, Canada. The term Wizard World is a registered United States trademark of Wizard World Inc of Los Angeles, California, USA. The term Dungeons & Dragons is a registered United States trademark of Wizards of the Coast LLC of Renton, Washington, USA. The term Postman Pat is a registered United States trademark of Woodland Animations Limited of London, United Kingdom. The term YTV is a registered United States trademark of YTV Canada Inc of Toronto, Ontario, Canada.

This book represents the personal views and opinions of the authors/contributors and Zepo Publishing, LLC is not associated with, endorsed by, or in any way affiliated with these trademark holders.

* * *

This is an unofficial and independent publication and is not authorized, licensed, approved, or endorsed by the British Broadcasting Corporation (BBC) or any parties affiliated with Doctor Who.

Doctor Who, including all characters, logos, names, and related elements, are the property of the BBC. This book is not associated with, endorsed, or sponsored by the BBC in any way.

The content of this book is presented for the purposes of commentary, criticism, analysis, and review, and is intended to fall within the boundaries of fair use and other applicable limitations and exceptions to copyright.

DEDICATION

Nick dedicates this book to
Jennifer Adams-Kelley, John Curtis, Eric Fettig,
David Fisher-Hewett and the members of the Earthbound
TimeLords, the Federation, and the Milwaukee Time Lords
Doctor Who clubs.

Without all of you helping to create a community and fandom,
this book would not exist.

ON THE COVER

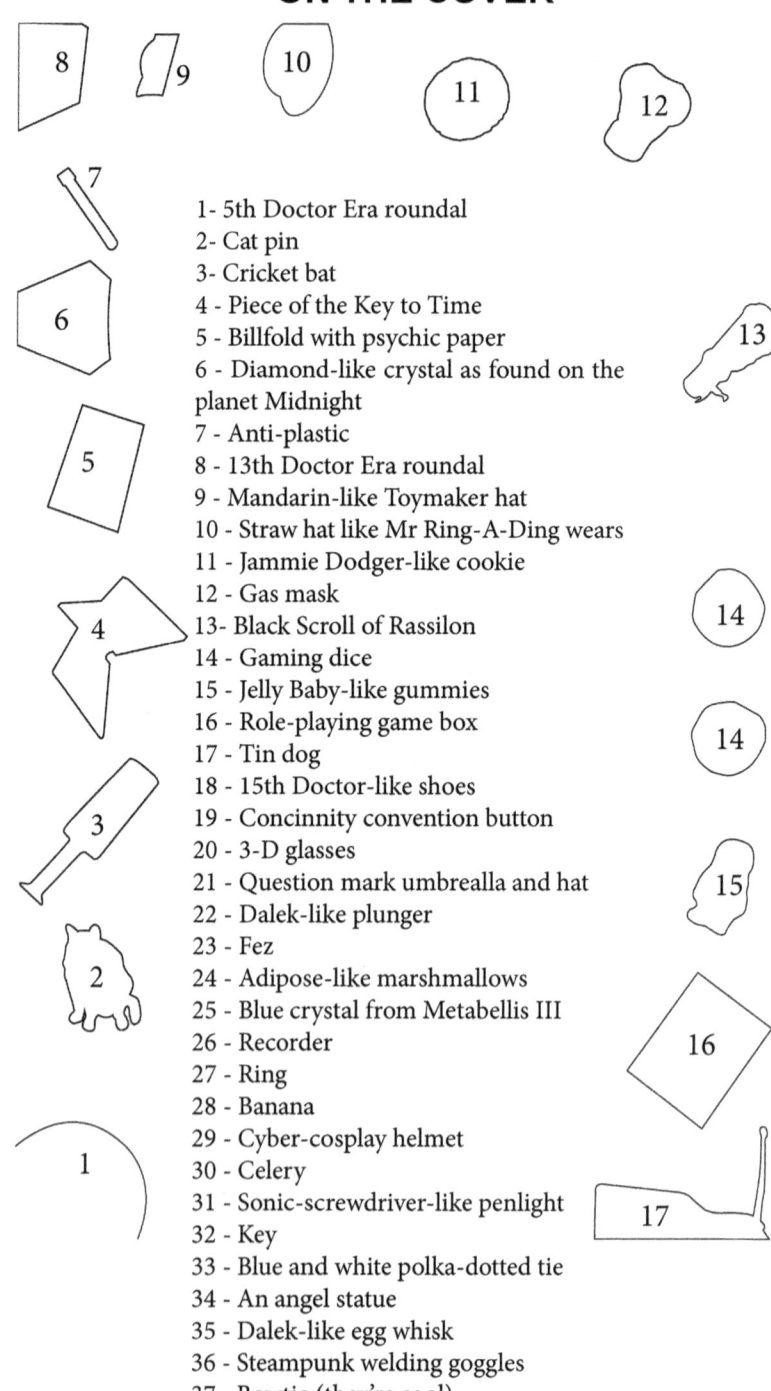

1 - 5th Doctor Era roundal
2 - Cat pin
3 - Cricket bat
4 - Piece of the Key to Time
5 - Billfold with psychic paper
6 - Diamond-like crystal as found on the planet Midnight
7 - Anti-plastic
8 - 13th Doctor Era roundal
9 - Mandarin-like Toymaker hat
10 - Straw hat like Mr Ring-A-Ding wears
11 - Jammie Dodger-like cookie
12 - Gas mask
13 - Black Scroll of Rassilon
14 - Gaming dice
15 - Jelly Baby-like gummies
16 - Role-playing game box
17 - Tin dog
18 - 15th Doctor-like shoes
19 - Concinnity convention button
20 - 3-D glasses
21 - Question mark umbrealla and hat
22 - Dalek-like plunger
23 - Fez
24 - Adipose-like marshmallows
25 - Blue crystal from Metabellis III
26 - Recorder
27 - Ring
28 - Banana
29 - Cyber-cosplay helmet
30 - Celery
31 - Sonic-screwdriver-like penlight
32 - Key
33 - Blue and white polka-dotted tie
34 - An angel statue
35 - Dalek-like egg whisk
36 - Steampunk welding goggles
37 - Bowtie (they're cool)

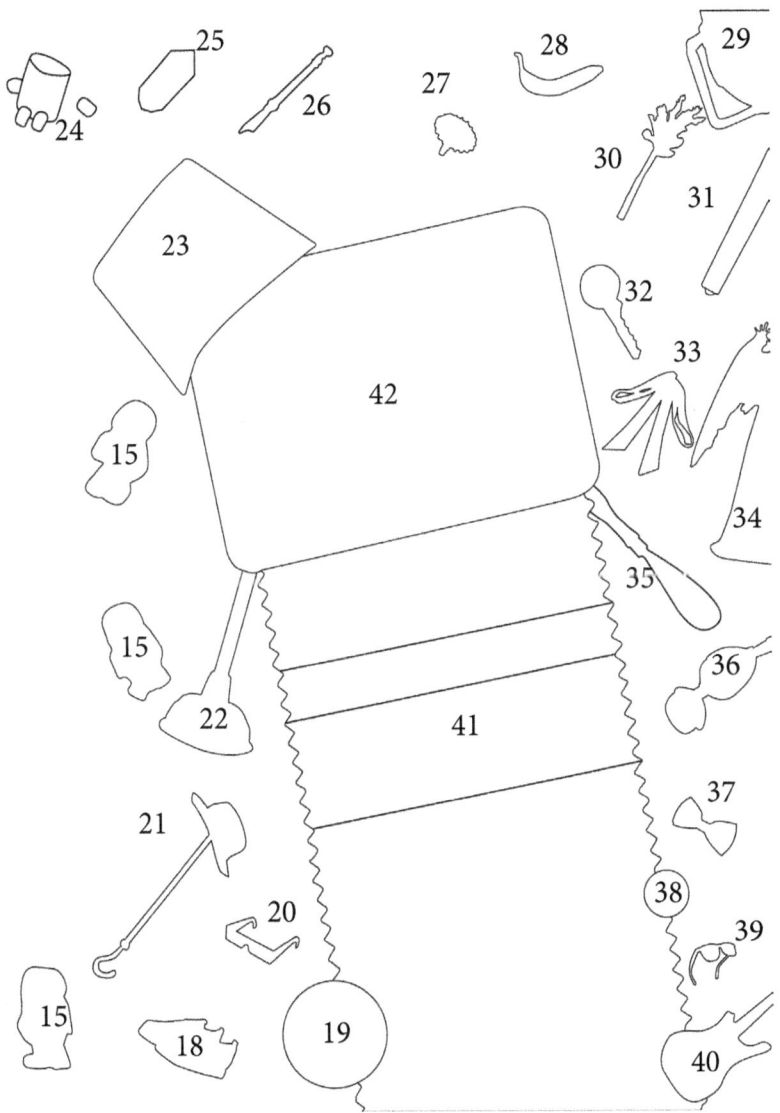

38 - Press Gang Fan Badge
39 - Sonic-like sunglasses
40 - Electric guitar
41 - Convention ribbons in the colors of the 4th Doctor's scarf
42 - Convention badge that looks similar to a spaceship that's bigger on the inside

CONTENTS

DOCTOR WHO 1
THAT FANTASTIC MOMENT 3
AN IMPORTANT NOTE ON HISTORICAL ACCURACY 6
LEGAL DISCLAIMER 6
EMMA ABRAHAM 7
HEATHER ACKROYD 9
BILL ALBERT .... .12
MICHEL "SISKOID" ALBERT. 16
NADIA ASFAR 19
MEG ATKINS 21
JAY BADENHOOP. 24
MARK BAUMGARTEN 27
CASSIE BEYER .... .29
RYAN BLAKE 32
ARNOLD T. BLUMBERG. 34
PAUL BOOTH 37
KEITH BRADBURY 40
BEN BRIGHOUSE 42
BOB BRINKMAN 44
BARBARA BROWN 46
CHRISTOPHER CEBULA 48
WALT CIECHANOWSKI 51
T. AARON CISCO. 53
TERRY COOPER 55
UMUT ÇEVIK 57
FRANCHESKA DAVIS 61
TIMOTHY DAVIS 62
TAYLOR DEATHERAGE 63
KEN DEEP 66
JOHN DERRICK 69
J. DIETENBERGER 72
MELANIE DOWEIKO 74
BEN ELLIS 76
HEATH FARNDEN 77
SCOTT FELLOWES 78
JAN FENNICK 81
JOHN FREEMAN 83
BOB FURNELL 85
HARRY GEROSTERGIOS 87

CINDY GYGAX	89
ERIC HILDEMAN	94
STEVEN WARREN HILL	96
EDWARD HOCHMAN	99
RANDY HOLNDONER	101
KERRY HURD	104
NANCY HUTCHINS	106
PAULETTE IMHOFF	108
GAYLAND JENKINS	109
SIMORGH JOURABCHI	110
AUDREY KANTHACK	111
ASSAD KHAISHGI	113
ALEX KINGDOM	116
CHRIS KOCHER	119
TERI KOEBEL	121
BETH KORMAN	123
ELIJAH KRALING	128
DENNIS KYTASAARI	130
DANIEL LAVERY	131
TJ LUBINSKY	133
SHAUN LYON	135
DERWIN MAK	137
CHARLES MARTIN	139
PATRICK MASSOELS	140
JAMIE MATHEWS	142
BRIAN MATTOCKS	144
CHRIS McAULEY	145
RUSSELL McGEE	148
JEFFREY MILLER	151
PETE MURPHY	153
ROB NISBET	155
NANCY NORBECK	158
AVERY O'SHAUGHNESSY	161
INGRID OLIANSKI	163
MIKE OLSON	165
JOSHUA ONG	167
JENA PANTANO	169
ANDREW PEREGRINE	171
BRANDON PETERS	174
JOEL PIERSEN	177
GARETH PRESTON	179

AMBER RADEN	181
FAIZ REHMAN	184
CHRIS RETTERATH	187
ALEXANDRA ROSENBAUM	189
ROSS RUEDIGER	191
JAMES RYAN	194
BRIAN SAA	195
NICHOLAS SEIDLER	198
LIBBY SHEA	203
GRAEME SHERIDAN	205
NICKY SMALLEY	206
GENE SMITH	208
NICK SMITH	210
STACEY SMITH?	212
BOB STAHLEY	213
ATHENA STAMOS	214
KATHY SULLIVAN	217
LEE THOMPSON	219
WILLIAM THOMPSON	221
BRAD TRECHAK	223
RUDY TRIZNA	225
LISA TRUANT-TAN	226
JASON TUCKER	230
LARRY VANMERSBERGEN	232
VAL VERSE	234
DAVID WALKER	235
PHILIP WARD	237
ROBERT WARNOCK	240
IAN WHEELER	242
FANTASTIC FINAL THOUGHTS	245
THE PURPOSE OF THIS BOOK	247
SOME FUN STATISTICS	250
THE QUESTIONS (ANSWER THEM YOURSELF)	252
HOW TO CELEBRATE YOUR DOCTOR WHO FANDOM	253
DOCTOR WHO EPISODE GUIDE	255
EDITOR BIO	276
HOW TO BE A HELPER	276
HOW TO CITE THIS BOOK	277
OTHER ZEPO PUBLISHING BOOKS	278

FOREWORD

My first *Doctor Who* experiences were in the mid-1970's when my father was on sabbatical in the UK. It worked for my math brain and my love of great storytelling. I turned on the reboot with mild curiosity and skepticism, only to be blown away. I watched with my kids, one hiding behind the sofa, the other curled in my lap, panicking over the Catkind nuns (Cat nuns!) and the "Empty Child." (Gas masks!)

As a director, I responded to a little-discussed episode, "Gridlock." I wanted... no, I needed... to know how they made it. How did they pull this off with so little money? How much did they spend on those visual effects to make them so epic? (I later did learn some of the secrets and was even more awed).

As I watched Christopher Eccleston and David Tennant embody the character and I revelled in the depth of the stories, I knew I wanted to work on the show. This became a mission. It took me six years of interviewing and cajoling before I landed the directing gig on the Series 8 finale, "Dark Water"/"Death In Heaven." It was as challenging and satisfying as I could ever imagine. To date, I've directed eight episodes – each different, each challenging, each rewarding, and each one part of the great fabric that makes up the joy that is *Doctor Who*.

So, how did the Doctor become one of the great mysteries of the Universe: Why is it the longest running science fiction show in the history of television?

Ask a fan. You will hear over a thousand reasons, each one an episode.

Time Travel: When the episodes can span all of time and space, this is a recipe to never be boring. Each week is a surprise – where will you be and what will you encounter? And what will it teach you about love and fear and kindness?

Regeneration: What a brilliant concept – that the Doctor does not die, they regenerate to a new body (within limitations). It has allowed a series of brilliant actors to play the role. What ripe materials for fans' passions – fearing, then embracing, each reincarnation. The series continues but refreshes itself with each new Doctor.

Companions: The Doctor travels with a variety of humans. What better eyes to view the galaxies, the histories, the futures, and the monsters, than one of us?

And the Doctor: A two-hearted alien who weekly battles monsters and tries to save universes while attempting to understand people – and themself.

It's all heart and soul — wrapped in huge adventures and big ideas.

This is a book by viewers and fans. It begins to answer the impossible question: where do I start in this epic universe? And how have others done it?

Of course, it's intimidating, but what a payoff.

Inside this book you will find some ideas on how to get started within the grand universe of so many episodes. You can start at the beginning. You can start at the stand-alone episodes that are fan favorites. Me, I randomly dove in. The beginning mattered less than the journey.

Step into the depths, the kindness, and the creativity of the world of *Doctor Who*.

Two hearts bring double the passion and twice the adventure.

Enter the eternal world of *Doctor Who*. I'm wagering you won't regret the journey.

— Rachel Talalay, 2025

DOCTOR WHO

It would be hard for someone interested in science fiction or media to never have heard of *Doctor Who*. The UK television series first aired on the BBC on 23 November 1963. It is a drama program meant to bring families together and has the mission to both educate and entertain. It is a story about a time and space traveler with the ambiguous name of the 'Doctor' exploring the universe with his family and friends. They travel in a spacecraft disguised as a blue police public call box. The Doctor is an alien from another world that appears human and helps people discover their true humanity with a focus on kindness and caring. The series quickly became one of the most popular series on television and was especially a hit with British children.

The show's storytelling is innovative. Adventures can happen in the past, present, future, or even other dimensions where history or the rules of physics might be different. The opportunity to tell any story is possible within the framework. In 1966, rather than changing the lead actor without acknowledgement, the series decided to write the change into the fabric of the show, establishing the Doctor's ability to "regenerate" into a new body and continue their adventures. This had never been done on television before, and it remains a cornerstone of the show's lore. The alien-ness of the Doctor and their power of regeneration has allowed many actors of different genders and backgrounds to all take the lead and represent the main character thus allowing the adventures to continue for generations of viewers. The core requirement being only that the main character be an intelligent person with a kind heart(s) willing to help those in need and do the right thing.

The series began worldwide distribution as early as a year after its debut and was soon distributed to other English-speaking countries such as New Zealand, Australia, and Canada. Soon after the series got wider distribution and was even dubbed into other foreign languages. It first aired in the United States in the early 1970s. By the early 1980s, repeat viewings on PBS and interest by American college students allowed the show to become a cult hit by its 20th Anniversary. The series ran continuously in the UK until 1989, when the original series ended. A co-production in the USA between the BBC, Fox TV and Universal saw a TV movie release in 1996, but interest was not strong enough to have a series permanently return. In those intervening 'Wilderness Years' the show lived on in books, comics, audio adventures, role-playing games, and even fan-made videos (a merchandising trend that had already started in the 1960s but expanded much wider). The show returned to regular broadcast in 2005 when the BBC resurrected the series and positioned it as the cornerstone of family television. This era is sometimes stylized by fans as "New Who" or "NuWho" with the earliest run of the series being called "Classic Who." Regular broadcasts continue into 2025, via an international co-distribution streaming model between the BBC and Disney.

The key to this success has been the fact that the show has not rebooted itself but simply keeps continuing the Doctor's adventures allowing the series to weave a strong and vivid history for itself. The show has also had numerous spin-offs to include *K-9 and Company, Torchwood, The Sarah Jane Adventures, K9, Class,* and *The War Between the Land and the Sea.* All of these stories are told within that connected framework that has become known as the "Whoniverse."

Doctor Who began as a black and white TV show, and by 1970 it made the jump to color. Almost all technical innovations within television can be experienced by following this single series. The series eventually added stereo sound, broadcasted some episodes in 3-D, transitioned to widescreen format, welcomed high definition, added surround sound, and transitioned to ultra-high definition 4K. More innovations are sure to come.

The show's excellent storytelling and creative ideas have won it a fanbase from its earliest appearance. British school children could be heard screaming "exterminate" in the school yard and imitating Daleks once these mechanical creatures first appeared in 1963. In the 1970s the first fan clubs and fanzines appeared and were shared. Ever since then the show has always had a presence of people devoted to it.

THAT FANTASTIC MOMENT

One of the great joys within a fandom is when one meets others with the same passionate interest. The excitement that people share when they realize they both enjoy the same thing fills them with happiness. Smiles are exchanged. Friendships are forged. Conversations are shared – some of which may last hours. Those are often some of the best and strongest friendships that people experience in their lifetimes. It is a fantastic moment when fans first meet each other and connect.

This moment is always particularly enjoyed "in the wild" when one encounters a new acquaintance only to discover that you share a common joy. It is fun when the topic somehow comes up and you discover that an acquaintance has a similar interest. This often leads to instant friendships and understanding. Socially and personally, this holds value to most people.

Television and film fandoms are fortunate that there are special events available that help them meet with others of the same interest. Conventions, meet-ups, and fan clubs exist devoted to celebrating the interest. This is especially true for the fandom of the BBC television series *Doctor Who*, which has numerous special events that occur around the world that celebrate the "Whoniverse." The show continues to capture people's interests and imaginations. The fandom is already closing in on three-quarters of a century of the series bringing people together.

One of the things that makes *Doctor Who* special is its supporters. The fans appreciate the moral integrity and emotional strength of the character of the Doctor. The show itself is a celebration of change for the better, new discoveries, tolerance, acceptance, helping others, doing what is right, and being selfless in the best of ways. It celebrates adventure for the sake of learning, caring for the purpose of improvement, and kindness for the reason of friendship. Fans often choose to live by the Doctor's example as they try to evoke the same characteristics as the lead character and work to make the world a better place in their own way. No fandom, or any group of like-minded people, is perfect – and most Whovians (*Doctor Who* fans) will acknowledge this – but most of these fans continually strive to improve themselves and the world.

When this book was first discussed with the editorial team, we were reminded that not every viewer of *Doctor Who* may consider themselves a "fan" or feel like they connect directly to a greater fandom. Many people define "fandom" as participating in events and conventions or intentionally seeking out others solely to speak about that single interest. We must remind ourselves that all of us engage in the interests that we enjoy in our own way. For the purpose of this book, simply enjoying the program is enough to be included in the group of *Doctor Who* viewers that we consider fans and aim to include.

We hope to celebrate this amazing group of people who we consider fans (whether involved in organized fandom or not), in the way that they often talk among themselves and how they share their own stories. With this book, we look inside and see how these fans answer the questions that they often ask each other.

We kept this project simple. We asked every interviewee the same four common questions. These are questions that fans often ask each other when they meet in person and get to know one another. Almost every *Doctor Who* fan has heard these questions before. Yet, in the many years of the fandom, these answers and stories seem to have never been recorded and compiled in a book. We hope sharing these answers puts smiles on faces, jogs memories, and creates new moments of joy and happiness for the reader. It is also important to document these memories and stories and preserve a record of the fandom that captivated the interests of so many people around the world.

Respondents were recruited by emails, social media posts, convention panels, fan clubs, fliers at related fan events, and personal invitations. There were no restrictions on responses. We did not aim for any specific demographic distributions (age, gender, location where one lives, length of time being a fan, ethnic background, how they discovered the show, and so forth). Responses came from those who chose to respond regardless of background. The only reasons anyone may not have been included would be because they never heard of the project, they chose not to send a response, or because unfortunately the required release form for the interview was not provided.

Answers include the written word derivations and spellings in the English dialects as shared with us. No submission was excluded for the answers being brief. It was felt that inclusion in the book was important to the respondent and also demonstrated the diversity of the types of answers that we received. We love all the answers, because they truly help one understand how a wide variety of *Doctor Who* fans experience the series.

Enjoy the effort of these *Doctor Who* fan contributors. In the words of the Ninth Doctor, we think these stories are "Fantastic!"

AN IMPORTANT NOTE ON HISTORICAL ACCURACY

The responses are presented as we got them, with only minor edits made for grammatical continuity of the text (for example "Dr. Who" or "DW" changed to "*Doctor Who*"; "9th" changed to "Ninth"; "D&D" expanded to "*Dungeons & Dragons*"; or dates arranged by day-month-year, and so forth). Minor wordsmithing was necessary in a few cases to enhance readability. What is reported here are individual fan's memories as they recall them and in some cases may not be factually or historically correct. For example, specific TV stations, dates, episode titles, and so on, may not be remembered correctly. Likewise, a fan's viewpoint may not match the correct or exact details of an event. To preserve the contributor's expression of their memories, we have not corrected any details from the answers they provided. This is to keep the fan's voice and viewpoint front and center, and document exactly how the fans would answer these questions.

LEGAL DISCLAIMER

These stories are based on personal memories and opinions. They may contain mistakes or details that are not historically or factually accurate. The creators of this publication disclaim any and all warranties implied or otherwise and are not responsible for any errors or omissions in these accounts. All content is provided "as is" for informational and entertainment purposes only.

EMMA ABRAHAM

WHAT WAS THE FIRST EPISODE/STORY OF DOCTOR WHO THAT YOU SAW?

I don't remember my first episode, but it would have been on WTTW (PBS) in 1975.

TELL US HOW YOU THEN BECAME A FAN OF THE SHOW.

I enjoyed the show immediately and began collecting older episodes as camera copies, like so many of us did. I attended a room party held by Paul Cordsmeyer at a con in Chicago and he wanted to run *Doctor Who* episodes, so I brought my VCR and tapes. He subsequently invited me to work at his next con, Omnicon, in Ft. Lauderdale in February 1981. By pure serendipity, I ended up being minder for actors Jeremy Bulloch (Boba Fett in *The Empire Strikes Back*) and Elisabeth Sladen (*Doctor Who*'s Sarah Jane Smith). I was already running a Chicago fan club called The Disciples of Rassilon, so also working Who cons pretty much cemented me into the fandom.

TELL US YOUR FAVORITE MOMENT IN YOUR DOCTOR WHO FANDOM EXPERIENCE.

On one of my trips to London, JNT (*Doctor Who*'s producer John Nathan-Turner) invited me to attend a pantomime theater performance with him and Gary Downie. Not sure if that was my favorite moment, but it was definitely the most surreal. Working with Lis Sladen was always pure joy as well. People say you always love your first doctor the most, but while that's not true of me, I DO love my first COMPANION (Lis Sladen's Sarah Jane Smith) the best, always.

IF YOU WERE TO INTRODUCE SOMEONE ELSE TO THE DOCTOR WHO SERIES, WHAT EPISODE/STORY WOULD YOU TELL THEM TO START WITH AND WHY?

Depending on the age of the person I'm dealing with, I'm often afraid to go old school since many younger people can't look past cheap effects. So I often start new people with "Blink," which might not be a TYPICAL episode, but is brilliant and understandable by almost anyone.

HEATHER ACKROYD

WHAT WAS THE FIRST EPISODE/STORY OF DOCTOR WHO THAT YOU SAW?

I couldn't tell you the very first episode I saw. I watched it from when I was very little - probably three or four years-old - with my Dad. I know it was Patrick Troughton and I remember flashes of scenes. I also have a very strong memory of seeing the TARDIS land in a field and a strange white-haired man falling out of it (Pertwee at the beginning of "Spearhead from Space") and me turning to Dad and saying, "That's not the Doctor!" I also remember having nightmares about Daleks and Cybermen chasing me in my backyard. The nightmares never stopped me from settling down with Dad to watch the next episode, though. The ABC (Australian Broadcasting Commission) never did reruns of the Troughton episodes, although they did repeat them from Pertwee on. So, it wasn't until decades later that I got to revisit those older episodes and I fell in love with Patrick Troughton's Doctor all over again.

TELL US HOW YOU THEN BECAME A FAN OF THE SHOW.

For many years I was pretty much a solitary fan. Not many of my school friends were into the show - or Science Fiction in general - and so I just watched the show and watched all the reruns. When I moved to the US in 2003 at age 36 I brought my entire VHS collection of *Doctor Who* stories. I had everything for which full video existed - no reconstructions. My American husband, the reason I moved, had seen random episodes of *Doctor Who* through PBS during the 1980's and 90's, and so we spent 18 months watching all the way from "An Unearthly Child" through to "Survival." When *Doctor Who* started up again in 2005 we both watched it. But I had never been to any conventions or joined online groups.

I wasn't much into social media, but I did succumb and joined Facebook eventually and it was a FB friend who introduced me to a video that had been put out by a small group of people who did "I Am the Doctor" as a virtual orchestra in 2011. Back then this sort of thing wasn't at all common, and it was one of the first orchestras where participants made individual recordings that were combined into the finished video. At the end of that video there was a link to indicate interest for their next project, and I immediately sent an email. It was the Doctor Who Fan Orchestra, run by the amazing Stephen Willis, and the first time I did any fan activity for *Doctor Who*. I played clarinet and sang for all the DWFO projects after that, from #2 "This is Gallifrey"/"Vale Decem" through to #10 "Donna's Suite" during 2011 to 2016. That led me to *Doctor Who* discussion groups on Facebook, which led me to attend a local *Doctor Who* convention that started up in 2015 and ran annually for a few years. Attending the conventions introduced me to even more fans, and some of us formed our own FB group (Meanwhile in the TARDIS) to celebrate *Doctor Who*.

TELL US YOUR FAVORITE MOMENT IN YOUR DOCTOR WHO FANDOM EXPERIENCE.

It's hard to pin down an absolute favourite. I have a selection.

Going to London to see the Proms in 2013 with fellow DWFO members from around the world and meeting with Ben Foster and Murray Gold was definitely a highlight.

The first time I met a Doctor (Colin Baker and Sylvester McCoy were at my first convention) and finally getting to talk about how much they meant to me growing up.

Being overcome with emotion when seeing Katy Manning for the first time, and her giving me a huge hug.

I think, though, that above all the individual experiences it's the feeling of community among fans that keeps me invested. For the most part it's a very warm and friendly fandom.

IF YOU WERE TO INTRODUCE SOMEONE ELSE TO THE DOCTOR WHO SERIES, WHAT EPISODE/STORY WOULD

YOU TELL THEM TO START WITH AND WHY?

    This very much depends on what sort of person they are. Where possible, I think it's good for people to check out the first episode "An Unearthly Child" because it does an excellent job of introducing the concept and premise of the show. However, for those who may not have the patience for a black and white episode from 1963, I would generally steer them to one of the opening stories of the modern Doctors. Whenever the Doctor regenerates they tend to get reintroduced, so those stories are good jumping-on points.

BILL ALBERT

WHAT WAS THE FIRST EPISODE/STORY OF DOCTOR WHO THAT YOU SAW?

Iowa Public Television was one of the very first stations in America ever to carry *Doctor Who*! It was 1974 and I was 11 years old. On Saturdays, I would stay at my grandparents and after *The Lawrence Welk Show* and before switching to *Emergency* they'd promo this new series with a photo of this outrageous man with this frilly shirt and cape standing in front of a helicopter marked UNIT. It certainly was like nothing else I'd ever seen before, and my 11-year-old imagination was interested.

The first story we got was "Ambassadors of Death." While I can't say for sure, I saw it the first time around. I remember that story and "Inferno" were the two stories that really got me hooked.

TELL US HOW YOU THEN BECAME A FAN OF THE SHOW.

The Ambassadors, dressed in space suits, can kill by touch. The Doctor enters an office and sees the body of a man laying on a desk. While the Doctor is examining the man for signs of life an Ambassador walks up behind him and calmly reaches over the unknowing Doctor's shoulder…

End of episode 4.

What? Wait a minute! They stopped there? He's going to kill the Doctor?

The Earth is cracking open. There's no hope for mankind and the Doctor is desperate to escape. He's at the TARDIS console in a shed trying to get it working. The doors open and a wall of lava floods into the shed…

End of episode 6.

No way is he getting out of that one!

Those cliffhangers had me hooked. It was brilliant storytelling, and my preteen and teenage imagination was always trying to figure out what was going to happen next. I sat with Terrance Dicks at a convention and told him about their impact on me and he said how he always knew it was never a question of if the Doctor was going to survive but how. Some good advice that I keep in mind trying to create cliffhangers for my own work today.

Dicks did enjoy telling him how there were many nights while the credits were rolling, I'd call my brother who I knew was watching at his house. He'd pick up the phone and just ask "Did you see that?"

I knew absolutely nothing about it, and, at the time, there was no way to research this strange British show. Years later when I finally got pen pals from England that gave me another cliffhanger.

He's the Third Doctor? How do they do that?

To this day, despite all of them, he's still my Doctor.

TELL US YOUR FAVORITE MOMENT IN YOUR DOCTOR WHO FANDOM EXPERIENCE.

I was in an elevator at a convention when the doors opened, and Elisabeth Sladen walked in. She smiled politely, I smiled back but was so starstruck with Sarah Jane Smith I couldn't think of anything to say.

The doors closed and the elevator went down when suddenly I gasped and checked my coat pockets. She looked at me in surprise and I explained I had just realized I had left my card key in my room. She laughed and said not to worry. I admitted that was the third time that day I'd done that and the lady at the register probably wasn't even going to ask me what I needed. She'll just hand me another one. Lis Sladen patted me on the shoulder and said she was sure I wasn't the only one to do that as the doors opened on the ground floor and she wished me luck.

Just a brief, wonderful encounter for a fan.

Another favorite moment came in 2022 when I made my first trip to England. I went to an event called 'A Day At Devil's

End' in the town of Aldbourne where "The Daemons" had been filmed. Walking those grounds where the Doctor and the Master had battled was pretty awe inspiring. One of the guests was Terry Molloy who had played Davros in "Remembrance of the Daleks." He asked the crowd where we had come from and after several answers he pointed at me.

"Iowa, Midwest, USA."

Everyone else's hands dropped when he looked at me and said, "You win." I hadn't expected it but being the only American there gave me some brief celebrity. Lots of people came to me after that and asked about being a fan of the show. I may have stood out a bit too much with my American sense of humor. There actually was a couple getting married in the church that day and as they were leaving nearly 500 hundred of us gave them a round of applause. Someone in the crowd said the couple could relax that there were no devil worshipers holding a ceremony in the crypt under the church. I looked over, smiled and said, "We hope."

Absolute silence.

Think I'll go have a pint.

There were two other wonderful moments too. Ten years ago, I was making short films at a local Public Access station. I managed to get permission to actually do a documentary at that year's Chicago TARDIS convention. Doing documentaries can sometimes be harder than the films I wrote, cast, produced, directed, and edited. There's very little planning for most of them. Other than jotting down a few questions it's just showing up, sitting down, and hoping something interesting happens. I found a spot that was kind of out of the way, for a while I considered having people sit behind the sofa in the lobby, set up the camera and started hoping someone would sit down. I ended up with so much footage I had to cut some really great comments.

For a long time, I had really bad self-discipline as a writer. I'd think about a story for weeks on end and then sit down and write like a maniac for a weekend. I'd spew out everything I'd hoped for then go back to thinking about it for another month. It's a bad way to get anywhere as a writer. I finally decided to change my ways and try to be more professional. This was it. I was going to write a serious novel. Still being a novice and a bit shy I figured it might as well be *Doctor Who*. For four months I wrote new material every day. Some days I'd write pages, some days I'd add a comma, but *Doctor Who: Shadows of the Past* was finished, and I was pretty proud of it. At the time the BBC book range was accepting unsolicited manuscripts, so I figured I'd go for it and off it went. I crossed my fingers and waited, and waited, and waited. No less than a few weeks before the announcement that the series was coming back, and the BBC book range was being closed, I got a very polite and short rejection letter. Here's the big question. Was it rejected because they didn't like it or because the range was cancelled? I'll never know, but it got me into the habit of writing regularly and all the books and scripts since then owe a bit to *Doctor Who*.

IF YOU WERE TO INTRODUCE SOMEONE ELSE TO THE DOCTOR WHO SERIES, WHAT EPISODE/STORY WOULD YOU TELL THEM TO START WITH AND WHY?

There is a guy at work and he and his wife are big fans of the new series but not very familiar with the original series. I gave them the DVD of "The Dæmons" to watch. I gave them the same advice I always give people about watching the originals, "Do not binge watch. These were told in a completely different era and style that can take a bit of getting used to. Watch two or three episodes, take a break, then watch more."

I chose "The Dæmons" because of the mix of the Doctor and the Master. They are mortal enemies fighting each other but they keep it classy, struggle to outdo their enemies, yet don't come face to face until the last half of the final episode. The writing doesn't take the easy way out.

MICHEL "SISKOID" ALBERT

WHAT WAS THE FIRST EPISODE/STORY OF DOCTOR WHO THAT YOU SAW?

I'm on the cusp of adolescence, spending summers in Texas – shared custody across borders – and I catch this weird sci-fi program. It stayed with me, but I didn't catch a title or anything. Must have been a couple years later, during the school year because I'm in Atlantic Canada, and I catch the very same program on Maine's PBS station, beamed in from across the river. Déjà vu! Once again, I'm told that Eldrad MUST live.
And so "The Hand of Fear" was my first episode of *Doctor Who*. Twice. Things would never be the same.

TELL US HOW YOU THEN BECAME A FAN OF THE SHOW.

From "The Hand of Fear" (second time), it wasn't much of a stretch for a science boy like me to look things up in *TV Guide* and make it a weekly habit. But true fandom requires more, and when I caught an episode of "Planet of the Daleks" on YTV (a youth-centric Canadian cable station), we were suddenly able to watch *Doctor Who* every day. And I say "we" because the whole family got into it. It was broadcast around dinner time. We were at that age when, to my mom's despair, we preferred to eat in front of the television, or else ran from the dinner table as quickly as we could, scarf down our still reasonably priced baloney. My sister would do Dalek gun sound effects and never forgave Jon Pertwee for regenerating into Tom Baker. When we got our first VCR (late into the '80s), I recorded all those episodes – everything from "Spearhead in Space" to "The Twin Dilemma" (what a finish) – and carried the tapes with me into the 2000s when I started replacing them with DVDs. And those allowed me to do screen grabs, which went into making thousands of cards for my own Unauthorized Doctor Who Collectible Card Game. So, while I discovered

Doctor Who as PBS omnibi, those YTV reruns were what really started my adventure into Who fandom.

TELL US YOUR FAVORITE MOMENT IN YOUR DOCTOR WHO FANDOM EXPERIENCE.

I'm not a convention goer, so while I've done a lot to celebrate my Who fandom – the card game, excessive blogging, hours and hours of podcasting – and met and worked with many other fans as a result, loving a television show is still a fairly insular, self-screen kind of thing, unlikely to result in "moments". But the one truly interactive part of my fandom was playing a few "seasons" of the *Doctor Who Role-Playing Game* (I own them all, but in this case, Cubicle 7's). Destroying Venetian sirens by blasting "Bohemian Rhapsody" from an iPod (years before "The Vampires of Venice"!), fighting aliens behind the scenes at Woodstock, seeing Susan regenerate and include her as a companion to our Time Lord the Shepherd, re-staging "The War Machines" in our home town (it's got a radio tower!), revealing our longest-standing companion was a Son of Fenric all along… These are moments that stay with you because you were an active participant. Barring the opportunity to hop into the TARDIS yourself, you can't do much better than that.

IF YOU WERE TO INTRODUCE SOMEONE ELSE TO THE DOCTOR WHO SERIES, WHAT EPISODE/STORY WOULD YOU TELL THEM TO START WITH AND WHY?

That "if" should really be a "when", because I've quite often introduced *Doctor Who* to others. The new series made that easy, of course. For most new audiences, a modern program is easier to get into than a foreign market's vintage television. So I usually say "Rose" because Russell T Davies really did introduce every concept at a pace that could be absorbed by new viewers easily and efficiently. It might not be my favorite era of the show, especially in retrospect, but that first season is an especially good primer for the show, farting aliens or no, and it's easy to tap into the era's overt emotionalism. (You haven't lived until someone produces heaving sobs in your living room while watching the end of "Doomsday"). For those who then want to discover Classic Who, I have a list of introductory episodes for each of the Doctors/eras – "The Aztecs," "The Invasion," "The Dæmons," "Pyramids of Mars," and so on – a sampler of strong stand-alone stories that showcase each era's feel, generally without spoiling hellos and goodbyes. If they like any of them, it could send them on their own adventure through part of the canon. Or the entire canon, at the risk of tipping into obsession, like it did me. But I didn't turn out so badly, did I?!

NADIA ASFAR

WHAT WAS THE FIRST EPISODE/STORY OF DOCTOR WHO THAT YOU SAW?

The six-minute-long story "Night of the Doctor" about 11 years ago before the 50th Anniversary special. Although I have seen clips from the Eleventh Doctor stories, "Night of the Doctor" was the show that really set my interest and love for *Doctor Who*, especially for the Eighth Doctor stories.

TELL US HOW YOU THEN BECAME A FAN OF THE SHOW.

After watching "The Night of the Doctor" and the 50th Anniversary special ("The Day of the Doctor"), I began watching Peter Capaldi's run. While Capaldi was giving it his all especially in "Heaven Sent", most of the stories were lackluster in my opinion. I wanted to explore more of the Eighth Doctor's stories, so I found out that Paul McGann was still portraying the Eighth Doctor through a series of audio adventures produced by Big Finish and I fell in love! I miss seeing that jovial, eccentric side of the Eighth Doctor that I had seen in the movie, but I was intrigued with listening to his darker side a lot more. Again, as I mentioned before, I did enjoy Capaldi's take on the Doctor because he takes after the bitterness from Hartnell's portrayal, Pertwee's suave and proper look (especially with Capaldi's magician cloak), and Troughton's childlike moments of excitement.

TELL US YOUR FAVORITE MOMENT IN YOUR DOCTOR WHO FANDOM EXPERIENCE.

Definitely interacting with the fans and of course the stars of the series. However, the most recent incredible fandom experience I had was while attending my first Chicago TARDIS event this year. I had the chance to moderate my first panel speaking greatly of the Eighth Doctor, and had the pleasure of speaking alongside Sonny McGann, who plays Alex Campbell the Doctor's great grandson and who is also the son of Paul McGann, who portrays the Eighth Doctor. Just being at the table speaking about my favorite Doctor and interacting with the panelists and audience members really made me feel like I was part of an accepting fandom, even for an introvert like myself!

IF YOU WERE TO INTRODUCE SOMEONE ELSE TO THE DOCTOR WHO SERIES, WHAT EPISODE/STORY WOULD YOU TELL THEM TO START WITH AND WHY?

The first few episodes that would come to mind if I were to introduce someone to Doctor Who are either "Rose" or "An Unearthly Child", but the story I would recommend to someone is "The Eleventh Hour". After learning about Matt Smith's departure and watching the 50th Anniversary Special, I wanted to explore more of the Eleventh Doctor. As I watched Smith in his debut, I was intrigued in seeing Smith's childlike and protective personality. This is something that defines who the Doctor is, especially when interacting with his soon-to-be companion Amelia (Amy) Pond as he was donned the name "Raggedy Man" by the seven-year-old past self. That is another reason why I would suggest that episode to someone who would be interested in beginning the *Doctor Who* series, mainly focusing on the relationship between companion and the Doctor, a father figure, a friend.

MEG ATKINS

WHAT WAS THE FIRST EPISODE/STORY OF DOCTOR WHO THAT YOU SAW?

The first episode I saw was "The Girl in the Fireplace." I had been sent to bed one night and came down under some pretext or another (it was just an excuse to not go to bed). Mum and Dad were watching it and I remember the scene where Mickey and Rose were on the tables as I lay down on the rug and the Doctor came in 'drunk,' allowing me my first look at the character that would be my love of the next almost two decades. My parents let me stay and see the end, astounded, as I had never been so quiet!

TELL US HOW YOU THEN BECAME A FAN OF THE SHOW.

For years I wasn't involved in the "fandom" exactly; I was still a kid after all. There was a *Doctor Who* society at school, but I was too nervous to join. I was, however, an avid *Doctor Who Adventures* reader and even won a *Blue Peter* badge for my *Doctor Who* fanfiction! Back before I even knew what fanfiction was!

TELL US YOUR FAVORITE MOMENT IN YOUR DOCTOR WHO FANDOM EXPERIENCE.

I have been very lucky as a *Doctor Who* fan in the last few years. I've met some wonderful people and made some amazing friends because of the show. I even met one of my best friends because he made the mistake of having a TARDIS bag for the first day of university!

I've met six Doctors, a handful of companions, and even an incarnation of both the Master and the Rani. I've been complimented by Matt Smith and hugged by Katy Manning, but my favourite moment as a *Doctor Who* fan was meeting Ncuti Gatwa. But first, some back story.

In July of 2024 they announced a production of *The*

Importance of Being Earnest. I have always been interested in queer history and Ncuti had already become my favourite Doctor, so it was too perfect for words. I bought two tickets (for myself and the aforementioned bestie) and started planning.

I'm not usually very crafty but I had this idea to make Ncuti a scrapbook. I collected messages and art and memes from across the fandom and put them all together for him. I also got together some other fun things, like a 'My Job is Doctor' T-shirt, some keychains, and even a TARDIS key! I compiled everything into a nice blue (obviously) gift box and took it to the theatre. As we had arrived late, I gave the box to a member of staff to look after and was told it would be delivered to Ncuti, which I thought was perfect!

After the play, my bestie and I went to the stage door because we wanted to meet Ncuti! He spent a while chatting with fans and when it was our turn I asked him about the present (my exact wording was "has anyone given you a big blue box" which made him laugh and I was oblivious until much later that he thought it was a TARDIS joke) and he hadn't had it! I was so upset! I honestly thought it had gotten lost or something, so I explained what I had done and he made a note of my name on his phone and promised to look into it.

I rang up the theatre a couple of days later and learned that presents left with the stage door were stashed away somewhere but had been collected. At this point you would be forgiven in thinking that's where the story ends – I know I did -- but that's when something really special happened.

Fast forward to Christmas Day and we were sitting down to open presents, about an hour before the Christmas special was due to air. I was opening my present from my dad (a very nice Fifteenth Doctor Build-A-Bear) when my phone buzzed with two Instagram notifications. It was Ncuti. He had messaged me to thank me for the presents I gave him and even sent me a little video. I was over the moon – it made all that work completely worth it.

Then, about six months later, I was at the cinema. I had watched "The Interstellar Song Contest" that morning and was now seeing the new *Lilo and Stitch*, which obviously meant my phone was off. I turned it on and was swamped with notifications. They had recently announced the release of the Barbie dolls and I had made some jokes in some fan forums that he should have worn the shirt I gave him as it had a Barbie theme. As it turned out, Ncuti had the same idea. Alongside his post about the dolls he included a picture of himself wearing the T-shirt and had tagged me with a caption about how much he loved the *Doctor Who* fans.

It truly meant the world to me and was easily the most amazing thing I've ever had happen. Ncuti has absolutely bought himself a fan for life!

IF YOU WERE TO INTRODUCE SOMEONE ELSE TO THE DOCTOR WHO SERIES, WHAT EPISODE/STORY WOULD YOU TELL THEM TO START WITH AND WHY?

I don't have a specific go-to for this one. I try to tailor the episodes I show people to their tastes and interests. That being said, my policy has always been that if you can't make it past the burping bin you don't deserve this show!

JAY BADENHOOP

WHAT WAS THE FIRST EPISODE/STORY OF DOCTOR WHO THAT YOU SAW?

I am not sure. I grew up in Milwaukee, Wisconsin. *Doctor Who* aired on a commercial station a few years before it was distributed to PBS stations. This was the late 1970s and I was a young kid then. I remember seeing "Genesis of the Daleks" with Tom Baker early on a Saturday morning, but I may have seen a few Pertwee episodes before that. It was taken off soon after. The first episode I saw on PBS was on WTTW Chicago on cable TV, late on a Sunday night. "Seeds of Doom" with Baker and Elisabeth Sladen's Sarah Jane Smith. I could only stay up late on vacations, so the next episode I saw was months later, "Keeper of Traken." I loved the updated opening theme and learned the Doctor had a different look and different companions. The Master was a classic archvillain. The next one I saw was "Earthshock," still with Adric, but Peter Davison's Doctor. Impressed with the Cybermen, but confused why a different actor was the Doctor? I discovered science fiction fandom with X-Con and met Mike Stutzman, President of Starfleet Academy, a *Star Trek* fan club in Milwaukee. The convention showed several *Doctor Who* episodes, including "Logopolis," "Castrovalva," and "The Three Doctors," which introduced me to the concept of regeneration and the show's extensive mythology.

TELL US HOW YOU THEN BECAME A FAN OF THE SHOW.

I was hooked by the show's concept of a time traveling alien, the Daleks, and Davros. The show's concept is the most versatile premise for a science fiction series ever devised. It can explore Earth history and any science, science fiction, fantasy, or technology concept. The TARDIS can go anywhere and anytime. The Doctor picks up and drops off different companions and periodically regenerates his (or her) body, which frees the series from the career lifespan of any one actor, or group of actors. They even got around the initial restriction of 12 regenerations of a Time Lord (13 Doctors). The series is centered around time yet is timeless and can go on forever. I co-founded The Milwaukee Time Lords club in 1989. The club kept *Doctor Who* fandom active during the lean years while the series was off the air and the club is still going strong 37 years later!

TELL US YOUR FAVORITE MOMENT IN YOUR DOCTOR WHO FANDOM EXPERIENCE.

Doctor Who fandom in the USA exploded in the mid-1980s after the worldwide broadcast of "The Five Doctors" in 1983. I attended many *Doctor Who* conventions including ones organized by Creation Conventions and Spirit of Light, predecessor to the modern Chicago TARDIS. The Chicago cons were huge, with dozens of actors and behind-the-scenes guests from the series. As Milwaukee Time Lords' Vice President and newsletter editor, I was able to interview many of these guests as one of the "fan press." I had the privilege of getting to know many stars of the show personally. I also met my wife Christy through the Milwaukee Time Lords. We have been married 31 years! Those are my favorite fan experiences.

IF YOU WERE TO INTRODUCE SOMEONE ELSE TO THE DOCTOR WHO SERIES, WHAT EPISODE/STORY WOULD YOU TELL THEM TO START WITH AND WHY?

That is a very difficult question because there are so many. Tom Baker was my first Doctor and still my favorite. "Pyramids of Mars" might be his best. "An Unearthly Child" episode one only (must see the pilot), "The Dalek Invasion of Earth" (great action), "The Time Meddler" (first episode with another Time Lord), "Tomb of the Cybermen" (Troughton's Doctor at his best), "Spearhead from Space" (first Pertwee), "Carnival of Monsters" (one of the series' best scripts), "Genesis of the Daleks" (allegory to Nazi Germany and reinvents the Daleks),

"The Sunmakers" (one of the best satirical stories), "City of Death" (best humor and use of time travel), "Earthshock" (great Cybermen story and explains the end of the dinosaurs), "The Caves of Androzani" (the Doctor's life in peril), "Vengeance on Varos" (satire with Sil as a slimy villain), "The Curse of Fenric" or "Battlefield" (Sylvester McCoy's best stories). Any story written by Robert Holmes before "The Trial of a Time Lord." From the new series, the best episodes were written by Steven Moffat, so any of his stories would be a good choice.

MARK BAUMGARTEN

WHAT WAS THE FIRST EPISODE/STORY OF DOCTOR WHO THAT YOU SAW?

"The Sontaran Experiment," Part Two (back in 1978 when my local PBS station aired it the first time)... so 10 episodes into its broadcast.

TELL US HOW YOU THEN BECAME A FAN OF THE SHOW.

The second episode I saw was "The Genesis of the Daleks," Part One (how could I not become a fan instantaneously!). I started reading everything I could on *Doctor Who*. I had a friend who ran small conventions where I watched Jon Pertwee episodes. Then in 1981, I started attending Omnicon, a *Doctor Who* convention held in South Florida. Over eight years of attending this convention, I went from punter, to volunteer, to staff. I met Patrick Troughton, Jon Pertwee, Peter Davison, Colin Baker, Nicholas Courtney, and many, many others over the years. I even went on the very first Doctor Who Cruise in 1988 run by my friend Dan Harris with Sylvester McCoy, Nick Courtney, John Nathan-Turner, and Gary Downie.

TELL US YOUR FAVORITE MOMENT IN YOUR DOCTOR WHO FANDOM EXPERIENCE.

In 2012, I created a podcast called MarkWHO42 with two friends. Since then, it has been on two separate online radio stations and has featured over 200 guest interviews with *Doctor Who* actors, writers, and monster performers, along with some *Star Trek, Farscape, Babylon 5*, and comic book creators as well, winning a Spacie Award along the way. The show is no longer just *Doctor Who*, but as it is my passion, I make sure we have plenty of content. We just spent nine episodes reviewing Ncuti Gatwa's second season meaning we did more shows than the BBC did!). Anyway, being invited to conventions all over the country to spread the *Doctor Who* gospel is really what I cherish most. Up and down the state of Florida, and places like Atlanta and Dallas, I moderated panels and interviewed big names (as I do on my show) as well as sold *Doctor Who* merchandise, being an authorized dealer of Big Finish audios. I think the most special one was in 2016. I was invited to participate at Geekinomicon in Oklahoma City where they threw a 20th Anniversary celebration of the 1996 TV movie. I was there and on stage with Sylvester McCoy, Paul McGann, Daphne Ashbrook, Eric Roberts, Jeremy Radick and Yee Jee Tso! It was a privilege to be invited to such an event!

IF YOU WERE TO INTRODUCE SOMEONE ELSE TO THE DOCTOR WHO SERIES, WHAT EPISODE/STORY WOULD YOU TELL THEM TO START WITH AND WHY?

That's a very hard question. If it were Classic Who, I'd start them with "Robot," since Tom was my first, and I find this era to be an amazing one. Jumping on as Philip Hinchcliffe and Robert Holmes took over as producer and script editor is going to be a real treat to a newbie. If it were Modern Who (can't call it New Who… it's 20 years old now), I'd probably pick the Moffat era (don't boo me) with "The Eleventh Hour," which totally feels like it was made as a jumping on point purposely, which makes sense. Didn't *Doctor Who* popularity go through the roof in the United States with that story (rhetorical question)? If not that story, then "Deep Breath" as I believe Peter Capaldi is the Classic Doctor in Modern Who, in as much as his Doctor could totally be put in the classic series and work perfectly! No wonder that he is my favorite Doctor!

CASSIE BEYER

WHAT WAS THE FIRST EPISODE/STORY OF DOCTOR WHO THAT YOU SAW?

     I watched it as a child and have no memory of what my first story might have been. For whatever reason, however, a single scene in "Enlightenment" stuck in my head (when Turlough is trapped in the vacuum chamber getting slowly sucked into space).

TELL US HOW YOU THEN BECAME A FAN OF THE SHOW.

     For several years I completely forgot about the show. I mostly only know I watched it as a kid because Mom told me much later.
     Then, when I was 13, I started having a lot of health problems. It was around this time I found *Doctor Who* again. I'm not sure why I latched on to it as strongly as I did. Perhaps it filled in a gap in science fiction for me. This was the mid-1980s, so there was no *Star Trek: The Next Generation*, and I was not a fan of the original *Star Trek*.
     But I had lots of time to fill. I couldn't do sports anymore. I couldn't walk the mall. So, I did solitary things, like writing stories and doing art. And I fell in love with *Doctor Who*. I scoured bookshops for books, both the novelizations and the behind the scenes stuff. It wasn't easy in the 80s in America to find them.
     I confess I was really obnoxious about it. I mean, I was 13, and 13-year-olds are kind of obnoxious by nature. (If you're 13 and reading this, I can promise when you're an adult and look back at your tween/teenage years, you're going to think the same.) But I was obsessed. I constantly wanted to talk about it, but I knew of no other fans, so I just constantly yabbered about it to anyone willing to put up with me.
     But there was still that "Enlightenment" episode. I didn't

have a name for it, just that one scene. I searched and searched for it. I got through what I thought was Davison's entire run and never saw it. I suspect I literally got every episode except that one. It was *years* before I finally saw it.

It's not even a favorite episode of mine.

Davison, however, is my favorite Doctor. I imagine my earliest episodes were Tom Baker, because that's the case for everyone my age, but I have no memory of them. Turlough, incidentally, is also my favorite companion, although I can't believe that episode is what endeared him to me.

TELL US YOUR FAVORITE MOMENT IN YOUR DOCTOR WHO FANDOM EXPERIENCE.

I was at the costume contest at Gen Con, and NuWho had been on for about three years at that point. A four-year-old came on stage dressed as David Tennant, and the whole audience melted from the adorableness.

"Well," I said, "the Doctors *are* getting younger every year!"

This is a convention of nerds, so I expected a bit of laughter, as opposed to most venues, where I wouldn't expect anyone to recognize anything from *Doctor Who*.

Instead, the entire audience broke into laughter. Several hundred people. And that was the first time I realized how big NuWho was.

IF YOU WERE TO INTRODUCE SOMEONE ELSE TO THE DOCTOR WHO SERIES, WHAT EPISODE/STORY WOULD YOU TELL THEM TO START WITH AND WHY?

For NuWho, I would absolutely suggest starting with episode one, "Rose." I love the way that story was written so you needed no knowledge of *Doctor Who* to enjoy it and it introduced some basic concepts of the show. (The easter eggs for us Classic Who folks were also great.)

I think a lot of my favorite episodes really work best if

you have at least a basic understanding of the show.

For Classic Who, the specific episode is less important. I think the Tom Baker and Peter Davison episodes are the most accessible. I like Davison more than Baker, so that would color my choice too.

RYAN BLAKE

WHAT WAS THE FIRST EPISODE/STORY OF DOCTOR WHO THAT YOU SAW?

This has been lost to the mists of a temporal haze really. I have a clear recollection of the handshake between the Master and the Fourth Doctor at the end of "Logopolis" Part Three, but this is competing with the regeneration of the Fifth Doctor turning into the Sixth. No one else in my family is really a *Doctor Who* fan, so when I ask them if either was part of The Faces of Doctor Who repeat series, they just look at me as if I were the insides of a Dalek…

TELL US HOW YOU THEN BECAME A FAN OF THE SHOW.

I fully realized I was a *Doctor Who* fan when I was in high school. This was the very beginning of the Wilderness Years, and I went with a friend to see the MOMI (Museum of Moving Images) *Doctor Who* exhibition. We were both closeted Whovians, mostly because this was just before it was cool to be a geek and our high school was particularly brutal about that sort of thing. I remember that it brought everything into such sharp focus, all the costumes and props and stories, the Doctor was not gone… only sleeping. Soon after, the Virgin New Adventures came out and the story began again.

TELL US YOUR FAVORITE MOMENT IN YOUR DOCTOR WHO FANDOM EXPERIENCE.

Well, it's a tie between the aforementioned Virgin novels and the announcement of the Eighth Doctor TV movie. I literally jumped for joy when the trailer dropped (I spent that year seriously ill so I hadn't really had access to any news outlets) so it was a genuine surprise. "These shoes fit perfectly" still makes me smile every time I hear it…

IF YOU WERE TO INTRODUCE SOMEONE ELSE TO THE DOCTOR WHO SERIES, WHAT EPISODE/STORY WOULD YOU TELL THEM TO START WITH AND WHY?

Probably either "Rose" or "The Eleventh Hour" both are more or less immaculate intros to the series and don't require much of an explanation of anything else. Both say who the Doctor is, what they are about, and hint at the legacy just enough to intrigue without conclusion. Eleven's intro is marginally better but mostly because the heavy lifting of the new format had been accomplished by Russell T Davies.

ARNOLD T. BLUMBERG

WHAT WAS THE FIRST EPISODE/STORY OF DOCTOR WHO THAT YOU SAW?

It's complicated. I remember once, when I was little, my mother was flipping TV channels and saw a guy with a scarf who also had curly hair like me. She suggested I might like the show – similar hair was the criteria, I guess? I also recall seeing the ending of "The Armageddon Factor," with the repeating time loop, and all of "The Leisure Hive," both times thinking I was watching a standalone British sci-fi film of some kind. But I was a *Star Trek/Star Wars* kid, and that was enough for me.

Then one night in 1987, I turned on Maryland Public Television (MPT) and saw a bizarre man in an eye-burning patchwork coat and a girl in a physically unlikely pink leotard (she kept me watching, I'm not going to lie) battling silver cyborgs in "Attack of the Cybermen." Not the best story to spark your fandom? Perhaps. But for me, it was a revelation (no, we're not still talking about Peri). For me, all the flaws that dedicated fans often see in that story were the very reasons I couldn't stop watching. It was filled with detail, history, references – and it was confusing. I knew this was something that was part of a bigger picture, a larger universe of storytelling, and I wanted to know what that story was. I looked in the TV Guide and saw that the very next day, the Washington DC PBS station (WETA) was also showing this thing called *Doctor Who*. So I turned it on that Sunday afternoon and saw an older man with white hair and a slightly more subdued outfit helping an Earth-based paramilitary organization figure out the mystery of some returned astronauts in "The Ambassadors of Death." It was in black and white, it was clearly years earlier... but it was the same show, and yes, still the Doctor... somehow! I realized just how vast this universe was that I had fallen into, and how much more there was to see and know.

The trip of a lifetime had begun.

TELL US HOW YOU THEN BECAME A FAN OF THE SHOW.

The local comic shop had a wall of Target novels, an occasional issue of the *Doctor Who Magazine*, and comic books from Marvel that featured informational articles I would only later realize were woefully inaccurate. But the road lay ahead, the die was cast... or should I say, the coordinates were set. I started throwing myself into researching everything I could about the show and its mythology, picking up those great hardcovers by Peter Haining (also not entirely accurate, but oh well), watching the show twice weekly (until WETA dropped it one sad day), and instantly becoming a *Doctor Who* fan.

What started for me as a mild curiosity on a PBS station has turned out to be quite a great spirit of adventure, and it transformed not just my personal but my professional life. I've designed books about *Doctor Who*. I've written, edited, and contributed to books and articles about *Doctor Who*. I've published books about *Doctor Who* as ATB Publishing (five so far, more to come!). Those projects enabled me to become a guest at *Doctor Who* conventions where I've met heroes, made friends, and became a part of a wonderful fan community. I've collected *Doctor Who*. I read *Doctor Who*. I listen to *Doctor Who*. I watch *Doctor Who*. It will always be a part of my life.

TELL US YOUR FAVORITE MOMENT IN YOUR DOCTOR WHO FANDOM EXPERIENCE.

I've always joked that I came by my choice of "favorite Doctor" honestly, because unlike the general assumption that one's favorite is usually the first Doctor they saw, mine is Peter Davison's often breathless, crickety Fifth Doctor. Possibly my favorite moment in my fan experience involves him as well. At one of the conventions where I was a guest, I had the privilege of sharing the green room with Davison and Colin Baker for a few minutes late one day. Davison was fretting about having to perform at that night's cabaret, a then-regular feature of that convention. He had no planned act and didn't know what to do.

He was almost panicky about it, as he was too good an actor not to want to do something good, but he was worried that what he came up with wouldn't be good enough. I told him everyone would just be happy to see him on stage, and whatever he did would be fine; Baker said much the same. Between the two of us, we calmed him down and eventually steered him to a simple solution – the old gag about volunteering to read a poem for the audience, doing it silently, then saying "thank you" and walking off. A quick silly joke, and we guaranteed him that everyone would be delighted. And they were. And that was the day I helped the Fifth Doctor face his greatest challenge – stage fright! Well, not really, but it was very nice – a sort-of alternate "The Three Doctors."

IF YOU WERE TO INTRODUCE SOMEONE ELSE TO THE DOCTOR WHO SERIES, WHAT EPISODE/STORY WOULD YOU TELL THEM TO START WITH AND WHY?

This one is also pretty complicated, and my answer has evolved as the show itself has evolved. We're way past the point where it's as easy as saying "Well, start with the modern era and go from there," because so-called 'modern' Who has been through so many changes at this point that there are very distinctive – and distinctively different – eras since 2005. I wouldn't point a new viewer in 2024 to the classic show; that would wait for them to be interested enough to seek it out on their own. And I wouldn't suggest "Rose" anymore, my usual go-to in the past, because it has itself aged quite a bit in style and approach that a newcomer might see it as a relic much like a 'classic' story. So, with all this in mind, I would suggest that a new viewer start with "The Church on Ruby Road," meet the latest Doctor, and see if the most recent style of Who clicks with them. From there, it's up to them!

PAUL BOOTH

WHAT WAS THE FIRST EPISODE/STORY OF DOCTOR WHO THAT YOU SAW?

First age I watched *Doctor Who*: four or five. I'd just moved to the Chicagoland area in the mid-1980s; well, I say "I moved" but really my parents did and I was just along for the ride. You have to be when you're three years old. My father was born in the UK and was ten when "An Unearthly Child" first premiered. He even remembers watching it from behind the sofa!

It was 1984 when we moved and I think it was probably the next year that my father realized that the local public television station – WTTW, Channel 11 – showed episodes of *Doctor Who* late at night on Sunday evenings. These were full stories – not half hour episodes, but the start-to-finish ninety-minute serials. They never showed them in order, so I didn't know if the Doctor was a wide-eyed curly-haired crazy alien or a tall aristocratic man with an amazing bouffant.

I was four, maybe five years old and we would watch those classic Tom Baker and Jon Pertwee stories together. But the first one I remember watching was "Planet of Evil." And I remember being scared – Out. Of. My. Mind!

TELL US HOW YOU THEN BECAME A FAN OF THE SHOW.

I wasn't a fan after "Planet of Evil."

That's a lie. I mean, I was a fan, but I was also five years old and I don't know if you can really call it "fandom" if you can't tie your own shoes. I was a fan of many things then, including *Postman Pat*, chicken nuggets, and sippy cups. When I watched "Planet of Evil" (and all the other episodes on WTTW) I certainly loved them and I eagerly waited for them to come on. I'd set up my parents' VHS player (remember those?) to tape them late at night and I would watch them on Monday after school.

When I was a young teenager in the 1990s, I discovered that my local library had *Doctor Who* books. Probably the first time I would have thought of myself as a 'fan' was when I read through Peter Haining's *Doctor Who: A Celebration* and Lesley Standring's *The Doctor Who Illustrated A–Z* and realized there was a much longer history of *Doctor Who* than I had originally thought. When my mother went to a local flea market (which included a bookseller that sold used books), I sent her with a list of Target novelizations, and over the years, I read and collected them all. The bookstore near me would special order books for me and I fell in love with Jean-Marc Lofficier's *The Doctor Who Programme Guide*, *The Terrestrial Index*, and *The Universal Databank*.

But did I think of myself as a "fan?" I don't think so. I don't think I had the language then.

When I did first think of myself as a fan was 14 May 1996 – the premiere of the *Doctor Who* TV Movie. I blocked off my entire evening, told my family "not to disturb me under any circumstances!" and for eighty-nine minutes, I was in heaven.

TELL US YOUR FAVORITE MOMENT IN YOUR DOCTOR WHO FANDOM EXPERIENCE.

I'm a professor at DePaul University and one of the greatest moments of my life was when I was given permission to create a class about *Doctor Who*. The class came out of many conversations I had about *Doctor Who* during the 50th Anniversary, because all of my colleagues know how big a fan I am. Plus, I had been conducting academic research on *Doctor Who* fandom at the time, including interviewing fans at Chicago TARDIS and Gallifrey One, and there were a number of students who just wanted to talk about *Doctor Who* with me.

The first time I taught the class it went very well, and the class gelled. It was like they had been waiting for something like this their entire lives. I think back to when I was eighteen years old and, if there had been even the hint of the mere possibility that there could be a class about my favorite TV show, I would have moved across the country to attend. But the class itself is not my favorite moment in *Doctor Who* fandom. The class was great, and since I started it, I've been able to teach it as a study abroad class, which has included some amazing moments like having stars of the show talk to my class, getting to tour sets, and even taking the students to see filming.

But my favorite moment in my *Doctor Who* fandom emerged after that initial class. A few of the students came up to me after class was done and asked if they could keep watching *Doctor Who* with me, even when they didn't get graded for it! They wanted to keep learning about the show! So in 2014 – ten years ago now – we started DePaul Doctor Who Club. And it is still going strong today! The students in the club speak at the Chicago TARDIS and Gallifrey One conventions. They watch episodes and interview guests. And it's become a highlight of my time at DePaul.

IF YOU WERE TO INTRODUCE SOMEONE ELSE TO THE DOCTOR WHO SERIES, WHAT EPISODE/STORY WOULD YOU TELL THEM TO START WITH AND WHY.

Whenever someone asks me about where to start with *Doctor Who* episodes, I always ask them what their favorite movie, book, or TV show is. Depending on what the answer is, I can usually point to an episode that has a similar vibe. Want horror? Try "Blink." Want comedy? Try "The Lodger."

But if I'm drawing out of my memory, I usually recommend "The Eleventh Hour" (for New Who) or "Ark in Space" (for Classic Who). Both give a light-hearted, fun episode with a turn towards the serious. And both are superbly indicative of the possibilities that *Doctor Who* allows.

KEITH BRADBURY

WHAT WAS THE FIRST EPISODE/STORY OF DOCTOR WHO THAT YOU SAW?

"Robot" (Tom Baker), Part One. It was the first episode aired on the Champaign/Urbana PBS station back in the early 1980's.

TELL US HOW YOU THEN BECAME A FAN OF THE SHOW.

I was a HUGE fan of *Star Wars* (saw it in theaters), watched *Star Trek, Space: 1999, Quark, Battlestar Galactica,* and *Buck Rogers in the 25th Century*. In the early 80's, there was almost no new sci-fi on TV until *Star Trek: The Next Generation* in 1987. *Doctor Who* was definitely filling that void!

TELL US YOUR FAVORITE MOMENT IN YOUR DOCTOR WHO FANDOM EXPERIENCE.

I was such a huge fan of Tom Baker, but I had almost no exposure to any of the "behind the scenes" information. When "Shada" was released on VHS, it was my BIGGEST fan moment. After more than a decade of reruns, I finally had a new *Doctor Who* story with my favorite Doctor, and I fell instantly in love with this story, even if it was incomplete!

I don't remember exactly when I learned that the BBC had destroyed many of its original black and white stories from the first two Doctors, but when the internet became a "thing" in the late 1990's, I started exploring how to make a website and created an early fan-centric *Doctor Who* site. I think many of us believed that the internet opened up opportunities to help locate these missing stories. Also, growing up as a kid who saw *Star Wars* in the theaters, I had all the toys I could possibly want, but there was nothing available for *Doctor Who*. I started using the internet to find *Doctor Who* product manufacturers in the UK, hoping to score some of these collectibles. Dapol, the manufacturer at the time of the *Doctor Who* action figures, told me that I would need to purchase approximately $1000 worth of goods for them to supply me. That is when I had the bright idea to order one for myself and sell the rest on my website. I placed the order, and within a week of listing these items for sale, I had to order more. In 1998, Who North America was born. We began as an online company, but as time progressed, more and more people wanted to visit. Now we have a retail facility and a "museum of merchandise," comprised of all those "one for me" items I have been setting aside over the years. We have had the opportunity to have actors appear at our facility and events, including Sophie Aldred (Ace), Caitlin Blackwood (Young Amy Pond), Peter Davison (Fifth Doctor), Sylvester McCoy (Seventh Doctor), and Nicholas Briggs (voice of the Daleks). And that is how a childhood fan obsession over a TV show turned into a labor of love!

IF YOU WERE TO INTRODUCE SOMEONE ELSE TO THE DOCTOR WHO SERIES, WHAT EPISODE/STORY WOULD YOU TELL THEM TO START WITH AND WHY?

One of the absolute best stories to introduce someone to Classic *Doctor Who* is the story "The Time Warrior" with Jon Pertwee. You get to discover the Doctor right along with Sarah Jane Smith. First Sontaran story, a good period costume drama without an over-reliance on outdated special effects, and a fun story to boot!

BEN BRIGHOUSE

WHAT WAS THE FIRST EPISODE/STORY OF DOCTOR WHO THAT YOU SAW?

My first episode was "Destiny of the Daleks," on its original run I assume. It obviously has quite an impact on me because, for years afterwards, I dreamt about it with quite some frequency – not the stuff with the Daleks, mind you, but the business with the Doctor and Romana in the cave. Weird, eh?

TELL US HOW YOU THEN BECAME A FAN OF THE SHOW.

To be honest; I am not certain… but I remember caring about the show and the Doctor enough that I got particularly upset when the Watcher "killed" the Doctor. In my defense, I was only five and I didn't understand regeneration yet, but it'd take a long time for me to become a fan of the Fifth Doctor too. At primary school we did areas of study called "topics," sometimes as a whole class (the Victorians, Europe, and Romans for example), and sometimes individually as "personal topics," which we chose the subject for ourselves. I remember doing one on insects, and, more importantly, one on the monsters of *Doctor Who*. So, I must have been a big fan then. I think I was nine. I was particularly mesmerized by those stories that I'd never gotten to watch. I still remember drawing Axons, the Mummies, and Morbius. Anyways, I have been a fan ever since. Though still I occasionally question whether I am a fan or not. I mean, what makes someone a fan? But as I have been running three interrelated role-playing games set in a little corner of the #Whoniverse that we call the #Mikrosverse for nearly two years now, I guess that shows a level of dedication worthy of a fan.

TELL US YOUR FAVORITE MOMENT IN YOUR DOCTOR WHO FANDOM EXPERIENCE.

Probably when I went to see the 50th Anniversary Special

("The Day of the Doctor") at my local cinema. The cheer that it got as it started was a pleasure to behold, and I'm not normally into that sort of thing at all. It was just great to be there with a room full of fellow fans who were so excited to see an episode of the show.

That, or our three Mikrosamandrella (the name of our Time Lord) role-playing game campaigns.

IF YOU WERE TO INTRODUCE SOMEONE ELSE TO THE DOCTOR WHO SERIES, WHAT EPISODE/STORY WOULD YOU TELL THEM TO START WITH AND WHY?

"The Eleventh Hour." I see it simply as the best jumping on point, the best first episode for showing what the show is about, without needing lots of foreknowledge. One of the best Doctors, not my favorite, but definitely up there. And importantly, it has a whole load of story hooks to have new fans wanting to come back for more in hope that their questions get answered. That scene on the hospital room where the Doctor warns the Atraxi off Earth – *chef's kiss*! The perfect "I-am-the-Doctor" moment!

BOB BRINKMAN

WHAT WAS THE FIRST EPISODE/STORY OF DOCTOR WHO THAT YOU SAW?

"Terror of the Zygons," still a favorite of mine. I remember it quite clearly. WEDU in Sarasota, Florida was just starting to run the series, and that was the first episode shown. We were in Florida for Christmas vacation and had dinner at my grandparents that night. I got to go into their bedroom and watch the show while the adults sat in the living room and chatted. There are so many parts of that night burned into my brain.

TELL US HOW YOU THEN BECAME A FAN OF THE SHOW.

I was a fan prior to ever seeing an episode. The boyfriend of my older sister let me read several of the Pinnacle novelizations and I immediately fell in love with them. So much so that, upon finishing those books, I immediately began writing my own story over a summer. It wasn't until the next year, when I was 10, that I met someone my age who watched *Doctor Who* but... still I had never seen it. Instead, I was devouring the Target novelizations as quickly as I could get them. When I finally saw an episode (the above mentioned "Terror of the Zygons") I was utterly enthralled. The next week the station ran "The Pyramids of Mars" – still my favorite episode – and I've not looked back since.

I ended up joining the Doctor Who Fan Club of America (DWFCA), and they had a small convention in Chicago that I gleefully attended. I made great use of their 800 number (1-800-CALL-WHO) and likely annoyed the crap out of them with all of my phone calls and questions.

TELL US YOUR FAVORITE MOMENT IN YOUR DOCTOR WHO FANDOM EXPERIENCE.

For the 20th Anniversary there was a major convention,

Spirit of Light's Doctor Who: The Ultimate Celebration convention in Chicago. I got to go and it was utterly mind-blowing! I spent at least half the convention trying to find Tom Baker and get his autograph, or maybe even a photo, but to no avail. Finally, on the final night, it was raining as we all walked to the last panel discussion and still raining when we left again. Not wanting to get too wet, I ducked under someone's umbrella. Looking up, it was Tom Baker! I gawped at him for a moment and said, "I can't believe I'm under your umbrella." With a hint of laughter he answered, "Nor can I."

That moment was utterly magic. I had no pen, my camera was out of film, there was no souvenir of the meeting to be had, but it didn't matter. I got to meet Tom Baker, who was already my favorite Doctor, and that locked him in as my favorite for life.

IF YOU WERE TO INTRODUCE SOMEONE ELSE TO THE DOCTOR WHO SERIES, WHAT EPISODE/STORY WOULD YOU TELL THEM TO START WITH AND WHY?

That's a tougher one. I think I'd introduce them with the revival series rather than the classic, as attention spans and television pacing have greatly changed. I think I'd start them with "Rose," letting them discover the series in a way that even we fans didn't get to – blind. "Rose" is a great introduction to the Doctor for a modern audience, and their not knowing all the lore and backstory would help them enjoy the mystery. Once they get to Matt Smith's introduction, and they first encounter the prior faces of the Doctor, then I'd begin showing them some of the classic episodes. By that point they'd have an appreciation for the show and hopefully be more curious about the Doctor's history.

BARBARA BROWN

WHAT WAS THE FIRST EPISODE/STORY OF DOCTOR WHO THAT YOU SAW?

It was on a Friday in April 1983, a Tom Baker story involving Cybermen on a planet of gold ("Revenge of the Cybermen"). My brother was watching this awful cheesy 1970s British Sci-Fi series with horrible special effects, and I kept on telling him to turn the channel, but he wouldn't. "Turn this awful program off!" Begging and pleading had no effect, so I finally sucked it up and grudgingly began watching. And then the Cybermen appeared on the screen, and I was entranced. There was something so wonderfully art deco-ish about them. I began to get caught up with the characters and watched until the end.

TELL US HOW YOU THEN BECAME A FAN OF THE SHOW.

By the time the story "The Android Invasion" aired, I was actively watching the show. I even got a top similar to the one Sarah Jane wore in the story: Sailor collar with a scarf. In November 1983, I saw an ad in the *UWM Post* (I was a University of Wisconsin - Milwaukee student at the time) about the formation of a *Doctor Who* fan club, The Renegade Time Lords, so I joined. My brother and father joined shortly after. I met a lot of friends with common interests. When The Milwaukee Time Lords split from the campus club in 1989, we joined that as well. Although my dad passed on in 2018, my brother and I are still members of the Milwaukee Time Lords.

TELL US YOUR FAVORITE MOMENT IN YOUR DOCTOR WHO FANDOM EXPERIENCE.

There are several hilarious stories, but the earliest was my first *Doctor Who* convention. It was during the drought summer of 1988 in St. Paul, Minnesota. We were all poor college students. We drove up in two cars, and there were ten people staying in our room. The lucky people got the beds -- the rest of us were in sleeping bags. A lot of people were in costume, so when this lady in a Tahitian costume sat next to me at the cabaret, I thought nothing of it. I talked to her a bit, and she said it was part of something her husband had planned, and that they hoped they would pull it off. Then her husband introduced Jon Pertwee on the stage, she came up to Jon Pertwee, put a lei around his neck, and said, "I bet this is the first time you've ever been lei-ed in St. Paul." The crowd roared with laughter. Then Jon took her hand and made off to the nearest exit. Only it was a fire exit, and Jon set off the fire alarm. The crowd was laughing so much, we practically peed our pants. It took the hotel about 20 minutes to turn off that alarm, and we were laughing the whole time.

IF YOU WERE TO INTRODUCE SOMEONE ELSE TO THE DOCTOR WHO SERIES, WHAT EPISODE/STORY WOULD YOU TELL THEM TO START WITH AND WHY?

This is a tough question to answer. I guess it would depend on their personality and age. Some good stories to start someone with in the original series are: "Pyramids of Mars," "The Deadly Assassin," "The Talons of Weng-Chiang," "City of Death," The Master-Regeneration Trilogy ("Keeper of Traken," "Logopolis," and "Castrovalva"), "Earthshock," "The Caves of Androzani," or "Curse of Fenric." With the new series, it'd be: "Rose," "The Empty Child"/"The Doctor Dances," "The Girl in the Fireplace," "The Fires of Pompeii," "The Planet of the Ood," "Blink," "The Waters of Mars," and "Heaven Sent." Tough to pick one.

CHRISTOPHER CEBULA

WHAT WAS THE FIRST EPISODE/STORY OF DOCTOR WHO THAT YOU SAW?

"The Sontaran Experiment" on Channel 10 (WMVS, analog era) at 2:00PM on Saturday, 09 April 1983.

TELL US HOW YOU THEN BECAME A FAN OF THE SHOW.

My mother and I were channel surfing and came across this guy in a long coat, fedora, and really long and colorful scarf, using a whirring tool, trying to repair some equipment on a lush, green hillside. My mother turned to me and said, "Chris this is stupid; I think you'll like it!" (And the rest, as they say, is history.)

I began calling Channel 10 about this strange series with different program lengths and was eventually asked to come to the station to get fliers for distribution at the University of Wisconsin - Milwaukee (UWM) or Marquette University promoting a showing of "The Five Doctors" at Park Avenue (a bar on the corner of Water Street and Clybourn Avenue in downtown Milwaukee) on 22 November 1983. By the time I took the bus and arrived at the station's studios in the Milwaukee Area Technical College's (MATC), holder of the station's licenses, downtown campus, two other people had already picked up fliers and were distributing them. The Volunteer Director asked me to call all the viewers whose names they had collected about the series (remember, this was before the internet or e-mail); she figured this would take three days, but I completed the task in one afternoon.

The Volunteer Director was so impressed that she asked me to consider volunteering for a customer service position called Viewer Services Volunteer, answering telephone calls and letters (again, this was before the internet or e-mail) about the station's programming. I volunteered for over 40 years and was also the station's *Doctor Who* expert, until MATC (Milwaukee Area Technical College) decided in February 2024 that volunteers were a security threat to their network and an insurance liability.

As a UWM student in 1984, a group of us formed a student organization called the Renegade Time Lords (RTL); we would show *Doctor Who* videos on Friday nights in the Student Union. Unfortunately, the Union began losing our room and video equipment reservations; some members began bringing their own equipment to meetings. It was also becoming increasingly difficult to meet the university's requirements that only students could be officers and maintaining the minimum number of office hours in a room shared with four other student orgs.

In 1989, Founding President Ed Hochman proposed forming the Milwaukee Time Lords (MTL), a *Doctor Who* club not associated with the university, which celebrated its 35th Anniversary on 16 August 2024. I am a Founding Member of both RTL and MTL, have held all five MTL officer positions at one time or another, currently serving as Parliamentarian, Video Equipment Coordinator, and Events Committee Chairman.

TELL US YOUR FAVORITE MOMENT IN YOUR DOCTOR WHO FANDOM EXPERIENCE.

I flew to Boston in July of 1984 to see Tom Baker. At some time while volunteering (again I forget when), Tom Baker came to Milwaukee to promote the series; I volunteered to pick him up from General Mitchell International Airport and deliver him to the WMVS studios. The staff were OK with this because they were too busy doing their jobs; I was thrilled to meet the star of my favorite show in person!

IF YOU WERE TO INTRODUCE SOMEONE ELSE TO THE DOCTOR WHO SERIES, WHAT EPISODE/STORY WOULD YOU TELL THEM TO START WITH AND WHY?

I would recommend "The Five Doctors." It contains all the elements of *Doctor Who* (e.g., Gallifrey, Time Lords, multiple incarnations of the Doctor, the TARDIS, companions, UNIT, the Master, Daleks, Cybermen, etc.).

WALT CIECHANOWSKI

WHAT WAS THE FIRST EPISODE/STORY OF DOCTOR WHO THAT YOU SAW?

The classic series episode "The Time Warrior," with Jon Pertwee as the Doctor, the Brigadier, and introducing Sarah Jane Smith. The Sontarans were introduced in this story and never looked better!

TELL US HOW YOU THEN BECAME A FAN OF THE SHOW.

With the Doctor transported to a medieval setting with an alien baddie that wanted to change history, I was hooked from the get-go. I devoured every episode I could watch. One PBS channel showed them nightly, episode by episode (which my dad taped on the VCR for me) and another showed omnibus stories on Saturday nights, usually with pledge breaks.

My fandom made me a bit of an Anglophile and I jumped at the chance to go on a school trip to England, Wales, and Ireland in 1989, where I got to see a Dalek face-to-eye stalk!

TELL US YOUR FAVORITE MOMENT IN YOUR DOCTOR WHO FANDOM EXPERIENCE.

I've been privileged to write for the *Doctor Who Roleplaying Game*, which led to me being a guest at a local *Doctor Who* convention in 2013. I got to hang out with two Doctors, several classic companions, Davros, and a Cyberman!

IF YOU WERE TO INTRODUCE SOMEONE ELSE TO THE DOCTOR WHO SERIES, WHAT EPISODE/STORY WOULD YOU TELL THEM TO START WITH AND WHY?

If we're talking classic series, I usually go with "Battlefield." I know it's cheesy, but it's got some of the best effects of the classic era, the Arthurian mythos reimagined, a fun catch-up with an old friend (the Brigadier), and a cute ending. It's the one I hooked my wife with!

If we're talking modern series, I'd go with "Rose." May as well start from the beginning, and the season does a great job of reintroducing *Doctor Who* to a new audience.

T. AARON CISCO

WHAT WAS THE FIRST EPISODE/STORY OF DOCTOR WHO THAT YOU SAW?

The very first episode that kidnapped my imagination and refused to return it was "Paradise Towers." Imagine being eight and discovering that the universe isn't just *Star Trek*'s final frontier or *Wonder Woman*'s lasso tricks but also includes a time-traveling madman in a box. There I was, staring at the screen, as the Seventh Doctor and Mel navigated a building that could've been designed by a committee whose only agreement was that they should disagree. It was less a paradise, more a lesson in what happens when architects take a holiday forever. But seriously, robots, monsters in the basement, warring gangs, a time traveling alien. It was like everything I liked, and didn't know I liked, in one amazingly gripping piece of television.

TELL US HOW YOU THEN BECAME A FAN OF THE SHOW.

It was an instantaneous and irreversible chemical reaction. No sooner had "Paradise Towers" ended than I began a relentless campaign to absorb all things Who. I borrowed, rented, and consumed VHS tapes with the fervor of a man who's discovered he can rewind time but only on tape. My DIY attempt at the Seventh Doctor's question-mark vest was a fashion catastrophe of cosmic proportions (so much so, that I wrote a book/memoir about the experience titled *Black Nerd Blue Box: The Wibbly Wobbly Memoir of a Lonely Whovian*) but even that didn't deter me. I'd discovered the universe of the Doctor, and no amount of schoolyard teasing could exile me from it.

TELL US YOUR FAVORITE MOMENT IN YOUR DOCTOR WHO FANDOM EXPERIENCE.

I imagine that choosing a single, favorite moment in the Who Fandom is like trying to find the best cup of tea in England;

near-impossible, but an absolutely splendid problem to have. I've got not one, but two absolutely groovy moments; the time I met Sophie Aldred and Sylvester McCoy. Recreating 1980s promotional photos with Sophie while dressed as the Doctor was surreal – like stepping into your own fan art. And interviewing Sylvester McCoy. Imagine having a casual chat with the laws of physics, only they're wearing a strikingly stylish vest and can talk about the weather. It was an exhilarating collision of nostalgia and star-struck glee.

IF YOU WERE TO INTRODUCE SOMEONE ELSE TO THE DOCTOR WHO SERIES, WHAT EPISODE/STORY WOULD YOU TELL THEM TO START WITH AND WHY?

Ah, the infamous "where to start" dilemma. It's like asking which door in an infinite corridor you should open first to find the exit (or the entrance, depending on your view of space and time). I'd propose "Rose" from the NuWho era for newcomers. It's like a soft reboot – a comfortable sofa from which to dive into the sprawling, often nonsensical, always fascinating narrative. It's short, sweet, and packed with enough mystery and adventure to hook anyone's interest. From there, depending on their reaction to timey-wimey stuff, you can either march forward into New Who or rewind to classic episodes where the effects were wobbly, but the storytelling was solid as a rock.

TERRY COOPER

WHAT WAS THE FIRST EPISODE/STORY OF DOCTOR WHO THAT YOU SAW?

My earliest memory of *Doctor Who* was most likely seeing 'The Green Death' story in 1973. I may have seen earlier ones, but this is the one that stood out to me. I was about four years old at the time. Although me and my family were living in London, both my parents are Welsh, so the story's Welsh setting might be a factor. The thought behind this theory is that my Dad wasn't a big fan of the show, but he probably tolerated watching it as it was set in Wales.

TELL US HOW YOU THEN BECAME A FAN OF THE SHOW.

At the time, a kid living nearby had a very large collection of *Doctor Who* Target novels. I'd borrow some from him regularly, and also from the local library. I remember the Cybermen ones (which had interior illustrations) being my favourites. They're my favourite Who monsters to date, and today, I earn my living illustrating books for Candy Jar Books in Cardiff, who publish quite a bit of Who related books.

TELL US YOUR FAVORITE MOMENT IN YOUR DOCTOR WHO FANDOM EXPERIENCE.

In 2008, I wrote *Kangazang!*, my first novel, which is a sci-fi comedy, published by Candy Jar. They suggested we do an audiobook version of it. They hired Colin Baker, who read the book beforehand and told me he really enjoyed it. He came into the studio and performed it over nine hours. As a Who fan, to hear my words and characters being spoken by the voice of the Sixth Doctor was mind-blowing. It's something that will stay with me forever. I even got him to say, "Whether you like it... or not!" Sixie was never my favourite Doctor, but Colin is the real deal. The nicest guy in the business.

IF YOU WERE TO INTRODUCE SOMEONE ELSE TO THE DOCTOR WHO SERIES, WHAT EPISODE/STORY WOULD YOU TELL THEM TO START WITH AND WHY?

I think I'd tell them to watch "An Unearthly Child" as it sets the scene, the Doctor, the TARDIS and so on. After that, I think one of the early Tom Baker stories would really expand on the unique formula and surreal setup that *Doctor Who* has in its DNA. Once Tom's Doctor has grabbed you, curiosity will do the rest, and like me, you'd get to experience all of the Doctors and begin to find your favourites. There really is nothing else like it in sci-fi, fantasy or storytelling. And even if there is, you can bet that *Doctor Who* did it first.

UMUT ÇEVIK

WHAT WAS THE FIRST EPISODE/STORY OF DOCTOR WHO THAT YOU SAW?

My first encounter with *Doctor Who* happened in the summer of 2009, when I was 14. Summer had only just begun, but I was already bored and looking for something to watch. That's when I stumbled upon a scene: Earth was being destroyed, and a man and a young woman were watching it with apparent delight. The moment was both shocking and intriguing. I found it so strange that I thought, "What on Earth are these people doing?" I decided to post something sarcastic about it on Facebook — but first, I needed to find out what I was actually watching. I stayed in front of the screen. Eventually, the episode ended, and the title "Doctor Who" appeared. As soon as I saw the name, I rushed to my computer and decided to do some research before making any judgments. I discovered that *Doctor Who* wasn't a film, but a long-running TV series, and what I had seen was the second episode of the revival, "The End of the World."

TELL US HOW YOU THEN BECAME A FAN OF THE SHOW.

If Earth was being destroyed in the second episode and those two (the Doctor and Rose) were so casual about it, there had to be something I was missing. So, I found the first episode and started watching. Living mannequins, a centuries-old alien, time and space travel – all of it fascinated me and hooked me immediately. I quickly caught up with the most recent episodes.

The show had already drawn me in, though I wasn't aware of it yet. To this day, I don't know exactly what affected me so deeply or why I kept watching. But I found myself eagerly waiting for the next episode. Around that time, "Planet of the Dead" aired – the first episode I watched almost in real-time.

Looking back, I realize I became a fan during that period, even though I didn't yet know to call it that. I didn't just watch the episodes – I researched the show extensively. What impressed me most was its long history. But there was almost no Turkish content online, and I wanted to learn more. I felt something had to be done about that. Soon after, I started following a Facebook page called "Doctor-Who Türkiye Grubu." I say "soon" because everything developed in just a few months. I shared what I had learned in the comments and engaged in discussions with others. Apparently, my posts caught the attention of the page admin, because out of the blue, I was invited to become a page editor. If one of the turning points in my life was starting to watch *Doctor Who*, the other was becoming an editor on that page. With my joining the team, we started taking action to move past the mindset of "Why doesn't this exist?" and "Why is no one doing this?" We began translating up-to-date news. We sought support from anyone who could help. We translated news, wiki pages from TARDIS.wiki, and even episode subtitles. Eventually, I even hosted online radio shows on various platforms.

TELL US YOUR FAVORITE MOMENT IN YOUR DOCTOR WHO FANDOM EXPERIENCE.

The most important moment came in 2012 when a few friends met up in Bursa. I wasn't there that day, but the joy they shared lit a spark in us: why weren't we organizing fan meetups like in other countries?

In 2013, our page received a message. A magazine called *Postkolik* wanted to feature *Doctor Who* in their November issue for the show's 50th Anniversary and asked for our help with the content. I didn't just help – I wrote a relatively long and detailed article. It was longer than they expected, but instead of cutting it down, they decided to give it more space. That article didn't just increase our visibility – it also opened new doors.

During that time, we continued our social media work and started thinking about events that hadn't been done before. Toward the end of 2014, an interesting development occurred. CNBC-e, which was then airing the show, had a TV magazine.

Before the 8th season premiered, they wanted to dedicate one or two pages to *Doctor Who*. I mentioned that I had written an article for *Postkolik* and could do something similar for them. They told me they were already aware of my writing and liked it – that's why they had reached out. So I wrote another detailed article, this time for CNBC-e Dergi. While chatting with the magazine editor, I learned they were planning a small viewing party before the season aired. I told them about an event we were planning in Istanbul. At first, they only offered social media support, but as time passed, the idea grew, and on 25 January 2015, we organized a major event at the channel's headquarters. That was the official beginning of our long-dreamed-of Istanbul gatherings. Later that same year, in July, we organized another event at a private university, supported by CNBC-e's social media and attended by İthaki Publishing. This proved that we could host events even without a broadcaster's help.

In 2016, after an event I had organized (but couldn't attend) at another university, we realized it was time to try something new – and we did. Around that time, due to some internal conflicts, I had to leave the page I had worked so hard on for years. I was alone now – but not abandoned. That was the day we rose from the ashes and founded "Doctor Who Merkezi." Despite all the challenges, we kept growing and evolving. In 2017, we hosted a meetup in an Istanbul café, and in 2018, we held a watch party at The Box Cafe, a *Doctor Who*-themed venue in Izmir. But our pace started to slow. We realized we were repeating ourselves. That prompted us to explore new paths and fresh ideas.

During this period, unofficial fan translations gradually gave way to official ones. Although it was never published, I translated "The Blood Cell" novel for İthaki Publishing. I've always done my best to keep my promises. Over time, I found myself alone; support dwindled – but I didn't give up. My efforts paid off. In December 2021, we organized a special "Flux" screening event with guest James Goss. Then came 2022 – the most important year of my life. I married the person I met through TARDIS.wiki translation projects and who had become my partner. We became a Whovian family. Because of that, I don't have just one meaningful memory with *Doctor Who*, but several. I couldn't choose just one to tell, so I tried to list them all, as they happened. Of course, these words cannot truly summarize 16 years.

I still watch *Doctor Who* with the same passion I had on day one, and I continue sharing what I've learned. I'm active on many platforms, but I spend most of my time on Twitter. These days, I'm expanding my *Doctor Who* collection and writing a book on the history of *Doctor Who* in Turkey. Maybe one day, I'll make a documentary too – who knows? Over these 16 years, I've seen the fanbase change countless times. There were moments when I felt stuck in a loop, overwhelmed. But every new fan I met, every person I guided in some small way, brought me closer to the show again.

IF YOU WERE TO INTRODUCE SOMEONE ELSE TO THE DOCTOR WHO SERIES, WHAT EPISODE/STORY WOULD YOU TELL THEM TO START WITH AND WHY?

I still get asked the same questions all the time: "I want to start *Doctor Who*, but where should I begin?" or "I want to introduce my friend to the show, but which episode should I pick?"

These have always been tough questions. Rather than exceptional episodes like "Blink" or "The Waters of Mars," I prefer recommending ones like "Rose" or "The Eleventh Hour" – episodes that launch a new era and capture the adventurous spirit of the show. Because while I love the show's vast mythology, what moves me most is that we're watching a journey that isn't about reaching an end – it's about the road itself.

FRANCHESKA DAVIS

WHAT WAS THE FIRST EPISODE/STORY OF DOCTOR WHO THAT YOU SAW?

My first episode was "The Robot Revolution" from Series 15.

TELL US HOW YOU THEN BECAME A FAN OF THE SHOW.

I became a fan of the show as I loved the concept of the constant change in the show and the interesting plots and storylines. My fandom grew through watching *Doctor Who* with friends.

TELL US YOUR FAVORITE MOMENT IN YOUR DOCTOR WHO FANDOM EXPERIENCE.

My favorite moment of my fandom was going to watch parties at my friend Libby's house and watching new episodes with friends.

IF YOU WERE TO INTRODUCE SOMEONE ELSE TO THE DOCTOR WHO SERIES, WHAT EPISODE/STORY WOULD YOU TELL THEM TO START WITH AND WHY?

I would tell them to start with the "Lux" episode as it was one of my favorites from the most recent season. I thought it was a fantastic story with memorable characters and moments.

TIMOTHY DAVIS

WHAT WAS THE FIRST EPISODE/STORY OF DOCTOR WHO THAT YOU SAW?

Tom Baker, around 1986.

TELL US HOW YOU THEN BECAME A FAN OF THE SHOW.

I always like sci-fi. It was a series that you could get at the time. Lots of stories had a deeper meaning to them when I look back at them.

TELL US YOUR FAVORITE MOMENT IN YOUR DOCTOR WHO FANDOM EXPERIENCE.

"The Five Doctors" ending.

IF YOU WERE TO INTRODUCE SOMEONE ELSE TO THE DOCTOR WHO SERIES, WHAT EPISODE/STORY WOULD YOU TELL THEM TO START WITH AND WHY?

"Rose," because of the excitement and because it was the beginning of the modern era.

TAYLOR DEATHERAGE

WHAT WAS THE FIRST EPISODE/STORY OF DOCTOR WHO THAT YOU SAW?

It was 2006, and I was sitting in the back of a Metra commuter train with my high school best friends. One of them excitedly reached over to tap me on the shoulder and asked, "Have you ever heard of *Doctor Who*?" The name seemed vaguely familiar to me (flashes of an old book I'd once found tucked amongst my dad's comic collection complete with a curly-haired, wide-smiling man wearing a colorful scarf popped briefly into my head), but I said "No," and he started in on a play-by-play of the Ninth Doctor's introductory episode. I was hooked instantly.

TELL US HOW YOU THEN BECAME A FAN OF THE SHOW.

Sci-Fi Channel had just acquired the rights to air the revival of *Doctor Who* in America, and once I had a chance to watch "Rose," I spent the rest of the spring and all of summer consuming any *Doctor Who*-related media I could get my hands on. I started streaming David Tennant's first season as the Doctor as it was aired in real-time. After I got over being spoiled and the grief that comes with regeneration, I latched on to this Doctor as "mine." That wouldn't become a permanent determination, but pursuing it led me to endlessly search YouTube for Classic Series episodes. I quickly built a list of favorite Fourth, Fifth, Sixth, and Seventh Doctor serials. I found the forum Gallifrey Base and engaged in late-night discussions with Whovians from all over the world. I shifted my fanfiction focus to reading and writing only in the *Doctor Who* fandom. I finally answered the question of which Doctor seemed like "mine" with the discovery of Big Finish and the continuing Eighth Doctor adventures. After all this, I was ready to search out where I could meet up with fellow Whovians in person, to cosplay, have character discussions, and just share our love for this niche fandom. This is how I ultimately found the convention Chicago TARDIS.

Two years after diving headfirst into the fandom, and with the very limited budget of a college student, I planned my first *Doctor Who* con experience. This would also be the driving force of me continuing my now-long cosplay journey beyond ever-niche Halloween costuming.

That first Chicago TARDIS I felt instantly at home. I sat in on panels with expert cosplayers, listened to one of my favorite companions, Elisabeth Sladen, talk about her show experiences live on stage, and met my first Doctor, Colin Baker, who still holds an incredibly special place in my heart. The weekend was topped off with a snuggly hug given to me by Lis Sladen in one of the last Sunday photo ops. She had nothing but sweet words to say, and it would be the first and last opportunity I would have to meet her. From that year on, I would make it an annual tradition to attend Chicago TARDIS, and I would add Gallifrey One to my travel itinerary just a few years later.

TELL US YOUR FAVORITE MOMENT IN YOUR DOCTOR WHO FANDOM EXPERIENCE.

In 2013, seven years after first immersing myself in the world of *Doctor Who*, I had an unbelievable opportunity that changed my life and allowed my passion for the fandom to become one of the most central things to me to date.

A college friend who was looking out for me as I was going through a difficult time, reached out to let me know that the small business he worked for desperately needed help with marketing and going on the road to conventions due to the recent pop culture con boom. Would I want a job? I was looking to switch careers and thought I could do much worse than making one of my main hobbies of existing in geekdom a full-time job. It was a little bit of time before I realized this small business was also the one that was behind Chicago TARDIS – the convention I saw as home for one weekend each year.

I had no idea how this turn of events would lead to countless adventures at cons all over the U.S. – helping out

Doctors and companions as they met other fans like me at various large events; fulfilling many dreams. It seemed very surreal then, and it still does now. I am grateful for a community that has embraced me through the collective love of a TV show that helped me better connect with my queer identity, made me feel seen in the hardest times, and whose themes transcend all of time and space.

IF YOU WERE TO INTRODUCE SOMEONE ELSE TO THE DOCTOR WHO SERIES, WHAT EPISODE/STORY WOULD YOU TELL THEM TO START WITH AND WHY?

It's hard for me not to look back at that day on the Metra train and have the urge to recommend any episode for a new fan to start with other than "Rose." The answer might be surprising for some, but the hook of the episode - the feeling of danger and instant adventure once you are put in the shoes of the companion - is hard to deny.

With the introduction of the Fifteenth Doctor and his emerging storyline, I am also tempted to recommend this as a starting point. The content of Ncuti's introductory season and portrayal of the characters have the potential to draw in a whole new audience who have yet to interact with the boundless world of *Doctor Who*. With their inclusion, I am excited about the new ideas and perspectives that are sure to pop up within the fandom.

KEN DEEP

WHAT WAS THE FIRST EPISODE/STORY OF DOCTOR WHO THAT YOU SAW?

I came across "The Pirate Planet" Part Three on my local PBS station Channel 21 WLIW. They aired the program as individual parts in the half hour time slot. I was completely lost and I didn't try watching again for a few weeks. It was visually very striking and it definitely made an impression on me.
Weeks later, I tuned in again. This time, it was "Warrior's Gate," I think. It was another visually stunning episode. I remember being confused again, but determined to stay with the show until I joined a story at Part One. My wait was short and "Keeper of Traken" Part One came across my TV set. This blew me away. A talking statue! An old man in a chair! A back story! A sort of *I, Claudius* in space. I'm in.

TELL US HOW YOU THEN BECAME A FAN OF THE SHOW.

Months later, I was at my local comic book shop. In the early 1980s, this was the hub of all geeky social life, shopping, and information exchange. There was a flyer on the bulletin board for a *Doctor Who* fan club. I asked the shopkeeper for a pencil and I scribbled down the address. To my surprise, it was in Oceanside, my hometown! The headquarters of the *Doctor Who* fan club was in MY town?
In the medieval times of the 1980s, if one wanted to find a location or directions, one would use a map. Made of paper! I dug out my handy Hagstrom and located the address. On an early summer afternoon I pedaled my Huffy to the address across town. In the hour it took (even at blazing speed), I imagined this glass and steel monolith that the *Doctor Who* fan club headquarters would look like. To my disappointment, it was just a house. A blue ranch with cars in the driveway. No signs. No USA Tour trailer. Nothing to betray the inner workings of this Gallifreyan Embassy.

I cycled home a bit bewildered and disappointed. The following weekend my parents, enablers, drove me into Manhattan where I attended my second or third convention. There in the hallway, the Gallifreyan Embassy, Long Island's *Doctor Who* fan club, had a table set up. I met the organizers and joined the club. I participated in anything and everything they had to offer. That was the start of my conversion from passive to active fandom. My company, the one that operates the L.I. Who convention, is named Gallifreyan Events to honor our club.

TELL US YOUR FAVORITE MOMENT IN YOUR DOCTOR WHO FANDOM EXPERIENCE.

After 40 years, it is tough to pin that down. I would say my set visit in 2017. The crew were in Germany filming "Smile." The friend who arranged the tour said I have good news and bad news. The bad news was that the cast and crew were away and we wouldn't get to meet Peter and Pearl, which would have made for a great picture followed by a hasty exit. The good news was that with the set going unused that day we would have extra time to look around and take pictures. An added bonus was they lit the set for us as if they were recording. The pictures look beautiful.

IF YOU WERE TO INTRODUCE SOMEONE ELSE TO THE DOCTOR WHO SERIES, WHAT EPISODE/STORY WOULD YOU TELL THEM TO START WITH AND WHY?

This question really depends on knowing your audience. A younger crowd might not want to see classic *Doctor Who* or even modern Who if it's only in standard definition. People who like quirky or eclectic television could start with the first Tom Baker series. It seemed to work for millions here in the states, where his first seasons were on endless cycles.

For a younger viewer, "Eleventh Hour" really is the start of something special. And that cast! All stars now, which could be a gateway for some. If your new-vian fancies the boys, I guess letting them see David Tennant in "Blink" might catch their attention.

JOHN DERRICK

WHAT WAS THE FIRST EPISODE/STORY OF DOCTOR WHO THAT YOU SAW?

I'll never actually know. By pure chance, I was introduced to the show on the night I was born. My parents had never heard of *Doctor Who* before they arrived at the hospital, but my mother's roommate was a fan, and a deal was struck over their shared television: my mom could watch whatever she liked, so long as each night the roommate could watch *Doctor Who,* which PBS was then airing episodically on weeknights.
(Ed. - With our help and the great website BroaDWcast.com, John has been able to identify that the first episode that he saw on the date of his birth was "Planet of Evil" - Part Four.)

TELL US HOW YOU THEN BECAME A FAN OF THE SHOW.

Admittedly, I have no memory of that first encounter with the Doctor and the TARDIS, though I suspect it imprinted deeply on my personality. Yet among my earliest memories is the magical night a few years later, when I was maybe four years old, when my mother and I were watching TV together and happened on *Doctor Who* on PBS again. To my knowledge this was the first time my mom had seen Who since the hospital, but when she told me the story of my first viewing, it felt like destiny. We kept watching, and I've never stopped since.

As I recall, the story that night was "Planet of the Spiders," and it made a rather perfect introduction to the series, featuring, as it did, Elisabeth Sladen's incredible Sarah Jane, Nicholas Courtney's wonderful Brigadier, and a regeneration. How fantastic, to understand immediately, the particular brilliance of the Time Lord concept, and to know right off the bat that the Doctor would be not just one favorite character, but a multitude. As an added bonus, the episodes were woven through with Buddhist concepts and themes, which would resonate even more strongly as I got older.

From that night on, I was a Whovian. I watched every episode I could find on PBS throughout the next several years, right up until it was canceled, shortly after the BBC had ended the series in 1989. I was crushed, particularly as the Seventh Doctor and Ace were my favorite TARDIS team yet. Thankfully, I'd already taped or collected a number of episodes on VHS. I had novelizations, action figures, and a board game, to revisit or create my own adventures throughout the Wilderness Years. I wrote fanfic, some of which got turned in as English class assignments or writing exams, for quite good grades, and some of which was eventually published in the *Friends of Doctor Who* newsletter and a charity anthology, *The Cat Who Walked Through Time*. Once the internet became a thing, one of the first things I did was find other Whovians in message boards and chat rooms, eventually becoming involved in an online *Doctor Who* role-playing group that would, much like that original hospital television coincidence, set new coordinates for my destiny.

TELL US YOUR FAVORITE MOMENT IN YOUR DOCTOR WHO FANDOM EXPERIENCE.

"The universe hangs by such a fragile thread of coincidences," the Eighth Doctor told us. *Doctor Who* found me by coincidence, and by an amazing chain of coincidences, it also led me to most of my very favorite people. A friend from my online *Doctor Who* role-playing group was also involved in a *Sliders* RPG, and we decided to run a crossover adventure together, which is how I met my friend Carrie. Carrie and I were also fans of a new show at the time, *Farscape,* and she introduced me to more Scapers, including Rachael. It would take Rachael and me seven years of friendship to realize we could, in fact, be more, but we got there in the end! Then we watched lots of *Doctor Who* together, along with many other things, and got married and had a kid, Calvin. Eventually we took a trip to Seattle, where we went to The Museum of Pop Culture, AKA MoPop, which I highly recommend, and I took pictures with a 1980s Dalek and Cyberman. A few years after

that, someone saw that Cyberman picture online and thought, "Anyone that excited to meet a 1980s Cyberman is someone I should talk to," and that's how Natalie entered our lives.

All of which leads, like the zoom-in from space at the beginning of "*Rose*" to my favorite singular moment to date as a Whovian: New Years 2022, watching "*Eve of the Daleks*" on the couch with Rachael and Natalie on either side of me and Calvin in my lap.

IF YOU WERE TO INTRODUCE SOMEONE ELSE TO THE DOCTOR WHO SERIES, WHAT EPISODE/STORY WOULD YOU TELL THEM TO START WITH AND WHY?

"Partners in Crime." The Tenth Doctor and Donna are another of my very favorite TARDIS teams, right up there with the Seventh and Ace, and that story is such a perfectly joyous confection. On the day my son was born, I knew I would show him *Doctor Who*. If I imprinted that first night for life, I'd give him the same chance. In the hospital, on my iPad, that's the one we watched.

J. DIETENBERGER

WHAT WAS THE FIRST EPISODE/STORY OF DOCTOR WHO THAT YOU SAW?

Probably Tom Baker -- "Horror on Fang Rock" or "The Brain of Morbius."

TELL US HOW YOU THEN BECAME A FAN OF THE SHOW.

Initially after "looking the other way" for the falling over trees and rock quarry backgrounds we all know too well – it was the simple narratives, plots of imagination, and saving-the-day scenarios that were alluring.

TELL US YOUR FAVORITE MOMENT IN YOUR DOCTOR WHO FANDOM EXPERIENCE.

Meeting Tom Baker in London – my looking the wrong direction – seeing a large shadow approach on the store wall in front of me – my turning around to see and hear the larger-than-life man with his booming voice stating "Well, hello there. Who would like a Jelly Baby?" and me gobsmacked and speechless for a millisecond moment.

IF YOU WERE TO INTRODUCE SOMEONE ELSE TO THE DOCTOR WHO SERIES, WHAT EPISODE/STORY WOULD YOU TELL THEM TO START WITH AND WHY.

First provide them a personal introduction to the "larger on the inside" TARDIS, regeneration and why, explain Time Lords and TARDIS companions, the timey-wimey time travels thing, the attempted "kill off" of the series in the 1980s – then . . .
Secondly – if they want to start with the classic series – Tom Baker and the above two mentioned episodes and possibly including "Logopolis" and/or Peter Davison's "Earthshock."
Thirdly – if they want to start with the new series,

probably the first episode of Matt Smith ("The Eleventh Hour") or Ncuti Gatwa's first season opener ("Space Babies").

MELANIE DOWEIKO

WHAT WAS THE FIRST EPISODE/STORY OF DOCTOR WHO THAT YOU SAW?

I started watching back when *Doctor Who* was still on Netflix and, as a completionist who likes to start from square one, I started with "Rose." I had heard a little about the show on Tumblr and my dad had been a fan back in Tom Baker's era, so he encouraged me to watch it when he saw it on Netflix, too. Little did I know how many square ones there were!

TELL US HOW YOU THEN BECAME A FAN OF THE SHOW.

I absolutely devoured everything that was on Netflix. The internet was my main outlet for fandom when I caught up to what was airing which, at the time, was Series 7 of New Who. Tumblr was huge back then. I ended up directly in the zeitgeist that was SuperWhoLock, which fed my need for crossovers. I followed *Doctor Who* blogs on Tumblr, read a ton of fanfiction on fanfiction.net and archiveofourown.org, and had both a Tenth Doctor and the Master (who was stuck on Earth as Sherlock from *Sherlock;* again, I love a good crossover) roleplay blog. I made a few very close friends through roleplay. I also handwrote a ton of fanfiction, some of which I published on the fanfic sites but most of which stayed in my notebooks. I shared them with my friends in synopses and short bursts of infodumping. I also shared them with my Creative Writing teacher in high school, who was also a massive Whovian and assigned us journal pages in her course. It wasn't until college that I made friends with people in person who were also fans of the show, and I'm still pretty close with some of the people I originally connected with over *Doctor Who*. It wasn't until after college that I went to my first convention (Chicago TARDIS!). While I've fallen out of the internet some, I'm now a member of DePaul University's *Doctor Who* club and I've been going to more and more conventions.

TELL US YOUR FAVORITE MOMENT IN YOUR DOCTOR WHO FANDOM EXPERIENCE.

I think most recently it's the moment I got to tell Billie Piper how much her run on *Doctor Who* meant to me and the fandom experience it birthed, and she seemed really excited when I told her I was in a *Doctor Who* club! But another favorite moment has been doing panels. There was one year when I was on like five panels at Chicago TARDIS and I had the best time!

IF YOU WERE TO INTRODUCE SOMEONE ELSE TO THE DOCTOR WHO SERIES, WHAT EPISODE/STORY WOULD YOU TELL THEM TO START WITH AND WHY?

I think that really depends on the person. Usually, when people ask me, I tell them that they can start at the beginning of any Doctor's run in New Who and have a full understanding. It can be overwhelming, looking at over 60 years of a show. If you're a completionist, like me, that's a huge commitment. It can also be difficult for people who are used to modern television to get into Classic Who, like trying to get into Victorian literature. There is so much media available to us now that if something doesn't catch our interest within a few episodes, we might not continue with it. Not only that, but with so many choices comes decision fatigue. Sometimes I just won't watch anything when I feel so overwhelmed by choices like this, so you can see how this would be a barrier for entry!

BEN ELLIS

WHAT WAS THE FIRST EPISODE/STORY OF DOCTOR WHO THAT YOU SAW?

"The Five Doctors."

TELL US HOW YOU THEN BECAME A FAN OF THE SHOW.

After watching "The Five Doctors" I had so many questions. Why were all these men who look nothing alike called the Doctor? What was the deal with the robot that looked like a salt shaker? Who is Sarah Jane Smith and that robot dog? I did my thorough research looking for everything I could find out about this Time Lord from Gallifrey.

TELL US YOUR FAVORITE MOMENT IN YOUR DOCTOR WHO FANDOM EXPERIENCE.

In 2016, after the CONsole Room convention was over, I had the privilege to sit in the hotel bar with Anneke Wills. Over a couple of glasses of wine, she told me about her friendship with Roger Loyd Pack and how she was so happy whenever she and Michael Craze got to be guests at a convention together.

IF YOU WERE TO INTRODUCE SOMEONE ELSE TO THE DOCTOR WHO SERIES, WHAT EPISODE/STORY WOULD YOU TELL THEM TO START WITH AND WHY?

I would suggest the story "Rose." It's a great introduction to what the role of the companion is and it's a great introduction of who the Doctor is.

HEATH FARNDEN

WHAT WAS THE FIRST EPISODE/STORY OF DOCTOR WHO THAT YOU SAW?

Not sure if it was the first but the earliest I can remember is "The Curse of Fenric."

TELL US HOW YOU THEN BECAME A FAN OF THE SHOW.

I remember watching as a child in the late 1980s/early 1990s, and loved aspects of the Doctors at that time: Tom's scarf, hair, and Jelly Babies; Peter's cricket vest; Sylvester's pork pie hat; and K-9.

TELL US YOUR FAVORITE MOMENT IN YOUR DOCTOR WHO FANDOM EXPERIENCE.

One of my favorite moments is from the David Tennant era, when Donna proclaims to be "Part Donna, part Doctor." Definitely made me laugh.

IF YOU WERE TO INTRODUCE SOMEONE ELSE TO THE DOCTOR WHO SERIES, WHAT EPISODE/STORY WOULD YOU TELL THEM TO START WITH AND WHY?

Any series is fine. If you want to start from right at the beginning or the current series, just start from the first episode from that series.

SCOTT FELLOWES

WHAT WAS THE FIRST EPISODE/STORY OF DOCTOR WHO THAT YOU SAW?

"The Seeds of Doom," 1976. I have vague memories of a giant green octopus on the roof of a big house and didn't realise it was from this story until many years later, but then I was only four at the time.

TELL US HOW YOU THEN BECAME A FAN OF THE SHOW.

I didn't really become a fan until the 1980s when I started going to the big Panopticon conventions in Coventry. It wasn't cool at school to admit you were a geek unless you admitted to collecting Panini football stickers as well. But the power of a story that could go anywhere and do anything, slowly but surely dragged me into its orbit.

TELL US YOUR FAVORITE MOMENT IN YOUR DOCTOR WHO FANDOM EXPERIENCE.

So many… rolling a TARDIS console up a stairwell like a giant penny. Having to help with a crane to 'fly' a non-collapsible TARDIS police box from the pavement onto the first floor of the Leofric Hotel. Spending a night drinking and running across to a garage for Pot Noodles with John Nathan Turner, Gary Downie, and mates and finding out they were just the most fun to be with (despite the rumours that circled even then). Propping up Nick Courtney (the Brigadier) at more than one bar. Caroline John (Liz Shaw) offering to buy me lunch. Spending another lunch with the awesome Terrance Dicks and Barry Letts. Meeting people who I am still friends with so many years later… the fact that a *Doctor Who* convention (or any other comic con I've attended or worked) is so welcoming to everybody.

IF YOU WERE TO INTRODUCE SOMEONE ELSE TO THE DOCTOR WHO SERIES, WHAT EPISODE/STORY WOULD YOU TELL THEM TO START WITH AND WHY?

This was quite a difficult question and I ran through a mental check of my favourite Who stories to see what would be best to impress a newbie and welcome them into the fandom fold. "An Unearthly Child" (first episode awesome, other three dull), "The War Games" (epic, but too long), "Inferno" (a story where the Doctor loses, maybe not ideal), "Genesis of the Daleks" (Davros! But far too grim for beginners), "The Talons of Weng-Chiang" (somewhat problematic seen through today's optics), "The Caves of Androzani" (maybe but the Doctor is a passenger in the story rather than the driver).

But then I thought of another favourite, "The Masque of Mandragora."

The TARDIS lands in Renaissance Italy, unwittingly carrying with it a portion of evil Mandragora energy, which possesses an underground cult intent on dragging humanity and the world back to the dark ages.

This is a self-contained four-parter from 1976 that is nestled within a golden age of Who's history. At this point the show was riding a wave of popularity due to a number of factors. Tom Baker had made the character of the Doctor completely his own with his recognisable hat and scarf silhouette and paired with Elisabeth Sladen as Sarah Jane Smith, continued to prove why this is one of the most popular and loved Doctor/Companion combinations. To many, Sarah Jane will always have a special place in fan's hearts and is usually why she is rated the top companion (sorry Billie!).

At this time *Doctor Who* was mashing its sci-fi trappings with gothic horror to great effect with recent stories riffing on *The Mummy*, *Frankenstein* and *Jekyll and Hyde*. This story took inspiration from 1964's *The Masque of The Red Death* and was full of wonderful elements such as religious cults, astrology, science vs superstition, hooded monks, and everybody playing it with the gravitas of a Shakespearean play. The attention to period detail is the sort of the thing that the BBC excelled at with their costume dramas. The costumes themselves, reused from the 1954 film version of *Romeo and Juliet*, are elegant and beautiful. The sets are detailed and sumptuous with a new wood and stained-glass console room being introduced early on. Nowadays it would be called steampunk, but the set, a wonderful homage to Jules Verne, could be a lesson to today's show that sometimes understated conveys more than overblown.

All of this helps to raise everybody's game to a first-rate creepy historical adventure. The actors all turn in faultless performances with a young Tim Piggot-Smith amongst the cast. Tom is still playing the Doctor as a galactic Renaissance man of both action and words in the days before his characterisation devolved into a poor shadow of what had once been. Elisabeth Sladen is also given slightly more to do in the story, effortlessly playing Sarah Jane as the Doctor's best friend and the pair of them utterly believable.

The location filing in Portmeirion, Wales (and the home of *The Prisoner* in 1967), lends the production an authentic Italian flavour and even the special effects, bearing in mind this was 1974, are still pretty impressive. Even the villains are well realised with Norman Jones' Hieronymous making the most of his ambitious astrologer and leader of the Brotherhood (because monks in hoods are always creepy). The story also benefits from the Mandragora Helix itself being a formless Lovecraftian intelligence of evil, as opposed to a stuntman in a rubber costume, although its disembodied ominous voice strays close to parody. Add in the running joke about the Doctor missing Leonardo da Vinci and you've got the (almost) perfect adventure for anybody who wants to see a slice of Classic Who.

JAN FENNICK

WHAT WAS THE FIRST EPISODE/STORY OF DOCTOR WHO THAT YOU SAW?

The first episode I ever saw was Part One of "The Sun Makers" on 10 August 1978, broadcast as a repeat on BBC 1, in Stratford-On-Avon.

TELL US HOW YOU THEN BECAME A FAN OF THE SHOW.

Despite being an anglophile, I had never heard of the show so had no idea what I was watching. Just that it was science fiction, it was funny and clever, and it appealed to a 15-year-old me. This was long before the internet so it's not like I could look it up somehow. Fast forward to October of that year when a local syndicated station, WOR (Channel 9, Secaucus, New Jersey - so the New York City metro area), started airing the show from "Robot" onward (through "Invasion of Time"). The local TV reviewer in our local newspaper wrote a glowing review which included the history of the show, and that told me all I needed to know. When I got to college, I actually met other fans so it was no longer my personal guilty pleasure. I got to actually share it with people!

TELL US YOUR FAVORITE MOMENT IN YOUR DOCTOR WHO FANDOM EXPERIENCE.

I have a lot of favorite moments, and favorite periods of DW fandom, so it's very hard to choose. However, I think seeing "Day of the Doctor", the 50th Anniversary special, in a packed theater with my best friend (who I'd turned on to the show in college) and several other mutual friends was probably one of the most special. To experience that with such an enthusiastic crowd after decades of the show being a fringe thing was magical.

IF YOU WERE TO INTRODUCE SOMEONE ELSE TO THE DOCTOR WHO SERIES, WHAT EPISODE/STORY WOULD YOU TELL THEM TO START WITH AND WHY?

I'd probably start with "The Eleventh Hour" which I personally think is one of the best first episodes featuring a new Doctor in the show's history, if not THE best. It's a great jumping in point; it isn't bogged down with previous show history or characters. It's smart, it's funny, and it's designed to be an entry point. It's got just enough timey-wimey-ness to introduce a new viewer to the show's concepts without being overly complicated. It's got an engaging story, and of course, my favorite TARDIS team of the new series. It's not too scary, it's not political, and it's everything *Doctor Who* should be.

JOHN FREEMAN

WHAT WAS THE FIRST EPISODE/STORY OF DOCTOR WHO THAT YOU SAW?

My earliest memories of watching *Doctor Who* are from the final season of the William Hartnell era, such as "The Tenth Planet," but probably my most vivid early memory is the Dalek creature slipping under the door in "The Power of the Daleks," which haunts me still!

TELL US HOW YOU THEN BECAME A FAN OF THE SHOW.

While a fan of the show, it was the Doctor's adventures in Britain's *Countdown* comic that really stirred my interest. We didn't have a TV in the early part of the 1970s, until the tail end of Jon Pertwee's time on the show. I discovered the Doctor Who Appreciation Society and went to their second convention at Imperial College, London, and devoured various "Who" fanzines.

Strangely, it was actually my editorship of *Doctor Who Magazine* (DWM) that rekindled my interest in the series post-University – I didn't watch many of the Peter Davison and Colin Baker stories first time around, because I was busy doing other things and had limited access to TV! I was able to rewatch a lot of surviving classic *Doctor Who* episodes during my editorship, and meet actors and behind the scenes personnel, which spurred interest in so many aspects of the saga.

TELL US YOUR FAVORITE MOMENT IN YOUR DOCTOR WHO FANDOM EXPERIENCE.

Sitting down to breakfast at a US convention with Jon Pertwee and chatting about his work both in and outside of *Doctor Who*; interviewing Tom Baker in London's Soho (yes, we went to a pub); and Sylvester McCoy being so helpful with photographs. And the fans who supported DWM, of course – an amazing crowd!

IF YOU WERE TO INTRODUCE SOMEONE ELSE TO THE DOCTOR WHO SERIES, WHAT EPISODE/STORY WOULD YOU TELL THEM TO START WITH AND WHY?

Start at the beginning and enjoy. Early stories may seem dated and slow in comparison with today's stories, but I don't think you can really understand the character's success in all the Time Lord's guises without at least some "Classic" viewing!

BOB FURNELL

WHAT WAS THE FIRST EPISODE/STORY OF DOCTOR WHO THAT YOU SAW?

"Robot."

TELL US HOW YOU THEN BECAME A FAN OF THE SHOW.

My journey as a *Doctor Who* fan began in 1981 while living in Edmonton, Alberta, when I discovered the series through KSPS Spokane. The station aired half-hour episodes Monday through Friday, with full stories presented Saturday nights at 11:00PM. From the moment I tuned in, I was captivated by the show's unique blend of science fiction, adventure, and character-driven storytelling. Eager to immerse myself further, I joined the Doctor Who Information Network (DWIN), Canada's national fan organization, which connected me to a vibrant and growing community of fellow fans.

My enthusiasm soon expanded beyond passive viewership. I began collecting the Target novelizations of the episodes, scouring a local bookshop near my home for every title I could find. In 1982, I took my fandom a step further by founding my own fan group, The TARDIS Companions. That endeavor laid the foundation for future projects, including the establishment of two additional groups: The Time Meddlers in 1985 and the Telefantasy Appreciation Society of Canada (TASC) in 1987. These groups helped foster local fan communities and became hubs for discussion, screenings, and fan creativity.

My passion for organizing led to the creation of two full-scale conventions: Who Party West in 1987 and Who Party West III in 1990, the latter featuring guest star Nicola Bryant. Alongside these, I organized a series of mini conventions under the banner of TMOVsocials (1 through 9) and a special event, A Day with Anneke Wills. I also became involved in efforts to locate lost episodes of *Doctor Who* within Canada, a search that connected me with fellow fans and archivists dedicated to preserving the show's history. In 1996, I contributed to the documentary *Bidding Adieu*, focusing on the Paul McGann TV movie, working with Mark Gatiss on the project.

Throughout these years, I continued to express my fandom through publishing. I created several fanzines, most notably *Whotopia*, and in 1999 co-founded *The Doctor Who Project*, a fanfiction series that continues to this day. With over 200 stories published, the series remains a testament to the enduring creativity of *Doctor Who* fans. This lifelong journey has not only deepened my love for the show but also brought me lasting friendships and countless unforgettable experiences.

TELL US YOUR FAVORITE MOMENT IN YOUR DOCTOR WHO FANDOM EXPERIENCE.

Actually, there are several I could name but the two that I would say are: 1) organizing Who Party West III with guest Nicola Bryant in 1990; 2) watching the 1996 TV Movie at my apartment with a group of friends and former companion Anneke Wills (who portrayed the First Doctor's companion Polly).

IF YOU WERE TO INTRODUCE SOMEONE ELSE TO THE DOCTOR WHO SERIES, WHAT EPISODE/STORY WOULD YOU TELL THEM TO START WITH AND WHY?

I think I'd introduce a new viewer to the series with "The Caves of Androzani." This is probably the best all round story from the classic series with a great story, superb acting, and most adult in terms of subject matter and premise. Classic Who at its very best.

HARRY GEROSTERGIOS

WHAT WAS THE FIRST EPISODE/STORY OF DOCTOR WHO THAT YOU SAW?

I was probably around five years old when I saw my first *Doctor Who* episode. It was a Tom Baker episode and I want to say it was his first episode ever, which is "Robot." I watched this on our local PBS (Public Broadcasting Service) Channel 2. Channel 2 was one of the only one of five or so channels that came in on the TV back in the day. My parents were Greek immigrants, and they didn't speak English that well, but they allowed me to watch whatever I wanted, especially Channel 2 programming which included *Sesame Street*, *The Electric Company*, *The Joy of Painting*, and so forth.

TELL US HOW YOU THEN BECAME A FAN OF THE SHOW.

After watching my first episode, which I believe was Tom Baker's first episode "Robot," I was hooked! The scary robot that grew to be 50 feet tall didn't scare me. Somehow, I knew the Doctor (Tom Baker) would find a way to stop it, and of course he did! I watched many more episodes after, until the time came that Doctor regenerated! I had no idea what was going on. I thought it was just another weird thing that happened to the Doctor, much like when he turned into a cactus in "Meglos". But, it was true, there was a different actor playing the Doctor, but I ended up liking Peter Davison too, and every actor that followed!

TELL US YOUR FAVORITE MOMENT IN YOUR DOCTOR WHO FANDOM EXPERIENCE.

Looking back, I had never forgotten all the great episodes of *Doctor Who* that I enjoyed watching as a kid. This show pretty much represented my childhood! As an adult, and even as an artist, I began going to comic book conventions around 2013. At these conventions, I've been able to meet some of my *Doctor Who* heroes! I've met at least seven actors who have played the Doctor, including Peter Davison, Colin Baker, Paul McGann, Sylvester McCoy, Chistopher Eccleston, David Tennant and Matt Smith, including additional actors who've played their companions. My favorite experience has to be when I went to one of these conventions in New York. There, they had the TARDIS console from the *Doctor Who* TV movie (1996) starring Paul McGann. I was able to get a photo-op with Peter Davison, Colin Baker, and Paul McGann. For the picture, I asked them if I could pretend I was pushing the wrong button on the console and they were all trying to stop me. I told them each where to stand, they were great sports and completely played along. It's probably my favorite photo-op I've ever taken!

IF YOU WERE TO INTRODUCE SOMEONE ELSE TO THE DOCTOR WHO SERIES, WHAT EPISODE/STORY WOULD YOU TELL THEM TO START WITH AND WHY?

I have thought of this question many times, as I've introduced this show to several people over the years. I always tell them to start with the episode/story "The Five Doctors." If you were new to the show it's an episode that introduces you to five of the Doctors, their companions, and several of the Doctor's arch enemies, like the Master, Daleks, and Cybermen.

CINDY GYGAX

WHAT WAS THE FIRST EPISODE/STORY OF DOCTOR WHO THAT YOU SAW?

"Vincent and the Doctor."

TELL US HOW YOU THEN BECAME A FAN OF THE SHOW.

I recall as a teenager I saw an episode on PBS with Tom Baker as The Doctor. I only saw part of it as we had very poor reception out in the country. PBS only came in sometimes. However, at sometime in 2011, on a Saturday evening, my children were watching TV as I read a book in the next room. I heard familiar music. My children were being unusually quiet. I put my book down and went into the living room where I saw my three children transfixed by something they were watching. I looked at the TV screen and saw a thin man running around an old European village with an odd machine-like contraption strapped to his back. As he dodged being attacked by something he could only see while looking through the mirror, I sat down, immediately absorbed in the show. The episode was over far too soon. I recall making the connection as to which show I was watching when the closing music came on. I told my children that *Doctor Who* was a show I had tried to watch as a teen living in the boondocks and how frustrating it was. We discussed how cool the episode was and how very sad that Vincent ended up with the same eventuality as in real life. My daughter and I shed some tears as we discussed how we loved the show and hoped another episode would be on soon. I later looked it up online and was thrilled to share with my children that another episode would be on next Saturday! It became "Our Show." Every Saturday, my children and I would sit down together and thoroughly enjoy another episode in space and time with the Doctor – the Eleventh Doctor!

TELL US YOUR FAVORITE MOMENT IN YOUR DOCTOR

WHO FANDOM EXPERIENCE.

I have many favorite moments as a *Doctor Who* fan. Every one of them was when I was with my children watching the show. We not only watched great adventures in space and time, but we had something we all could talk about together every week. *Doctor Who* brought my family together in a new and exciting way! Our favorite Doctor was Eleven. We did go back and watch Nine and Ten but our Doctor will always be Matt Smith's Doctor. We loved Steven Moffat's writing. I know that other people have their opinions of his writing, however, as the daughter of a writer, I can appreciate artistic license.

IF YOU WERE TO INTRODUCE SOMEONE ELSE TO THE DOCTOR WHO SERIES, WHAT EPISODE/STORY WOULD YOU TELL THEM TO START WITH AND WHY?

Which episode would I recommend to someone who has never seen *Doctor Who*? That would depend on the person. I've converted a few friends. I usually recommend "Vincent and the Doctor," "The Girl in the Fireplace," or "Blink"! I recommend them because they're among my top five favorite episodes. I think that most episodes of Doctors Nine through Twelve would be of interest to most people. Sadly, as my children are all adults now, we haven't sat down together to watch *Doctor Who* in a few years.

KATIE HAINES

WHAT WAS THE FIRST EPISODE/STORY OF DOCTOR WHO THAT YOU SAW?

It's kinda funny because the first *Doctor Who* episodes I watched were before I was a fan of the show. In 2008, I watched "The Empty Child" and "The Doctor Dances" back-to-back in college with two friends of mine. I didn't know anything about *Doctor Who* but I loved what I saw. It was my boyfriend, now husband, who really introduced me to the show later that year. We binged the entire series and got completely caught up. I was absolutely devastated watching Christopher Eccleston regenerate (bearing in mind, I had no idea what regeneration was), and then was instantly enraged when I saw David Tennant pop up. My reaction was as follows: "Who the hell is that? Where's the Doctor! No! Bring the Doctor back! I want my Doctor back!"

Ever since then, I was hooked.

TELL US HOW YOU THEN BECAME A FAN OF THE SHOW.

I became a Whovian thanks to my incredible husband and my love of the show was always there, but the hyperfixation often fluctuated (no pun intended) between different fandoms. However, I will never forget where I was when I saw a message from Jodie Whittaker pop up on the BBC's YouTube channel at the start of lockdown in 2020. That whole video is forever tattooed in my mind and changed my life for good. Even now when I am feeling my worst, I remember "Be kind. Even kinder than you were yesterday, and I know you were super kind yesterday." Since I lived in the U.S. at the time and my fiancé lived in London, we binged all of Jodie's episodes over Zoom. Since then, the Thirteenth Doctor has become my second heart. I began cosplaying her, acting as her on TikTok, even going so far as to learn how to do a proper Yorkshire accident, so I could do fan voice over work as her. My love for the Thirteenth

Doctor reignited my love for *Doctor Who* as a whole and now I genuinely cannot imagine my life without it. The Doctor reminds me to always stand up and fight for what is right, even if I might be absolutely terrified to do it. *Doctor Who* has helped me find my chosen family, some of my closest friends, the love of my life. Even in the darkest of times, the Doctor has never failed to give me hope.

TELL US YOUR FAVORITE MOMENT IN YOUR DOCTOR WHO FANDOM EXPERIENCE.

I've genuinely been lucky enough to have some incredible fan interactions in the Whoniverse. From winning a costume contest as the Thirteenth Doctor, to officiating my best friend's wedding as the Doctor, to Ray Holman letting me hold Jodie Whittaker's actual costume, to getting thrown into the pool at Gallifrey One in full cosplay. But there are two moments that always stand out in my mind.

One was when I was talking to a lovely couple at Gallifrey One. We were just talking about the Thirteenth Doctor's era and how it had impacted us. That led to them talking about their relationship and it was clear to me how absolutely in love they were with each other. I don't remember what prompted me to do it, I think it might have been their wedding anniversary, but I took their hands and recited Jodie Whittaker's speech about love from Demons of the Punjab. They both started to cry and hugged me.

The other was a little girl who approached me at Chicago TARDIS. and asked for my autograph. I said "You know I'm not Jodie Whittaker." She smiled at me and said "I know." It was so humbling and sweet.

IF YOU WERE TO INTRODUCE SOMEONE ELSE TO THE DOCTOR WHO SERIES, WHAT EPISODE/STORY WOULD YOU TELL THEM TO START WITH AND WHY?

I say you can go one of two ways with this one:

(1) Series 1, Episode 1, "Rose." Simply put, it's a perfect introduction to the show and you NEVER skip Nine.
(2) Season 1, Episode 1, "An Unearthly Child." Go back to the very start. Yes, it will take a good long while, but if you wanna start at the beginning, start at the beginning.

ERIC HILDEMAN

WHAT WAS THE FIRST EPISODE/STORY OF DOCTOR WHO THAT YOU SAW?

I'm not sure which episode was exactly my first. I want to say it was "Robot," the first Tom Baker adventure. But really, it may have been something from the Jon Pertwee era. Back then (and here we're talking about 1984 or so), WMVS would regularly cycle through Jon Pertwee and Tom Baker episodes, and would start over when the episodes ran out. Somewhere along this non-stop cycle was when I jumped on board. It was an obscure thing and seemed to be all mine. Later I learned there were various other classmates of mine who were into the show as well.

TELL US HOW YOU THEN BECAME A FAN OF THE SHOW.

I largely became hooked when Tom Baker's humor shone through. *Doctor Who* was particularly witty back then, and although the special effects were laughable, I found the storylines to be fun. Baker's personality behind the Doctor was infectious. The character of Sarah Jane Smith was captivating, as were the various other companions who came afterward. I found myself watching *Doctor Who* whenever I spotted it on TV listings in the local paper, and followed Tom Baker into the Peter Davison era, the Colin Baker era, and even a little bit of the Sylvester McCoy era.

TELL US YOUR FAVORITE MOMENT IN YOUR DOCTOR WHO FANDOM EXPERIENCE.

There are so many. But ultimately, I'd have to say my favorite moment was when Romana regenerated, and Lalla Ward became the new actress portraying her. We got a glimpse of her in the "Key to Time" series, and fortunately she stuck around. She was stunning! And the bit about female Time Lords being able to choose their own shape was lighthearted and fun. (I later learned that the great Douglas Adams had a hand in that.) I fell in love with Romana at that moment and have remained a fan of Lalla Ward ever since.

IF YOU WERE TO INTRODUCE SOMEONE ELSE TO THE DOCTOR WHO SERIES, WHAT EPISODE/STORY WOULD YOU TELL THEM TO START WITH AND WHY?

I already did this with a friend of mine. She'd gotten me into various things, from comic books to *Buffy the Vampire Slayer*, but had only heard about *Doctor Who*, and was curious. I procured the episode "Robot" (I think via Netflix, back when they only sent DVDs through the mail) and we watched it together, beginning with Tom Baker. I figured bringing people along the same path I took to fandom was a tried-and-true method. Well, I was right. She remains a Whovian to this day.

STEVEN WARREN HILL

WHAT WAS THE FIRST EPISODE/STORY OF DOCTOR WHO THAT YOU SAW?

The truth is, I can't be certain. I know it was in 1975, on WTTW-11 in Chicago. Since we know what episodes aired thanks to the website broaDWcast.org (which collects *Doctor Who* airdate information globally), I have narrowed it down to the most likely possibility, which is "The Sea Devils", Episode One, on Monday, 17 November 1975. (It may have been a different part of "The Sea Devils"; in other words, I may have discovered the show in mid-story. That's something I may never know.) I watched it faithfully from that point until Monday, 12 January 1976, after which WTTW moved the airtime from weeknights at 6:30PM, which was an acceptable time for 9-year-old me, to weeknights at 10:00PM, which was past my bedtime. The bedtime rule took *Doctor Who* away from me and there was nothing I could do about it, otherwise I would have seen stories such as "Doctor Who and the Silurians" and "The Ambassadors of Death" in their original color. I didn't see any *Doctor Who* again until Monday, 24 July 1978, when WPTV in West Palm Beach, Florida aired a 'test' of "The Hand of Fear" (the omnibus edit, which means all four parts edited together) in a two-hour prime time slot. I was privileged to already know what *Doctor Who* was, but this was nevertheless the first time I saw Tom Baker as the Doctor, and I believe my memory of the show had faded enough in the two and a half years I hadn't seen it. I failed to realize I was seeing a different actor! (I had no idea whatsoever of regeneration.) Miami public television station (WPBT) began airing episodic *Doctor Who* starting with "Robot" on Monday, 07 May 1979, and I was already a veteran devoted fan.

For a number of years in the mid-1980s, I was an active member of the *Doctor Who* special interest group on CompuServe, and later participated somewhat in rec.arts.drwho on Usenet and on some mailing lists. When the World Wide

Web was introduced, I created a popular website called the Doctor Who Image Archive, which still exists but hasn't been active for years. I became a moderator, then an administrator, and finally the chief administrator of Shaun Lyon's Outpost Gallifrey *Doctor Who* forum, and when he shut down that forum, I created Gallifrey Base, still popular today with thousands of active members. I led a group of writers on a mission to create the ultimate history of *Doctor Who* in the USA, which was published as *Red White and Who: The Story of Doctor Who in America* in 2017, and have been involved as a staff member in conventions in the Chicago area since 1990; I am currently the program director for Chicago TARDIS.

TELL US HOW YOU THEN BECAME A FAN OF THE SHOW.

Although my previous answer does explain it, I want to go a bit further, because although I considered myself a very devoted fan of *Doctor Who* already by 1976, it was mostly 'solo' – I didn't have any collective fandom experiences until many years later (except for getting a few school friends to watch the show in 1975/76 and then play 'Doctor Who' on the playground at recess). When I started my junior year of high school in autumn 1982, I made some friends who were *Doctor Who* fans, and I remember circulating a questionnaire among them after Peter Davison's debut in "Castrovalva" first aired on WTTW Chicago on Sunday, 24 April 1983, to see what they all thought of the new Doctor (some liked him, some didn't). In July 1983, I attended my first *Doctor Who* convention, with Tom Baker being the guest. I had just turned seventeen. So now I was dipping my toes into the wider world of fandom, and I continued to attend some conventions (usually with a friend), until traveling to one in St Louis in 1986 and meeting a fan club there that I ended up joining and taking an active role in – they were called The Federation. That was me going from the shallow end of the pool to the deep end, and I've been heavily involved in *Doctor Who* fandom ever since.

TELL US YOUR FAVORITE MOMENT IN YOUR DOCTOR

WHO FANDOM EXPERIENCE.

I've got so many great memories, having been in fandom for such a long time, so I'm going to pick an outstanding moment that is still quite recent (at the time I'm writing this, of course). On Saturday, 25 November 2023, as emcee of the Chicago TARDIS *Doctor Who* convention, I had the overwhelming (and very emotional) privilege of introducing director Rachel Talalay to a roaring crowd just before and just after we screened her episode "The Star Beast," which had premiered earlier that day in the UK. Being there in that moment was unforgettable.

IF YOU WERE TO INTRODUCE SOMEONE ELSE TO THE DOCTOR WHO SERIES, WHAT EPISODE/STORY WOULD YOU TELL THEM TO START WITH AND WHY?

My answer to this question changes with the times, although I always give two answers. One of them is a constant: "An Unearthly Child," the very first 25-minute episode from Saturday, 23 November 1963. It's one of the best and most intriguing pieces of television ever made, and it's only fitting that a potential new fan should take 25 minutes of their time to see how it all started for the entire world. My second answer has changed many times, and currently is probably overdue for another change, since it's now 14 years old! "The Eleventh Hour" is hard to beat for an introductory story with a Doctor that seems effortlessly irresistible from the moment he first appears, and a supporting cast that carries a lot of recognition and appeal that arguably started right here.

EDWARD HOCHMAN

WHAT WAS THE FIRST EPISODE/STORY OF DOCTOR WHO THAT YOU SAW?

"The Sontaran Experiment."

TELL US HOW YOU THEN BECAME A FAN OF THE SHOW.

I was a personal friend of Howard Weintrob at the time, and he would stay home Saturday evenings so that he could see *Doctor Who*. I asked him what *Doctor Who* was. He had a problem explaining it, and said you'll have to see it. I did, and it was okay, so I asked him for the background story behind it. He didn't know, but it made me remember going to the TV set years ago when I was young (maybe ten years old) and I turned on the channel early in the morning. I saw a clip of *Doctor Who* at that time and turned it off as it didn't interest me. But something told me to go to the bookstore. I started to buy the Target books of every *Doctor Who* episode and I found myself hooked. All I had to do was wait to see it on TV.

TELL US YOUR FAVORITE MOMENT IN YOUR DOCTOR WHO FANDOM EXPERIENCE.

Seeing John Levine at one of the first Milwaukee Time Lord meetings. He came there as Sergeant Benton. Humorously, one of our members didn't recognize him at first and was going to throw him out.

IF YOU WERE TO INTRODUCE SOMEONE ELSE TO THE DOCTOR WHO SERIES, WHAT EPISODE/STORY WOULD YOU TELL THEM TO START WITH AND WHY?

I started with the classic series, so some key episodes. Maybe have someone start with the first and last episode of Number One, or the first episode of the Second Doctor and maybe the last two episodes of the Second Doctor, and so on.

RANDY HOLNDONER

WHAT WAS THE FIRST EPISODE/STORY OF DOCTOR WHO THAT YOU SAW?

My first episode I can remember seeing was "The Androids of Tara", probably back in 1981, on WTTW-11 in Chicago.

TELL US HOW YOU THEN BECAME A FAN OF THE SHOW.

The show was nothing like I had ever seen before. I obviously loved science fiction at the time as *Star Wars* was huge. But that episode had me glued, seeing androids looking human, (nothing compared to today's standards), but at the time it had me mesmerized. As did Tom Baker (still my favorite Doctor) commanding every scene, having my full attention, and politely offering Jelly Babies! And a robotic dog?!? I'm in!!!

How the show was broadcast brought a different feeling to the screen that made it unique as if it was live. As a kid, I really enjoyed the episodes having the cliffhanger serial ending of "what happens next" and having to wait until next week to find out.

The episodes were broadcast on PBS in Chicago on Sunday nights at 11:00PM, which was WAY past my bedtime, but I would watch it with my older sister and occasionally get scolded by my parents for being up too late on a school night (but it was worth it).

I do have to admit that when Tom Baker regenerated, I did not accept it well at all. I was still a fan of the show, but it really upset me that someone else was taking the reins. It was silly, I know, but I was young, and because of it, I would not follow the show as much (no offense to Peter Davison). I discussed the change with my sister, but we both really enjoyed Baker. Once she stopped watching it, I lost my resource and urge for *Doctor Who*. I would still watch it on occasion and see others as the Doctor, including episodes from William Hartnell's era, which made me even more confused. Black and white episodes? From how long ago? And this is the Doctor? How many of him were there? What was happening? There was no internet back then and *Doctor Who* really seemed to be a cult following at the time in Chicago as hardly any of my friends watched the show let alone heard of it. So, finding out anything about the show was very limited for me. There was a long pause before I'd have someone to bring me back to where we are today.

TELL US YOUR FAVORITE MOMENT IN YOUR DOCTOR WHO FANDOM EXPERIENCE.

In 2017, my daughter came home from school saying that her science teacher had her watch a science fiction show during class. Yep, it was *Doctor Who*! Instantly, my childhood came back in a flash. I asked her if the Doctor wore a long multi-colored scarf, but she said no. It didn't surprise me, but it was worth a shot, right?

I vaguely remember hearing that the show was rebooted, but never really thought about it as college, work, and family kept me busy. But I was interested and so were the rest of the family, so we watched the episode. It was "Blink." This was my family's 'Big Bang' entrance into the *Doctor Who* Universe.

From watching that episode, we all decided to start with the "Rose" episode and watch an episode each night as a family. We have stayed loyal and up to date throughout the reboot series and have since gone to conventions wearing cosplay of our favorite characters from the series. As close as my family is, everyone does their own thing, yet *Doctor Who* always brings us together and is the one thing we can always agree upon to be involved in with no arguments other than what episode to watch and who was their favorite Doctor.

I decided to travel back to the beginning, starting with a young girl named Susan and her grandfather and his blue box. As an adult, it gave me an entirely new appreciation for the show now that the episodes, well most of them, were available now to watch at my leisure. The *Doctor Who* universe has also allowed me to meet fantastic new friends and collect over 1600 magazines, books, and comics of *Doctor Who* memorabilia. Two of my good friends recently became the new Guiness Book of World Records holders for the largest *Doctor Who* Memorabilia Collection. I take partial blame as our collections started when we began collecting *Doctor Who* books together. Oops!

IF YOU WERE TO INTRODUCE SOMEONE ELSE TO THE DOCTOR WHO SERIES, WHAT EPISODE/STORY WOULD YOU TELL THEM TO START WITH AND WHY?

It's hard to pick a single episode for someone new starting in the series considering there are over 60 years of stories to pick from. Both series have their own audience that it caters to.

The argument is do you introduce a newcomer to what they don't know pertaining to who/what the Doctor has faced in the past or do you risk them finding it hard to swallow the low budget effects that the Classic series started with? I still struggle with the rest of my family with the latter. As my son likes to remind me, "Those were made in the 1900s." Ouch!

I think I would have to start someone new with where my family began after their first episode – "Rose." The story piles 25 years into one crash course episode that provides the newcomer with enough to get them started on who the Doctor is while you and his new companion are lured in together for more adventures. It leaves more questions than answers, which you and Rose learn along the way. I think it provides a perfect beginning for a wild, timey-wimey ride with a Time Lord and his blue box.

KERRY HURD

WHAT WAS THE FIRST EPISODE/STORY OF DOCTOR WHO THAT YOU SAW?

Part Three of "The Talons of Weng-Chiang."

TELL US HOW YOU THEN BECAME A FAN OF THE SHOW.

In the late 1970s, my sister and I would regularly watch *Wild, Wild World of Animals* on WGBH, Channel 2 out of Boston. We sometimes would turn the TV on early, and we would catch the ending of a *Doctor Who* episode, which was being shown in episode format from 7:00PM to 7:30PM. Some of the cliffhangers looked kind of interesting, but when we saw Leela being eaten by a giant rat at the end of Part Three of "The Talons of Weng-Chiang," that was it – we were hooked. We watched it constantly after that, and have never looked back.

TELL US YOUR FAVORITE MOMENT IN YOUR DOCTOR WHO FANDOM EXPERIENCE.

While a member of a local *Doctor Who* fan club, I met my future wife. She became president of the club and we became better and better friends, volunteering for New Hampshire Public Television, and local conventions. We traveled together to *Doctor Who* conventions in New Hampshire, Massachusetts, Connecticut, and Pennsylvania. We have now been married over 37 years and still go to the Gallifrey One convention each February in California.

IF YOU WERE TO INTRODUCE SOMEONE ELSE TO THE DOCTOR WHO SERIES, WHAT EPISODE/STORY WOULD YOU TELL THEM TO START WITH AND WHY?

The Fourth Doctor adventure "The Ark in Space." It is a very well written story, with great characters and suspense, with some quirkiness.

NANCY HUTCHINS

WHAT WAS THE FIRST EPISODE/STORY OF DOCTOR WHO THAT YOU SAW?

"An Unearthly Child."

TELL US HOW YOU THEN BECAME A FAN OF THE SHOW.

I was working at college over the summer of 1988, and a local PBS station was airing the William Hartnell episodes. A friend came into the kitchen where I was having dinner, very excited because the "very first ever *Doctor Who* episode!" was going to be shown. I was only vaguely familiar with the show from when my younger brother had watched Tom Baker episodes, and I had no idea the character regenerated when the actor in the role changed. Curious, I watched the episode with her. The PBS station showed each 30-minute segment on weeknights, and it was easy to get into the habit of watching the episode while eating dinner. Another friend staying on campus that summer had a TV/VCR and a stack of VHS tapes with *Doctor Who* episodes she'd recorded. By the end of that summer, I was a thoroughly converted Whovian.

TELL US YOUR FAVORITE MOMENT IN YOUR DOCTOR WHO FANDOM EXPERIENCE.

I was having a birthday party at my house in 2008, when the fourth season was running. A friend who attended the party was able to download a copy of that week's episode, and we all piled into the living room to watch. The episode was "Turn Left," a pretty significant story that season. We were all screaming by the time it was over.

IF YOU WERE TO INTRODUCE SOMEONE ELSE TO THE DOCTOR WHO SERIES, WHAT EPISODE/STORY WOULD YOU TELL THEM TO START WITH AND WHY?

I would suggest starting with "Rose," because a lot of people are likely to find the style of the original series too outdated.

PAULETTE IMHOFF

WHAT WAS THE FIRST EPISODE/STORY OF DOCTOR WHO THAT YOU SAW?

"Robot" with Tom Baker.

TELL US HOW YOU THEN BECAME A FAN OF THE SHOW.

It was my sister's fault. She had a group of people over and told me there was a show on Public TV that I would really like. At noon, she turned it on, but there was so much people noise I couldn't hear the TV. I went home and tried to find it – for six months. Our Madison PBS station did not air the Doctor 'til later that year, and then at midnight in hour and a half show formats, instead of the episodic format Diane was watching.

TELL US YOUR FAVORITE MOMENT IN YOUR DOCTOR WHO FANDOM EXPERIENCE.

When I turned around and my 3-year-old son peeked around the hallway corner and said "I'm not watching," but he was. By then, *Doctor Who* had switched to daytime hours.

IF YOU WERE TO INTRODUCE SOMEONE ELSE TO THE DOCTOR WHO SERIES, WHAT EPISODE/STORY WOULD YOU TELL THEM TO START WITH AND WHY?

"Rose," the first Christopher Eccleston episode, because the opening Doctor's words are an enthusiastic "Run!" It immediately gets your attention.

GAYLAND JENKINS

WHAT WAS THE FIRST EPISODE/STORY OF DOCTOR WHO THAT YOU SAW?

"Robot."

TELL US HOW YOU THEN BECAME A FAN OF THE SHOW.

A friend in third grade introduced me to the show, went home and saw "Robot" on PBS.

TELL US YOUR FAVORITE MOMENT IN YOUR DOCTOR WHO FANDOM EXPERIENCE.

Meeting Tom Baker. He was everything I expected he would be. I also enjoy people asking me for a picture of my Fourth Doctor cosplay.

IF YOU WERE TO INTRODUCE SOMEONE ELSE TO THE DOCTOR WHO SERIES, WHAT EPISODE/STORY WOULD YOU TELL THEM TO START WITH AND WHY?

"Vincent and the Doctor" for younger potential fans and "Robot" or "Genesis of the Daleks" for older ones.

SIMORGH JOURABCHI

WHAT WAS THE FIRST EPISODE/STORY OF DOCTOR WHO THAT YOU SAW?

The first one I remember is "Robot." I had been Who-curious since seeing a bit of one of Pertwee's stories so I lobbied to get my bedtime changed so I could stay up to watch. I was about six at the time.

TELL US HOW YOU THEN BECAME A FAN OF THE SHOW.

It was love at first sight. Tom Baker moved into my heart to live rent free and I was a FAN. Being six, my main experience of fandom was making little stories of what the Doctor and Sarah Jane were doing. As I got older, I found other fans, like the Paul McGann Estrogen Brigade (PMEB) fan club and the Gallifrey One scene, and I've never been happier.

TELL US YOUR FAVORITE MOMENT IN YOUR DOCTOR WHO FANDOM EXPERIENCE.

Probably meeting Jodie Whittaker, the first female Doctor! Growing up, you play Doctor and Companion at home, and I always, ALWAYS got told "no" when I asked if I could be the Doctor this time, because "the Doctor is a boy." Jodie changed that for every little girl who falls in love with the Doctor.

IF YOU WERE TO INTRODUCE SOMEONE ELSE TO THE DOCTOR WHO SERIES, WHAT EPISODE/STORY WOULD YOU TELL THEM TO START WITH AND WHY?

Honestly, I love "The Woman Who Fell To Earth" as a jumping on point, but one time I played "The Pilot" for a pal and she was instantly smitten with Capaldi, so, your mileage may vary.

AUDREY KANTHACK

WHAT WAS THE FIRST EPISODE/STORY OF DOCTOR WHO THAT YOU SAW?

    The first episode of *Doctor Who* I saw was "The Unicorn and The Wasp" on PBS when I was in elementary school. David Tennant was playing the Doctor at the time, and I was taken aback by the show's special effects and Tennant's quirky, humorous personality. My family and I were hooked on the show after that and watching *Doctor Who* together became a regular weekend tradition for me, my dad, and my sister.

TELL US HOW YOU THEN BECAME A FAN OF THE SHOW.

    I became an even bigger fan of *Doctor Who* when Matt Smith took on the role of the Doctor. His kind demeanor, mixed with his charisma and charm, kept me invested in the series. Watching the show became a bonding experience for my family—one of the first shows we all consistently enjoyed together. Every new episode brought so much excitement, and it's a family tradition that holds fond memories for me. I also was a big fan of the YouTube Channel *charlieissocoollike* when I was in middle school. She is a big fan of the show, and I remember she would do weekly video recaps of the most recent episodes. It was like having another friend to talk about the show with, which added to my *Doctor Who* fan experience.

TELL US YOUR FAVORITE MOMENT IN YOUR DOCTOR WHO FANDOM EXPERIENCE.

    My favorite moment as a *Doctor Who* fan was when I was watching the episode "Night Terrors." It was during the fall and the creepy atmosphere of the episode made my sister and I so scared. We couldn't stop watching and we bonded over our fear that we had during the episode. That blend of suspense, excitement, and fun really captures what I love about the show.

IF YOU WERE TO INTRODUCE SOMEONE ELSE TO THE DOCTOR WHO SERIES, WHAT EPISODE/STORY WOULD YOU TELL THEM TO START WITH AND WHY?

If I were to introduce someone to *Doctor Who*, I would start with "The Eleventh Hour." It's the perfect starting point to the show because it introduces a new Doctor, played by Matt Smith, in a way that doesn't require prior knowledge of the series. It also introduces us to Amy, who I absolutely adore, and really showcases the bond that her and the Doctor will have moving forward.

ASSAD KHAISHGI

WHAT WAS THE FIRST EPISODE/STORY OF DOCTOR WHO THAT YOU SAW?

The first episode I saw was "The Curse of Peladon." I was visiting the UK in 1982 and it was part of a special season of reruns called Doctor Who and the Monsters. This included "Curse," "Genesis of the Daleks," and "Earthshock." I still have pretty vivid memories of some scenes from the stories, including the Dalek on top of the trench and the Cybermen marching through the freighter. Of course, rewatching those scenes recently shows that the memory was far superior to the reality. I didn't actually know what *Doctor Who* was at that time. It was only later that I realized what I had seen, once I was already an established fan!

TELL US HOW YOU THEN BECAME A FAN OF THE SHOW.

I do not actually think that watching that season made me a fan per se. But I very definitely know that when I read the novel of "The Keeper of Traken" (from the British Council library in Karachi) was when I first became familiar with *Doctor Who* as a concept. Terrance Dicks provided more than enough backstory for me to comfortably understand what was going on. Living in Pakistan, I did not really have much access to the show itself, so my fandom really developed through the books. Sometimes relatives bought them in the UK and sent them to me and sometimes the books appeared in the local bookshops in Karachi. As well as copies of *Starlog* and *Starburst* that came through the scrap paper market. I did have a small collection of video tapes that I watched repeatedly. The Peter Davison episodes were being shown in Dubai so I ended up with Parts One through Three of "Castrovalva," most of Part One of "Arc of Infinity" and Part Three of "Resurrection of the Daleks." My dad had picked up the video cassette of "The Caves of Androzani" when he was visiting the UK once. And a bootleg copy of "The Five Doctors" actually turned up in a local video store in Karachi! When my uncle was training in the UK, he was able to record most of the Sylvester McCoy run, so in terms of viewed episodes, he was definitely 'my' Doctor! Needless to say, things are much easier now being in the US and I have a complete DVD collection (now supplemented by a Blu-ray collection)!

TELL US YOUR FAVORITE MOMENT IN YOUR DOCTOR WHO FANDOM EXPERIENCE.

There's so many good memories, but I'll pick two. Chicago TARDIS 2012 was my first major convention. And I arrived at the welcome dinner at the same time as Sylvester McCoy! He was the first Doctor that I had actually seen a lot of stories of, thanks to my uncle working in the UK and sending back video tapes of most of his stories. So standing next to him seemed surreal. My second favorite memory was when I developed a costume of a Pakistani TARDIS and brought it to a later Chicago TARDIS. I was pretty nervous about it, but the reception was nothing but welcome and appreciation! It was wonderful to see the acceptance from my fellow fans, to explain the costume, and to show how the text on the costume is a translation of the wording on the TARDIS. It's also great to show it to South Asian guests from the show, who get a kick out of it (Sacha Dhawan was especially excited by it!). I've expanded to making ribbons and pins in Urdu, all of Who related stuff, natch, and people enjoy those too!

IF YOU WERE TO INTRODUCE SOMEONE ELSE TO THE DOCTOR WHO SERIES, WHAT EPISODE/STORY WOULD YOU TELL THEM TO START WITH AND WHY?

The easiest answer is "Blink." But I think I would probably recommend either "Spearhead from Space" or "The Eleventh Hour." Regeneration stories usually provide enough background for people to be able to get the hang of what is going on, and both of those are really good regeneration stories... excellently written and moving along at a cracking pace. Though given that Series 7 is my favourite season of all of Who of all time, I'm a bit biased there.

ALEX KINGDOM

WHAT WAS THE FIRST EPISODE/STORY OF DOCTOR WHO THAT YOU SAW?

The first *Doctor Who* episode I watched in full was "The Bells of Saint John" which I know might seem like a strange one. Me and my friends were playing an online game that evening and then they all left at the same time to watch the episode so I thought "Well, I may as well go and watch it too so I know when to go back online." After that, I was hooked. I also have vague memories of seeing "Planet of the Ood" and "The Unicorn and the Wasp," but I was too scared of the giant wasp to want to continue watching and it must have taken me seven years to get over it.

TELL US HOW YOU THEN BECAME A FAN OF THE SHOW.

It is tough to remember when I became a big fan of the show. For the rest of that series, I would watch and discuss with my friends, and I certainly enjoyed the episodes, but I wouldn't say I was huge on it. I do remember not enjoying the 50th Anniversary episode because of all of the callbacks and my twelve-year-old self at the time had no idea what was going on (I now love the episode.) It would have been the gap between the 50th and Christmas special that I began to go back and watch the rest of the new series and especially falling in love with the Eleventh Doctor, who is still my favourite now. Once I went to college in 2017, I was able to make more friends and chat about the show more and from then on I would say I was watching/talking about *Doctor Who* every day. I wouldn't say I really joined the fandom until the pandemic started though. As we all were finding things to do in the lockdown, I would join quizzes and zooms with fans (who are still close fans today). From there I would interact with more fans on social media, and once the world opened up, I started going to *Doctor Who* events. I have to say I found the fandom really open and friendly for the most part.

I know there are pockets of social media that aren't as friendly and a bit more volatile but I try not to get involved with that side of things. I have been incredibly lucky to have been a part of the fandom as it has not only given me work opportunities, but more importantly, it has given me friends for life, which is something I will be forever grateful to the show for.

TELL US YOUR FAVORITE MOMENT IN YOUR DOCTOR WHO FANDOM EXPERIENCE.

My favourite moment of being in this fandom has to be when I got the opportunity to go to the Gallifrey One convention in Los Angeles in the USA. For a bit of context, I am a wheelchair user who lives in the UK. To go on big trips like that, it takes a big effort and a lot of research and, on top of that, more money to make sure travel, accommodation and other things are accessible. So my friends set up a GoFundMe to help get me there which, even now, I am forever indebted to anybody that helped out. Luckily, the funds raised exceeded the goal and I was lucky enough to go. Getting the opportunity to hang out with people I am lucky enough to call my friends and just have a stress-free week (for the most part) was an experience I'll never forget and something I hold close to my heart. For those who haven't gone to Gallifrey One I would highly recommend it. It's like a long weekend full of *Doctor Who* where you get to meet people from all backgrounds and from different countries. But the one thing you all have in common is the show. If you get the chance to go, please do.

IF YOU WERE TO INTRODUCE SOMEONE ELSE TO THE DOCTOR WHO SERIES, WHAT EPISODE/STORY WOULD YOU TELL THEM TO START WITH AND WHY?

If I was to introduce someone to the show, I have to say I would show them "The Eleventh Hour." All Matt Smith bias aside, I do genuinely think this is a fantastic jumping on point for new viewers. Although it has small references to what had come before, it is not necessary to have seen the previous era to understand what is happening in this story. I also think Moffat's writing is a lot more breakneck than Russell T Davies'. From the first five seconds, we already have the Doctor struggling to pilot the TARDIS, which is a striking visual and immediately hooks you in. Apart from that, the chemistry between Matt Smith and Karen Gillian is fantastic straight away and you immediately get the dynamic between the two, which is a lot of fun. The pacing is also terrific, this 60-minute episode feels shorter than a regular 45-minute episode. Although you could say the villain is a little bit generic, I think Prisoner Zero works as a basic villain to set up the status quo going forward. I also believe that Series 5 is the strongest of the whole show, so if you want to get new viewers to watch why not start with the strongest run of episodes.

CHRIS KOCHER

WHAT WAS THE FIRST EPISODE/STORY OF DOCTOR WHO THAT YOU SAW?

"Warriors' Gate."

TELL US HOW YOU THEN BECAME A FAN OF THE SHOW.

I grew up a sci-fi and fantasy fan in the early 1980s, especially *Star Trek* and a show called *Voyagers!*, which featured two time travelers who journeyed through history to put things right when they went off course.

In the mid-1980s, my local public television station (WVIA in Scranton, Pa.) showed one *Doctor Who* episode every weeknight at 7:30PM. A friend at school talked about the show all the time, but I'd never really sat down and watched it, so one day (I can't remember why!) I tuned in to "Warriors' Gate." Man, what a confusing story to start with! It was unlike anything I'd seen before, and that intrigued me. Somehow, I missed "The Keeper of Traken," so I found a lot of "Logopolis" to be puzzling too. (Is that dude all in white the Master? Who is this Nyssa person? And are they really holding the universe together using the power of math?

Knowing nothing about *Doctor Who*, the regeneration at the end of "Logopolis" came as a shock – but again, it was intriguing enough that I kept watching through the Peter Davison era and beyond.

I've been a fan ever since, and that's led to some unexpected adventures: Editing a fiction fanzine (*Ninth Aspect*), writing for other fanzines and books (including the *Outside In* series and *A World of Demons: The Villains of Doctor Who*), attending the 50th Anniversary celebration in London (with that *Doctor Who*-loving classmate from way back when!), and becoming a regular panelist at the L.I. Who convention on Long Island. But as the cliché goes, fandom is also the friends we make along the way – and there have been many.

TELL US YOUR FAVORITE MOMENT IN YOUR DOCTOR WHO FANDOM EXPERIENCE.

There have been many great moments, but to pick one... I would say interviewing the Eighth Doctor himself, Paul McGann, for a virtual sci-fi convention that I helped to organize during the COVID-19 lockdown in 2020. He's been a favorite since the 1996 TV movie, and his numerous audio adventures from Big Finish only make me love him more.

IF YOU WERE TO INTRODUCE SOMEONE ELSE TO THE DOCTOR WHO SERIES, WHAT EPISODE/STORY WOULD YOU TELL THEM TO START WITH AND WHY?

It's probably the easiest answer, but "Rose" from the 2005 revival remains the best introduction – then work your way forward from there. Once you've finished that, pick through the best stories of the classic series, and don't be afraid to jump around to different eras and Doctors. If you're still enjoying it and have a sense of humor about some of *Doctor Who*'s dodgier moments, watch the rest of the original run. From there, try out the novels or the Big Finish audio adventures.

What makes *Doctor Who* the greatest television format ever: It can go anywhere and do anything – past, present, future, alternative and beyond. That means there are stories appealing to everyone. If this setup or plot isn't your cup of tea, just wait for the next one. You don't need to like all of it – and you'll never consume all of it – but that's not the point of the exercise. It's a big universe out there, and sometimes I envy the new fans who are just getting started.

TERI KOEBEL

WHAT WAS THE FIRST EPISODE/STORY OF DOCTOR WHO THAT YOU SAW?

"Rose."

TELL US HOW YOU THEN BECAME A FAN OF THE SHOW.

My parents watched *Doctor Who* when it was on PBS. When the show came back in 2005, it was not a question if I would watch it. They sat me down and said, "You'll like this." They were right.

TELL US YOUR FAVORITE MOMENT IN YOUR DOCTOR WHO FANDOM EXPERIENCE.

In 2009, about a week before the Midwest convention Chicago TARDIS, I had a fantastic idea. I would make a dress that looked like the TARDIS to wear to the con. Now, in the year of our Time Lord 2025, that might not seem like a novel idea, but believe it or not, I was the first person to create a TARDIS dress.

It was a modest creation, to be sure. It was a sweater dress from American Eagle with the "Police Public Call Box" sign and the "Pull To Open" panel printed on computer paper and safety pinned to it. The headband I made for the light was an old oversized Christmas light, a broken cupcake decorator stand, and some wooden dowels. I was thirteen, and this was one of my very first cosplays.

I was overwhelmed by the costume's great reception, but there was one person's reaction to that first TARDIS dress that I will never forget. You see, that year Phil Collinson, the executive producer of the show at the time, was a guest. I went to get my picture with him and he loved my costume so much that he asked to get a picture of us together for himself. I was flattered and didn't think much of it until I got my picture signed.

He asked me where he could find his photo. I told him and that was that. Or so I thought...

Cut to closing ceremonies on Sunday. I was seated in the front row as we said our goodbyes to the guests. Phil came out, and I noticed right away that he was holding something, a piece of paper and a sharpie. Then in front of the whole of Chicago TARDIS he said, "Is the girl who dressed like the TARDIS here?"

I nervously raised my hand, and he came to the edge of the stage and asked if I would sign the photo of us. I did, of course. I think I wrote something like "Thanks for coming!" It's a moment that I will never forget.

As the years went on, I had many versions of my TARDIS dress, eventually with fewer safety pins. It would become a staple of the *Doctor Who* cosplay world. It would become a Simplicity pattern and a dress at Hot Topic. I remember very clearly when the Hot Topic dress went on sale. I remember feeling both proud and a little... territorial, maybe? That was my idea in stores and on people around the world. I had somehow, by pure luck, safety pins, and hot glue, made something that changed the look of our fandom going forward.

It is a moment in my life I look back on fondly. It gave me stories I will always remember and friends that will last a lifetime. How many people can say that they got Alex Kingston to say that she'd been inside them? Not many, I'd wager, because I'm pretty sure she regretted it the moment she said it to me.

IF YOU WERE TO INTRODUCE SOMEONE ELSE TO THE DOCTOR WHO SERIES, WHAT EPISODE/STORY WOULD YOU TELL THEM TO START WITH AND WHY?

It depends on the person. If they have the time and the patience I would suggest "Rose" or "Blink." I like to show people "The Five Doctors" after they experience their first regeneration. But if they are new and unsure I think "Rogue" is a really good standalone story from the newest season.

BETH KORMAN

WHAT WAS THE FIRST EPISODE/STORY OF DOCTOR WHO THAT YOU SAW?

I have been trying to think of the actual episode that grabbed my attention, but, in all honesty, I just remember flipping channels and the local Milwaukee PBS station was showing its first round of Tom Baker episodes. We were hooked. I especially loved anything with Daleks, Cyberman, the Master, or the Brigadier. One of my favorite episode moments is when Tom Baker asks one of the Mummy robots guarding a room in "The Pyramids of Mars," "What will the other robot tell me is the exit?" It was brilliant because the lying robot would lie about what the truthful robot would say. The truthful robot would truthfully tell you what the lying robot would say. It was the little details in the scripts and its humor, intellect, complex scripts, and acting talents that really attracted viewers to the original series.

TELL US HOW YOU THEN BECAME A FAN OF THE SHOW.

My brother and I loved the show. In 1991 we were both studying abroad in London. We heard about a *Doctor Who* convention called Space Mountain that was happening in Shepperton, England. For three days, we took the train back and forth from London to Shepperton. By the third day, we had made tons of friends.

The best story I have from that event is that the convention hosted a trivia contest. Fortunately for my brother and I, we had some people on our team that could name every monster, planet, and story title. Each team was assigned an actor. We had Nicholas Courtney. Every time we got a question correct, our actor would move a few steps forward on a giant game board – it kind of resembled a Candy Land-type of board. (I wish I had photos.) Nick might have been a bit tipsy and stumbled off the board a few times! In the end, our team made it down to the two finalists. The two last teams had to do a relay race of sorts. We each had to act out a charades character. Fortunately, I had Tegan, so I made myself a plane, which was easily guessed. We had to knock down plates with a sponge, whistle with crackers in our mouths, and solve a jigsaw puzzle. Everyone except me seemed to have great difficulty with the puzzle (which I couldn't understand because the outside edges were round and the inside was the picture of a Triangle). I solved the puzzle in a few seconds. Nick Coutney went last. He had a lot of trouble with the puzzle. I hate to admit it, but I kept rotating the pieces with my fingers when no one noticed, so the round edges were on the outside. Finally, Nick saw it and clumped them together. We won a copy of an autographed Cyber script. It was all quite fun. Nicolas Courtney autographed my program book: "We Won!" He autographed my brother's book, "Like I said before, we won!" (My brother was not amused by that). My brother did, however, enjoy getting his copy of *Moon Boots and Dinner Suits* autographed by Jon Pertwee. Although Jon was not amused that my brother bought his copy from a London library rummage sale.

When next we saw Nicholas Courtney and Jon Pertwee at a Visions convention in Chicago, Mr. Courtney, saw us in the lobby, shouted and pointed, "We won!" We were quite surprised that he remembered us. Nick introduced us properly to his friend Jon, and from that point on we were buddies with them both. Jon told me a lovely story about how he was supposed to have the lead in the movie version of "A Funny Thing that Happened on the Way to the Forum." He told me that they replaced him with the larger name of Zero Mostel, but he was still paid well for the one-line smaller part he had instead. Although Jon Pertwee passed away shortly after, I believe that I saw Nicholas Courtney twice more at the Gallifrey One and Chicago TARDIS conventions. Each time I saw him, he pointed at me in a hallway and shouted, "We won!" Such a dear man. They both were.

It was also fun to be recognized by Richard Franklin and John Levene at those conventions. They both usually give me a big hug. As we often see the same actors and fan community at different conventions, it is like one big happy family. I remember hanging out in the hotel bar with Richard Franklin in Chicago and being invited to dinner with John Levine in L.A. The actors love to have fun with the fans. One actor in Chicago, who was in both *Star Wars* and *Doctor Who*, left a voice message on my brother's answering machine as a joke. He was so much fun! At the volunteer cast party, he told a bunch of us he would autograph *anything*. I jokingly gave him a tiny rubberband to autograph for my brother. My friend said "How about my butt?" He agreed to sign it. The two of them went out of the convention hall and came back giggling. We shall never know if it was signed.

It is really a nice feeling when the actors recognize the fans. Sophie "Ace" Aldred recognized me at the (Re) Generation Who convention and gave me a big hug. I was pleasantly surprised. The funny thing for me though, is an odd conversation I had in an elevator with Nicola Bryant about leggings. Somehow, she ended up being the first person that I told I was pregnant. It just slipped out in conversation. Oddly, Gene, who runs the Chicago TARDIS convention, was the second person to know. Eventually, I told my actual family.

Besides all these fan moments with the actors, the fans themselves are like a big family. One looks forward to seeing their convention friends every year. Even funnier, is when I moved to the Chicago area and went to a *Doctor Who* Fan club meeting. When I walked in the room, it was almost like being Norm on *Cheers*. People were like "Hey, we know you from Visions and Gallifrey One." How cool is that!

The show itself is great to watch, but I think that becoming a part of the fandom community and meeting the actors and other fans really solidified my love of the show.

TELL US YOUR FAVORITE MOMENT IN YOUR DOCTOR WHO FANDOM EXPERIENCE.

My brother and I had been attending the Gallifrey One convention since 1998 or 1999. Another great moment was when they did an amazing scavenger hunt for The Sixteen Swashbucklers of Gallifrey One event. Clues were given to locate a table area or convention staff member. Once we located them, they would present us with a question related to either *Doctor Who* or pirates. If we got the question correct, we got coins. If we got the answer wrong, we had to come back in two hours. It was really difficult for us because we didn't really know the staff at the time. I managed to make it to the finale first, and (with some help) won first prize! So, I won a free convention ticket for the next year. Someone won the second prize, then my brother and I went back at the very end before the Green Room closed so he could try to win third prize. But, he got the answer wrong. We were told to come back first thing in the morning and they would make sure he could try to answer the question. We were pretty excited and showed up really early. However, there had been some folks talking near the Green Room as we exited. It turns out, they had been waiting outside of the door to attempt third prize. So, when we came in the morning, we were standing in the hall waiting for a third prize attempt for nothing, as it had already been claimed. It was still tons of fun!

I also really enjoyed interviewing Patricia Quinn, most famous for her role as Magenta in *The Rocky Horror Picture Show* who also appeared in *Doctor Who*, for The Rogers Revue at the (Re) Generation Who convention. She was so much fun! All the fans were singing the Time Warp with her as she performed with some dancers dressed as belly dancing TARDISes.

IF YOU WERE TO INTRODUCE SOMEONE ELSE TO THE DOCTOR WHO SERIES, WHAT EPISODE/STORY WOULD YOU TELL THEM TO START WITH AND WHY?

I like to tell people that if they like old British comedies, and love sci-fi, they should start watching *Doctor Who* at Tom Baker, as most of the USA did. However, if special effects and newer more recent television is their preference, they should start at the reboot with Christopher Eccleston. Most fans have their own favorite Doctor or two that resonate more with them. So, although my two favorites are Tom Baker and David Tennant, I can understand why other fans have different favorites. I am quite fond of them all, really, for different reasons.

ELIJAH KRALING

WHAT WAS THE FIRST EPISODE/STORY OF DOCTOR WHO THAT YOU SAW?

The first episode I remember watching was "The Impossible Astronaut" on Netflix. The first episode on broadcast was "Journey to the Center of the TARDIS."

TELL US HOW YOU THEN BECAME A FAN OF THE SHOW.

I was in my junior high drama club and my friend kept going on about this show. So I checked it out. The thing that hooked me was the longevity of the show – it was coming up on its 50th Anniversary that year. Learning about the concept of regeneration and how the show changes but at its core is the same character in different iterations. During the build up to the 50th, I recall watching The Doctors Revisited on BBC America. They would follow up with a classic episode of *Doctor Who*. So, I got a little taste of each Doctor, while at the same time I was collecting the DVDs like The Beginnings boxset with "An Unearthly Child," "The Daleks," and "The Edge of Destruction." I also went back and started with Series 1 starring Eccleston and working my way up through Series 7 with Matt Smith.

TELL US YOUR FAVORITE MOMENT IN YOUR DOCTOR WHO FANDOM EXPERIENCE.

My favorite fandom experience was spending the 60th Anniversary of *Doctor Who* in the UK. I got to watch "The Daleks in Colour" on its broadcast on BBC Four while sitting in the hotel room with my pals Ivy and Kieran Highman (who was one of the colourists on it). He even uploaded the final edit from my apartment before we left for the UK from Minnesota! Also getting to watch "The Star Beast" live with friends in a private theater was a really cool memory. And my friend Reuben Herfinhahl offering to drive to the Beaulieu car museum to see the actual Whomobile and Bessie!

If I can add a bonus favorite moment, it was directing a theater stage adaptation of the *Doctor Who* story "Midnight" at my High School.

IF YOU WERE TO INTRODUCE SOMEONE ELSE TO THE DOCTOR WHO SERIES, WHAT EPISODE/STORY WOULD YOU TELL THEM TO START WITH AND WHY?

I would say start with "Rose," it's a great jumping on point. You are learning about the show and the character of the Doctor through the perspective of Rose. It doesn't lean on the lore of the series so much, which for a new fan they could find confusing at first.

DENNIS KYTASAARI

WHAT WAS THE FIRST EPISODE/STORY OF DOCTOR WHO THAT YOU SAW?

Part Two of "Genesis of the Daleks" on WTTW Channel 11 on Wednesday, 12 March 1980, somewhere in the middle of the airing.

TELL US HOW YOU THEN BECAME A FAN OF THE SHOW.

As a sci-fi fan, I saw Davros and quickly determined by the accents that the show was produced in England. As I was already a fan of Monty Python and other English TV programs, I added this to my viewing habits. The show moved to Sunday nights in the familiar movie format that following January, which made it easier to digest.

TELL US YOUR FAVORITE MOMENT IN YOUR DOCTOR WHO FANDOM EXPERIENCE.

Taking my love for Monty Python and *Doctor Who* and combining them with my friends in a performance of "The Six Doctors Lumberjack" in the costume contest at the TARDIS 21 convention in November of 1984.

IF YOU WERE TO INTRODUCE SOMEONE ELSE TO THE DOCTOR WHO SERIES, WHAT EPISODE/STORY WOULD YOU TELL THEM TO START WITH AND WHY?

For the classic series the best bet would be to start with the Fourth Doctor, Tom Baker, any story. His enigmatic charm should be able to hook them in. For those who like modern special effects, start with the new series (2005 and later) and start with the Ninth Doctor, Christopher Eccleston, from the beginning with "Rose." I would encourage them to embrace all of *Doctor Who*'s history from classic to new.

DANIEL LAVERY

WHAT WAS THE FIRST EPISODE/STORY OF DOCTOR WHO THAT YOU SAW?

My 'way in' is somewhat unusual. As a fan of *Blackadder* and *Mr Bean* I tuned into Comic Relief 1999 to watch Rowan Atkinson in "The Curse of Fatal Death!" About a month later, I was up one Sunday morning to watch this very strange man with big teeth and curls in "The Hand of Fear." Then I taped "The Deadly Assassin" and from there I was hooked. Before then, I knew what a Dalek was, and I recognised *Doctor Who* as Jon Pertwee.

TELL US HOW YOU THEN BECAME A FAN OF THE SHOW.

Things escalated quickly, thanks to the internet. I started buying *Doctor Who Magazine*, started a video collection, and continued watching the repeats. In October, my dad took me to my first convention where I met Sophie Aldred (who I recognised from *Words and Pictures*!) and Sylvester McCoy. I don't think I'd yet watched a Seventh Doctor story. I did buy my first copy of "The Five Doctors," which became an obsession, and a certain Jason Haigh-Ellery sold me "The Sirens of Time," the debut *Doctor Who* audio drama from Big Finish. I'm not sure I matched the right faces to the voices. During the Wilderness Years I became a huge Big Finish fan.

Over the years, I've attended many events, met so many people, and *Doctor Who* has opened many opportunities to me. I volunteer annually with the Whoovers in Derby, for Big Finish Day and Whooverville. In 2020, right before lockdown, I went to Los Angeles for the Gallifrey convention, so I got to explore Hollywood which I thought would never happen. Presently, I am a volunteer steward for the unofficial exhibition at Peterborough Museum.

TELL US YOUR FAVORITE MOMENT IN YOUR DOCTOR

WHO FANDOM EXPERIENCE.

At the Dimensions on Tyne convention in 2002, I got into the lift after a long day at the convention. Elisabeth Sladen was in there too. We went up to our floor. Elisabeth got out too. We walked along, said good night, and Lis stopped one door up. We were staying next door to Sarah Jane Smith. I was giddy with excitement. Elisabeth laughed, she was lovely.

IF YOU WERE TO INTRODUCE SOMEONE ELSE TO THE DOCTOR WHO SERIES, WHAT EPISODE/STORY WOULD YOU TELL THEM TO START WITH AND WHY?

If I were to introduce somebody to *Doctor Who*, I would pick "Remembrance of the Daleks." The Doctor is portrayed as a man with secrets, the Daleks are at war with each other, and being the end of Classic Who, the presentation is more action packed and modern.

TJ LUBINSKY

WHAT WAS THE FIRST EPISODE/STORY OF DOCTOR WHO THAT YOU SAW?

"The Ark In Space" end of Part One and Howard Da Silva preview teaser for Part Two seen in Florida on cable TV from WOR Channel 9 in New York.

TELL US HOW YOU THEN BECAME A FAN OF THE SHOW.

Tom Baker! Tom Baker! Tom Baker! Elizabeth Sladen and Howard Da Silva's voice! Tom was my anti-hero, accepting no bullshit from anyone – sometimes with a smile, sometimes very seriously, and always lovingly mercurial. Part of me and my personality is from my greatest influence – the incredible eccentric Tom Baker! I love being eccentric, I relish it! Thank you, Tom Baker!

TELL US YOUR FAVORITE MOMENT IN YOUR DOCTOR WHO FANDOM EXPERIENCE.

The first 12 Minutes of "Robot" from the face changing to Harry Sullivan getting tied up by the Doctor jump-roping!

IF YOU WERE TO INTRODUCE SOMEONE ELSE TO THE DOCTOR WHO SERIES, WHAT EPISODE/STORY WOULD YOU TELL THEM TO START WITH AND WHY.

If it were Joe Q. Public – or a "complete Non-fan" – "Genesis of the Daleks" (movie version). The morality lessons and comparisons to the darker parts of the human condition. As a nice Jewish boy – before I learned about my religion and spirituality – it helped me understand a fundamental comparison between Jewish survivors and the Nazi regime.

Now if I were showing a like-minded fan into sci-fi the show for the first time, I'd go with "The Robots of Death." If they were an action/suspense fan I would choose "Seeds of Doom" (Parts Three to Six) hands down!

SHAUN LYON

WHAT WAS THE FIRST EPISODE/STORY OF DOCTOR WHO THAT YOU SAW?

I was fourteen years old, and I'd never heard of the show, but I happened to discover it on our PBS station KCET in Los Angeles one day at the end of "The Hand of Fear." All I remember is the "mighty" Eldrad screaming at someone on a monitor, and then the Doctor tripping him so he'd fall into the abyss. Then he said goodbye to a woman I didn't know. So, Part Four of "The Hand of Fear" with Tom Baker and Lis Sladen. I think the first one I actually sat through completely, though, was "Destiny of the Daleks" with Tom and Lalla Ward.

TELL US HOW YOU THEN BECAME A FAN OF THE SHOW.

About two years after I'd seen my first few *Doctor Who* stories, I was volunteering at a convention called Equicon here in Los Angeles. There were a couple of people I knew from the CompuServe science fiction forums: a chap named Lee Whiteside from Arizona (who's still a friend of mine today) and a woman named Darbi Henderson, who was involved with our local club, the Time Meddlers. The club was having a small gathering in one of the rooms, and I remember being nervous about meeting new people, but I went to their gathering and dinner and then ended up at a room party (where they were watching "The Seeds of Death" on VHS)! I became a regular club member after that.

TELL US YOUR FAVORITE MOMENT IN YOUR DOCTOR WHO FANDOM EXPERIENCE.

I'm not sure I could ever answer this question with one specific answer, because I've spent the past forty years involved with this fandom. Our local fan club led to starting the Gallifrey One convention in 1990, which has been an enormous part of my life since then (I'm officially the program director and co-founder, but I'm basically the center of the entire show). Gallifrey One has given me so many wonderful memories and it's been such a treat to get to know every guest we've ever had to varying degrees, including being able to call many of them a friend. We had Janet Fielding for her first US convention in 15 years, Bonnie Langford for her first in 25 years, and Lalla Ward her first after 20 years. We were Paul McGann and Christopher Eccleston's first US *Doctor Who* event, Daphne Ashbrook's first-ever *Doctor Who* con, and the only US fan convention appearances for people like Steven Moffat, Derek Jacobi, Derrick Sherwin, Julie Gardner, and Murray Gold, among others.

If I had to pin down something from that long line of conventions, it's probably 2023, when we were able to have Jodie Whittaker joined by showrunner Chris Chibnall, whose tenure had been controversial, but the two were absolutely delightful together and I think Chris hadn't expected such a warm welcome. Stuff like that – and like our fans singing happy birthday to Chris Eccleston a few years prior – makes it all worthwhile.

IF YOU WERE TO INTRODUCE SOMEONE ELSE TO THE DOCTOR WHO SERIES, WHAT EPISODE/STORY WOULD YOU TELL THEM TO START WITH AND WHY?

I think this depends on the person. I'm very much an old-school *Doctor Who* fan, so I'd pick some of my favorite stories… "The Robots of Death" is a really good one, for example, because it's thrilling and suspenseful and the production design is magnificent. And because there's so much goodness that follows it, or precedes it (Tom Baker's tenure is always a good place to start)! But Classic Who isn't everyone's cup of tea in 2025, so for a more modern fan, I'd start them with "The Eleventh Hour," which I think is just about as perfect an episode as can be, and the entire season that follows is really engaging. There's a reason why Matt Smith's tenure on *Doctor Who* was the show's peak of popularity, after all!

DERWIN MAK

WHAT WAS THE FIRST EPISODE/STORY OF DOCTOR WHO THAT YOU SAW?

"The Three Doctors", Episode Four.

TELL US HOW YOU THEN BECAME A FAN OF THE SHOW.

I saw the title *Doctor Who* in *TV Guide* and knew nothing about it before watching my first episode, which was in the middle of "The Three Doctors". Arriving in mid-story was confusing, as were the end credits because three actors were billed as "Doctor Who"!

But this was 1978, and science fiction TV shows were very rare back then. All we had were *Star Trek* reruns, *Space: 1999*, *Star Blazers*, and a few Saturday morning children's shows. Most science fiction shows got cancelled quickly; anyone remember *The Fantastic Journey* or *Logan's Run*? What survived, for example, *The Six Million Dollar Man* and *The Bionic Woman*, were technically sci-fi, but to me, seemed too much like regular action adventure shows.

Despite not knowing what was really going on, I watched "The Three Doctors," Episode Four, the next week. The show hooked me quickly.

I started watching *Doctor Who* because it was science fiction, but I kept watching it because it was so different and eccentric compared to all the other shows. I was greatly amused by how the show compensated for its cheapness with imaginative stories, characters, and acting. To me, the cheapness was part of its charm. Only *Doctor Who* could get away with putting an actor in a chicken costume and calling him Kronos, a fearsome destroyer of universes in "The Time Monster."

TELL US YOUR FAVORITE MOMENT IN YOUR DOCTOR WHO FANDOM EXPERIENCE.

My favourite fandom moments are two related moments when I got to combine two of my great interests: *Doctor Who* and St. John Ambulance. In 2015, the British Consul General in Toronto hosted an event called 'An Evening of *Doctor Who*' as a benefit for the Hospital for Sick Children in Toronto. The local Doctor Who Appreciation Society set up a TARDIS with the St. John Ambulance logo on it. I had been in St. John Ambulance for twenty-three years at that time, so I wore my St. John Ambulance uniform and posed for a photo beside the TARDIS

Five years later, during the COVID-19 pandemic, the annual Chicago TARDIS convention went virtual. I had noticed that American *Doctor Who* fans put the St. John Ambulance logo on their TARDIS dresses and scarves and hats but didn't know what it represented. I suggested to the convention that I could give a presentation on the history of St. John Ambulance and the Order of St. John during the virtual convention. The convention agreed, and so I got to talk about the history of St. John and combine it with the history of *Doctor Who*. I appreciated the audience, who were all eager to learn about this very British and Commonwealth organization. Three years later, the international headquarters of the Order of St. John in London used the YouTube video of that presentation as a short way to explain the 900-year history of St. John.

IF YOU WERE TO INTRODUCE SOMEONE ELSE TO THE DOCTOR WHO SERIES, WHAT EPISODE/STORY WOULD YOU TELL THEM TO START WITH AND WHY?

It depends on what type of science fiction they like. *Doctor Who* is extremely diverse in the themes and tones of its stories. Since I tend to meet fans of soft sci-fi interested in social sciences, I would pick "Dot and Bubble" from 2024 because of its themes on society, privilege, and race.

CHARLES MARTIN

WHAT WAS THE FIRST EPISODE/STORY OF DOCTOR WHO THAT YOU SAW?

    I don't remember, but probably "The Ark in Space."

TELL US HOW YOU THEN BECAME A FAN OF THE SHOW.

    My friends put on a fan convention.

TELL US YOUR FAVORITE MOMENT IN YOUR DOCTOR WHO FANDOM EXPERIENCE.

    Meeting the Second Doctor, Patrick Troughton.

IF YOU WERE TO INTRODUCE SOMEONE ELSE TO THE DOCTOR WHO SERIES, WHAT EPISODE/STORY WOULD YOU TELL THEM TO START WITH AND WHY?

    "The Masque of Mandragora."

PATRICK MASSOELS

WHAT WAS THE FIRST EPISODE/STORY OF DOCTOR WHO THAT YOU SAW?

The very first episode that I saw was "The Day of the Doctor" which, in one episode, introduced me to both the Tenth and the Eleventh Doctors (as well as a lovely tease to the forthcoming Twelfth).

TELL US HOW YOU THEN BECAME A FAN OF THE SHOW.

Honestly, it was the way in which Steven Moffat told his story. So far, he may be my favorite showrunner in the rebooted series. He was able to portray the Doctor not just as a sci-fi action hero, but almost as a fairytale-esque legend. Matt Smith's portrayal is very grounded in being Amy Pond's imaginary friend, which I thought was just such a fun way to tell the story. And then you get the Twelfth Doctor, which is so delightfully weird as well as terrifying at times. Both actors' performances are what brought me in. Matt Smith was so fun and wacky and was a commanding hero. Then you have Capaldi, who almost gives me a Gandalf-ish vibe. I sometimes like to think that his adventures are what Gandalf would be up to in his long travels, which gave Series 8, 9, and 10 an almost Tolkien-ish vibe to me.

TELL US YOUR FAVORITE MOMENT IN YOUR DOCTOR WHO FANDOM EXPERIENCE.

I would say it is a tie: Capaldi's speech about war in "The Zygon Inversion" continues to give me chills whenever I watch it. Alongside this is Matt Smith's farewell speech to the Doctor just before he transforms. That said, the episode "Listen" may be my favorite episode as a whole. It is so terrifying as well as creative. I love that the Doctor is given the chance to be a bit goofy when undertaking his obsession for a creature of perfect hiding while also playing in a very relatable space. At times, we all feel like there is something following us and looking over our shoulder. It is a very real, very unnerving sensation that the show explored very well.

IF YOU WERE TO INTRODUCE SOMEONE ELSE TO THE DOCTOR WHO SERIES, WHAT EPISODE/STORY WOULD YOU TELL THEM TO START WITH AND WHY?

I would probably start them with "The Eleventh Hour" when Matt Smith's Doctor is introduced. I think it is a very clean introduction to the universe, it sets up not only the Doctor but the overall mythos behind his history and sets him up as a hero. From here, I think you can go both ways chronologically and not go wrong. Myself, I would watch all the way forward to "The Day of the Doctor," which introduces the past doctors very well. The intro to the War Doctor and his reincarnation I think blends well into the Ninth Doctor. From here, I would jump back and watch through his tenure and David Tennant's before connecting back with Matt Smith. (All this is the rebooted series, however.)

JAMIE MATHEWS

WHAT WAS THE FIRST EPISODE/STORY OF DOCTOR WHO THAT YOU SAW?

I believe the first *Doctor Who* sighting was "The Sontaran Experiment," but I wasn't really watching it. The first episode I watched was the end of "Logopolis," so I saw the Fourth Doctor leaving and the Fifth Doctor starting his adventures.

TELL US HOW YOU THEN BECAME A FAN OF THE SHOW.

My friend Peter was a massive fan of the Fourth Doctor, but honestly had no one else watching the show, so I leapt in, if only to give him someone to talk to about the show. I think I was twelve, maybe thirteen, years old. I did it to foster a closer friendship, ended up getting hooked on the show, and watching it Saturday nights on PBS alongside *Blakes 7*. Keeping in mind Peter was crushed as his long-time hero Doctor was gone, I was elated a new chapter was starting so I wouldn't have to catch up on the plots. It was the end of an era.

TELL US YOUR FAVORITE MOMENT IN YOUR DOCTOR WHO FANDOM EXPERIENCE.

From the show perspective it was "Earthshock," that cemented the show for me. After decidedly strange-to-my-12-year-old-brain episodes like "Kinda," seeing an almost straight up actioner like "Earthshock' hooked me in. Understanding the ending raised the stakes on the entire show. This was a watershed moment that showed the Doctor couldn't fix everything and didn't always win. A very different approach to American shows like *Knight Rider* or *The A-Team* where the good guys never suffered real consequences. It changed the entire show as it felt like the stakes from episode to episode were real and death of a major character was possible. The show would double down on this with Tegan leaving at the end of "Resurrection of the Daleks."

These moments marked Doctor Who as a very different show.

IF YOU WERE TO INTRODUCE SOMEONE ELSE TO THE DOCTOR WHO SERIES, WHAT EPISODE/STORY WOULD YOU TELL THEM TO START WITH AND WHY?

This is a hard one as I'm a classic *Doctor Who* fan who bridged into new *Doctor Who* but gradually lost interest during the Matt Smith run. I think it's a hard sell to get someone new into the old series, as the already ropey effects and sets are even more dated today. Honestly, I think I'd start an entirely new viewer off with the Eccleston episode "Dalek," as it reintroduces the classic villain in a subdued way and sets the tone for the modern series. From the classic episodes, Davison's "The Five Doctors" is a great introduction as it quickly introduces and establishes five regenerations of Doctors alongside their classic companions. I think it brings a viewer up to speed quickly, even if it is unfortunately an episode mostly devoid of Tom Baker.

BRIAN MATTOCKS

WHAT WAS THE FIRST EPISODE/STORY OF DOCTOR WHO THAT YOU SAW?

I know I saw earlier ones, but my first clear memory is "The Planet of Evil" in 1975. *Doctor Who* was way too scary in Season 13.

TELL US HOW YOU THEN BECAME A FAN OF THE SHOW.

"Destiny of the Daleks." 01 September 1979. That cliffhanger of Daleks bursting out of a wall thrilled me and scared me at age nine.

I never knew of fandom sadly until I was seventeen and went to my first *Doctor Who* groups and convention in 1988.

TELL US YOUR FAVORITE MOMENT IN YOUR DOCTOR WHO FANDOM EXPERIENCE.

Discovering I wasn't the ONLY fan as it did feel that way in a small town. And having the BBC and local press doing a feature on my huge *Doctor Who* room.

IF YOU WERE TO INTRODUCE SOMEONE ELSE TO THE DOCTOR WHO SERIES, WHAT EPISODE/STORY WOULD YOU TELL THEM TO START WITH AND WHY?

"An Unearthly Child" because (A) it is the first ever episode, and (B) because it's so damn good.

CHRIS McAULEY

WHAT WAS THE FIRST EPISODE/STORY OF DOCTOR WHO THAT YOU SAW?

"Battlefield," a BBC 2 repeat in 1993.

TELL US HOW YOU THEN BECAME A FAN OF THE SHOW.

Doctor Who has been a part of my life in ways that go beyond mere fandom; it's a journey that has shaped my creativity, my love of storytelling, and even my career. Looking back, it's a story of chance, discovery, and, of course, time travel.

It all began on 23 April 1993, when I was just eight years old. I was visiting my father in hospital, a time and place not particularly conducive to escapism, but fate had other plans. As I sat by his bedside, a TV in the corner of the room flickered to life, and there it was – *Doctor Who*. Specifically, it was a repeat of "Battlefield", an episode from the classic era that, despite being a bit out of the ordinary for a kid in the early 1990s, made an enormous impression. It wasn't the first time I'd seen a bit of *Doctor Who*, but this was the episode that made me feel it – the wild mix of mythology, adventure, and emotion. The Doctor, a character so unlike any hero I had encountered before, drew me in, and from that point on, I was hooked.

At the time, the show wasn't regularly on TV, so I had to hunt down my fix elsewhere. This led me to the local library, a treasure trove of *Doctor Who*-related material that ignited my passion for the show. My first finds were *Dalek Masterplan* by John Peel and one of "The Trial of a Time Lord" books by Pip and Jane Baker. These books not only expanded my understanding of the Doctor's universe but deepened my love for it. I remember being captivated by the way the Doctor's adventures were brought to life in words. These novelisations transported me to distant worlds, pulling me deeper into the mystery and grandeur of the show. But it didn't stop there. The allure of the Who universe was too strong to resist, and soon I discovered the Doctor Who New Adventures series from Virgin Books, and it was *Timewyrm: Genesis* by John Peel that really cemented my obsession. The series' exploration of new timelines, companions, and darker tones was exactly what my younger self craved. The stories were thrilling, and they left me wanting more – and more I got, as I devoured each new book with unrelenting enthusiasm.

Then, in 1996, the *Doctor Who* TV movie hit. I was still in school at the time, and it felt like the show I had grown up with had suddenly returned to me, just like magic. Paul McGann, with his intense, Byronic charm, became my Doctor, the perfect mix of mystery and elegance, while Eric Roberts' portrayal of the Master brought a new kind of menace to the iconic villain. It felt like a bridge – continuing the story I'd come to adore but also opening doors to a new era of *Doctor Who*. For a time, I held onto the hope that it was just the beginning of a new phase for the Doctor, but that was not to be.

Years passed, and as my tastes matured, the world of *Doctor Who* evolved with me. In 1999, the BBC aired "Doctor Who and the Curse of Fatal Death" for Comic Relief. It was a parody, a hilarious send-up of everything I loved about the series. Watching it was like rediscovering my passion for *Doctor Who* in a whole new light. It had the wit, the charm, and the chaos that I'd come to associate with the Doctor himself, but with an irreverence that felt so fresh and fun. This was a *Doctor Who* that understood itself – its quirks, its contradictions – and I laughed harder than I ever thought I would at a parody of the show I loved so much.

Then, in 2005, *Doctor Who* was resurrected, and I found myself as captivated as ever. Saturday nights became a ritual, eagerly anticipating each episode of New Who as the modern-day Doctors, starting with Christopher Eccleston, brought fresh energy and excitement to the show. It wasn't just nostalgia anymore – it was compelling, edge-of-your-seat storytelling that reawakened my passion for the series. As I grew older, I didn't just watch the show – I became a collector. I started buying the toys, not just for nostalgia, but as a celebration of this universe that had been a constant companion throughout my life. Each toy, each collectible, was a piece of the Doctor's world that I could hold in my hands.

Looking back on this journey, it's hard to believe how far it's taken me. From an eight-year-old watching "Battlefield" in a hospital room to writing short stories in the *Doctor Who* universe alongside luminaries like Jessica Martin, Terry Molloy, and John Peel, it has been an incredible ride. I can still remember the first time I received feedback from John Peel on a story I'd written – imagine, the man whose books had introduced me to the world of *Doctor Who* in the first place, now reading my work and offering his thoughts. It was humbling and exhilarating all at once, a validation of a dream that had started with the simplest of encounters.

TELL US YOUR FAVORITE MOMENT IN YOUR DOCTOR WHO FANDOM EXPERIENCE.

Becoming a writer in Who. Writing for *Doctor Who* has been a privilege I never could have predicted when I first stumbled upon the show as a child. It's a reminder that sometimes, the things we love as kids can grow with us, becoming not just a part of our past, but a shaping force for our future. And as I continue to write within the *Doctor Who* universe, I carry with me all the joy, wonder, and sense of adventure that the Doctor himself embodies – timeless, boundless, and ever-ready for the next adventure.

IF YOU WERE TO INTRODUCE SOMEONE ELSE TO THE DOCTOR WHO SERIES, WHAT EPISODE/STORY WOULD YOU TELL THEM TO START WITH AND WHY?

"Genesis of the Daleks." It's a superb story which not only introduces the Daleks but asks important moral and ethical questions. It also successfully combines horror with sci-fi.

RUSSELL McGEE

WHAT WAS THE FIRST EPISODE/STORY OF DOCTOR WHO THAT YOU SAW?

I grew up in rural Indiana in the '80s: with only three television channels, aluminum foil and rabbit ears, and... sadly... without my MTV. As a result, I didn't view an episode of *Doctor Who* until 1993, during the repeats of the series on the Sci-Fi Channel. You know, back when the Sci-Fi Channel was Sci-Fi and not the rubbish rebranded Syfy.

A friend of mine, David Britton had a satellite dish, and he introduced me to the worlds of *Doctor Who* with a viewing of Parts One and Two of "The Hand of Fear." And what an introduction to Classic Who! You had Sarah Jane, Tom Baker, and an over-the-top silicon-based baddie. "Eldrad must live!"

Unfortunately, I had to wait many years until "The Hand of Fear" was made available on VHS in the United States to see the conclusion of the story. Talk about a cliff-hanger.

TELL US HOW YOU THEN BECAME A FAN OF THE SHOW.

Well, although "The Hand of Fear" was the first story that I viewed, it was the 1996 Paul McGann TV Movie that made me a Whovian.

Paul McGann is my Doctor.

I became a fan in the Wilderness Years. Collecting *Doctor Who* wasn't easy at that time, most people didn't understand my passion for an outdated British sci-fi series with wobbly sets and low production values... but for me, it has always been about the stories. Those grand adventures, throughout time and space, with infinite possibilities.

After that I was hooked. I started collecting the show on VHS, taking full advantage of my discount from Suncoast Video, where I worked in college, and buying the books from Walden Books, which just happened to be right across the hall in the Terre Haute Mall.

I also collected the missing stories on audio via Napster and WinMX, purchased back issues of *Doctor Who Magazine* from my local comic book shop, and found Who North America, owned by Keith and Jany Bradbury, in roughly 1998 at the Ash Toy and Comic Book Convention in Indianapolis. I often joke with Keith because he became my "dealer"... feeding my passion for *Doctor Who*... affording me the opportunity to purchase things like Big Finish's "The Sirens of Time", the TV Movie Soundtrack, the Dapol action figures, and so on.

I also attended the Chicago TARDIS convention regularly and at the 50th Anniversary convention, I approached Jason Haigh-Ellery and asked him how I might become part of Big Finish Productions. I had just graduated from Indiana University and my master's thesis was a web series that was doing the rounds on the festival circuit and that caught Jason's interest. After a six-month audition process with Big Finish, I started working as an Audio Editor on a Third Doctor story in 2014, and the rest was history.

TELL US YOUR FAVORITE MOMENT IN YOUR DOCTOR WHO FANDOM EXPERIENCE.

That is hard for me... given I am a fan that has also had the rare privilege of being able to work on *Doctor Who*. However, there are two memories in particular that stick out for me.

One was while I was working on "Gallifrey: Time War" with Scott Handcock, whom I absolutely love and is a wonderful human. I was in the middle of editing a Dalek scene, when all of a sudden, Nick Briggs broke character and said, "Hello, Russell," in that modulating Dalek voice... it was brilliant!

The other story that I frequently share was when I worked on "Empire of the Racnoss." As you may remember in the TV story "The Runaway Bride," the Racnoss were introduced through the Empress. However, something you may not have considered is that the Empress never really moved in the television episode other than being transported from her ship onto the Earth.

Now you may be wondering, why is this crazy man bringing this up? Well, in "Empire of the Racnoss" there were no sound effects for the movement of the Racnoss, and this meant that I had to create all of the sound effects from scratch. Soooo, a friend and fellow Whovian, Nick Krohn, and I set about recording king crab legs moving, walking, and jumping on different surfaces. We used a baking pan for the ship/metal surfaces, a cinder block for pavement, and cat litter for a moon surface. We diligently recorded all of these sounds to create an army of giant eight-legged spiders of varying walks of life… quite literally.

We recorded all the sounds in a small studio about seven by ten feet wide over the course of eight hours. However, the one thing we hadn't considered was that by the end of that time, in that small studio space, without air conditioning, the crab legs would…well…begin to smell rather ripe.

In the end, the Racnoss sound effects were amazing, so job done… but never again!

IF YOU WERE TO INTRODUCE SOMEONE ELSE TO THE DOCTOR WHO SERIES, WHAT EPISODE/STORY WOULD YOU TELL THEM TO START WITH AND WHY?

No question. "Blink."

In fact, I use Steven Moffat's script from that story in the Introduction to Scriptwriting class that I teach at Indiana University each semester. It is brilliant writing and is a great way to introduce someone unfamiliar with the show to *Doctor Who*.

JEFFREY MILLER

WHAT WAS THE FIRST EPISODE/STORY OF DOCTOR WHO THAT YOU SAW?

The first episode I saw was the third Doctor's episode "The Mutants," which didn't impress me that much. The second episode I saw was the fifth Doctor episode "Black Orchid," which totally got me hooked. It included more aspects of time travel and gave a full introduction to the TARDIS, which I found very innovative. I was fascinated by this time machine that looked like a phone booth which could go anywhere in time and space. The fact it was larger on the inside was just icing on the cake that further piqued my interest and the excitement of exploration in me.

TELL US HOW YOU THEN BECAME A FAN OF THE SHOW.

My first experience with *Doctor Who* fandom would be joining the Earthbound TimeLords. It was a locally based group that I would attend with my 5-year-old nephew, who was also into the show. We would gather and watch black and white episodes, which were not previously available in the USA. The friendships I forged with some of its members have developed into life long relationships. Our shared love of the show would include role playing, conventions, cosplay, and gaming adventures of our own. Indeed, some of the best stories of my life.

TELL US YOUR FAVORITE MOMENT IN YOUR DOCTOR WHO FANDOM EXPERIENCE.

There are very many after almost 45 years of fandom. The one I am proudest of has to be for the 60th Anniversary. I was finally able to fully cosplay as my favorite Doctor (Peter Davison) and, after collecting thousands of *Doctor Who* collectibles, finally put them all on display in their own location in glass cases in an exhibit I call "The Whoseum." The soft launch happened in November of 2023 and I am so proud of my accomplishment of having fulfilled a lifelong dream of being able to share my fandom with my friends and family.

Tied for first would have to be when Big Finish sent out a casting call to appear on the cover of one of their CD covers. This would be the moment I became part of the *Doctor Who* franchise. The situation was further solidified when Paul McGann named several audio companions in the series episode "The Night of the Doctor" which further locked in the canonicity of the audio adventures. Then famed *Doctor Who* author Simon Guerrier afforded me and my husband the honor of giving our characters names and backstories. What a joy to have fleshed out *Doctor Who* characters.

IF YOU WERE TO INTRODUCE SOMEONE ELSE TO THE DOCTOR WHO SERIES, WHAT EPISODE/STORY WOULD YOU TELL THEM TO START WITH AND WHY?

This is always the most difficult of questions. What one story will introduce someone to a character that truly stands out from all other fictional characters. I'm always torn between classic and new *Doctor Who*, but I think a great stop is to encourage them to watch "Rose." It introduces the character well and gives a great introduction to the TARDIS. While somewhat silly at times, I fully encourage them to follow through by also watching "The End of the World" which plays right after. It introduces the time and space travel aspect of the show. It also gives good insight into the Doctor and Rose as characters and showcases some great makeup and creativity in the show.

PETE MURPHY

WHAT WAS THE FIRST EPISODE/STORY OF DOCTOR WHO THAT YOU SAW?

"Frontier in Space," Episode Six (on Saturday, 31 March 1973). I remember the Master introducing the Daleks at the end. My family watched *Doctor Who* so I was aware of how significant it was.

TELL US HOW YOU THEN BECAME A FAN OF THE SHOW.

I didn't become a "fan" of the show until I saw the repeat of "An Unearthly Child" (on Monday, 02 November 1981) in The Five Faces of Doctor Who season on BBC2. I regularly watched the first couple of seasons with the fourth Doctor but then I got into football (even more than what I originally was) and that took over every waking moment and I only watched *Doctor Who* if I caught it on TV.

TELL US YOUR FAVORITE MOMENT IN YOUR DOCTOR WHO FANDOM EXPERIENCE.

I joined the Lancaster Doctor Who Local Group in 1987. They had many escapades ranging from members fighting with each other and the police having to intervene to stop it (and that was after a meal out with Richard Franklin) to hurling abuse at the Preston Doctor Who Local Group after they had been verbally nasty to our Group Leader. Our group was given the nickname "Wholigans" from *Doctor Who Bulletin* (DWB) after a Panopticon Convention.

I also contributed to some desperately bad *Doctor Who* fanzines, *The Key* and *The Seventh Door* being a couple. I penned several really terrible novelettes in that time. One was *Timess*, the second in a series which had the great and original idea (NOT mine) of a future incarnation of the Doctor (and his companions Liz and Dodge).

I have also participated in the long-running Mikros

Doctor Who Role-Playing Game campaign.

IF YOU WERE TO INTRODUCE SOMEONE ELSE TO THE DOCTOR WHO SERIES, WHAT EPISODE/STORY WOULD YOU TELL THEM TO START WITH AND WHY?

"An Unearthly Child." I remember watching it in 1981 and thinking how amazing that episode is, and it still holds up.

ROB NISBET

WHAT WAS THE FIRST EPISODE/STORY OF DOCTOR WHO THAT YOU SAW?

My first memory from *Doctor Who* is from "The Mind Robber." I was eight years old at the time and don't remember much about the story at all. What I do remember is the statue of Medusa coming to life with the snakes beginning to move on her head. I'm fairly sure we didn't have a television at home then, so wherever I was watching, I was probably spellbound by the novelty of whatever was being shown. The stop-motion effect seems very crude now, but at the time it must have scared me enough to stick in my memory.

TELL US HOW YOU THEN BECAME A FAN OF THE SHOW.

Fast forward quite a few years to 1982. I was working then and commuting into Paddington station each day. In the W. H. Smith on the station concourse, I noticed the novelisation of "Warriors' Gate." I kept looking at it for several days. I had semi-regularly watched *Doctor Who* over the years and enjoyed it. "Warriors' Gate" was a story that had stuck in my mind. It had impressed me for being so different, but I hadn't fully understood the plot – and I certainly hadn't got a fancy VHS recorder at the time. I dithered. Wasn't it a kid's book? Would it be a waste of £1.25? Eventually I bought it. It must have been a good read because I started buying whatever Target *Doctor Who* books took my fancy. "Warriors' Gate" was written by "John Lydecker" a pseudonym for Steve Gallagher. Under another pseudonym, "Stephen Couper," he'd written *Dying of Paradise* and *The Ice Belt* (the trilogy completed in 2022 with *The Babylon Run*). I sought these out in the old Denmark Street Forbidden Planet bookshop and have loved reading sci-fi ever since. So, "Warriors' Gate" pushed me from being a watcher of the programme into being a fan and got me into reading sci-fi. My target books have vanished over the years, but I still have that slim, slightly browned, "Warriors' Gate" on my bookshelf.

TELL US YOUR FAVORITE MOMENT IN YOUR DOCTOR WHO FANDOM EXPERIENCE.

That's easy! I wrote several pieces of fiction for fanzines. At the time, these were (sometimes irreverent, but always fun) amateurly produced magazines, usually photocopied, with stories, illustrations, and articles on *Doctor Who*. One of the best fanzines was *Land of Fiction,* which was put together by Ian Atkins, and featured my story 'Apotheosis' over several issues. Years later, I'd had some success writing fiction for women's magazines (using my wife's name). I also won a writing competition run by *Writing Magazine*. The story was of a murder committed on a spacecraft. The magazine printed it along with a suitably embarrassing photo of me. Ian Atkins saw the story and remembered me. Ian, meanwhile, had been working for Big Finish and became the producer for their Short Trips series. My favourite moment in *Doctor Who* fandom was receiving an email from Ian asking if I'd like to submit a story idea which might be recorded. Imagine how I felt! That led to "Intuition," a story featuring Colin Baker's doctor and superbly performed by Stephen Critchlow. Subsequent recordings have allowed me to meet several of the *Doctor Who* cast, but the greatest moment for me was receiving that initial email. Thanks, Ian.

IF YOU WERE TO INTRODUCE SOMEONE ELSE TO THE DOCTOR WHO SERIES, WHAT EPISODE/STORY WOULD YOU TELL THEM TO START WITH AND WHY?

Not an easy question. Certainly, starting with "Warriors' Gate" would be too confusing. Perhaps I'd suggest Matt Smith's debut, "The Eleventh Hour." A new Doctor is a good access to the series. There are a couple of duds in that season, but there are the brilliant "Time of Angels," "Amy's Choice," "Vincent and the Doctor" as well as the cleverly constructed crack-in-the-wall/Pandorica story arc. It would also introduce a newbie to

Amy, Rory, and River. Once invested in these companions, they are bound to keep watching.

NANCY NORBECK

WHAT WAS THE FIRST EPISODE/STORY OF DOCTOR WHO THAT YOU SAW?

The very first story I saw was an episode of "The Brain of Morbius." I was 10 and it popped up midday on my local PBS channel during summer vacation. I was both intrigued and terrified by the opening titles, but it was the glowing, talking green brain that made me decide this was, perhaps, not for me.

Just a few years later, I was reintroduced to the show by a new friend who arrived at my school. Those years made all the difference – this time, I was hooked. I don't remember now which story I saw first with her, probably because we were fortunate enough to live near two PBS stations, one of which was showing Tom Baker and the other Peter Davison, though I know I saw "The Five Doctors" pretty early on, which really helped me get the full concept of the show very quickly. Either way, I now have a special fondness for "The Brain of Morbius" on behalf of my terrified 10-year-old self.

TELL US HOW YOU THEN BECAME A FAN OF THE SHOW.

That happened when my friend Marjorie arrived at my high school from Minnesota when we were in ninth grade. She was a devoted fan, and I quickly followed suit (to the alarm and confusion of my parents, who are not sci-fi fans at all). For most of my life – until I discovered LiveJournal in 2004, *Doctor Who* fandom for me consisted of me, Marjorie, and our friend Faye, who still lived in Minnesota but became a great pen pal. Marjorie and I would watch together, and Faye and I would write each other about it. It was small, but cozy, and I will admit that, while I love going to conventions and being around other people who get my love for this show, there are times when I really miss those small, cozy days.

TELL US YOUR FAVORITE MOMENT IN YOUR DOCTOR

WHO FANDOM EXPERIENCE.

Walking into my first convention – Long Island Doctor Who 4 in 2016 – truly turned me into a giddy fangirl. I wasn't sure what to expect, and I was only there for a single day, but it was an amazing moment of feeling like I had found the people I belonged with, in a way I'd never experienced before. It's a place where you can go into the vendor's room, pull out your phone to call up your spreadsheet with all your Target novels, and know that no one will think that's weird. And I'm here to tell you that, even when you know it's a fan-built labor of love that can't actually EX-TER-MIN-ATE you, being sized up by a Dalek in real life is an experience.

Three years later, at the same con in 2019, I had the opportunity to invite Paul McGann to be a guest on my podcast, Follow Your Curiosity. I was really nervous about asking, but I knew the worst possibility wasn't rejection – it was doing nothing and wondering for the rest of my life what would have happened if I'd asked. I couldn't live with that sort of potential regret, so I went for it. He said yes! It took a bit to find a time that worked, but we finally managed to connect over Zoom in mid-2020, during lockdown, and spent a delightful two and a half hours chatting about how he got into acting, his experience filming the *Doctor Who* TV movie, and a lot more.

It still amazes me that any of it happened, and I now make it a point to actively encourage people to go take the chance and ask in similar situations – you never know what may come out of it, unless, of course, you don't do it.

IF YOU WERE TO INTRODUCE SOMEONE ELSE TO THE DOCTOR WHO SERIES, WHAT EPISODE/STORY WOULD YOU TELL THEM TO START WITH AND WHY?

That really depends on how much time they have and whether I can get them to consider watching something that predates modern special effects.

If we have a short time period or a low tolerance for

vintage TV, I would show them "Blink" or "Vincent and the Doctor." Both give a really good feel for the show in 45 minutes, even though "Blink" is a Doctor-lite episode. Both are iconic in their own ways. If I know the person in question can deal with more of a horror angle, I'd go with "Blink," and if they're someone who looks for more of an emotional connection, I'd go with "Vincent and the Doctor."

If we have more time, or they're down with old-school TV, I'd probably go with "City of Death," because I love it so much. It has everything you could possibly want in a *Doctor Who* story. It's clever, funny, urbane, and it's in Paris! With Julian Glover and Catherine Schell and the Mona Lisa! A bit of John Cleese. Duggan is my favorite almost-companion ever, and there's a henchman named Hermann. And Leonardo da Vinci, sort of. Written by Douglas Adams. What's not to love?

AVERY O'SHAUGHNESSY

WHAT WAS THE FIRST EPISODE/STORY OF DOCTOR WHO THAT YOU SAW?

A friend recommended the show to me, so one day I pulled the show up on Hulu and started watching with "Rose."

TELL US HOW YOU THEN BECAME A FAN OF THE SHOW.

From "Rose" onward, I watched all the way up through Series 11. I fell off from watching it until I got to college and the gaming and sci-fi club there, MAGE, had a convention called Concinnity. That's where I met Nick Seidler and Chris Cebula, who were involved in Whovian fandom. I then got involved in organizing that con, which is where I sort of got involved in organized fandom. From there, I became the Doctor Who Chair in the club and organized viewing events at my university, getting more students involved and enjoying the show.

TELL US YOUR FAVORITE MOMENT IN YOUR DOCTOR WHO FANDOM EXPERIENCE.

My favorite experience with the fandom is attending the Chicago TARDIS convention. It allowed me to meet and listen to the *Doctor Who* actors and also meet and befriend other fans. Personal highlights include during the opening ceremony Sacha Dewan, who plays the Master in the series, took the time to stop and talk with a little child. His taking the time to engage even the youngest of fans brought joy to my heart.

IF YOU WERE TO INTRODUCE SOMEONE ELSE TO THE DOCTOR WHO SERIES, WHAT EPISODE/STORY WOULD YOU TELL THEM TO START WITH AND WHY?

If I had to convince someone, I'd probably start them with "The Empty Child"/"The Doctor Dances." If someone was willing to jump right in, I'd recommend the beginning of a Doctor with either "Rose" or "The Church on Ruby Road."

INGRID OLIANSKI

WHAT WAS THE FIRST EPISODE/STORY OF DOCTOR WHO THAT YOU SAW?

That is actually an impossible question to answer. I first watched *Doctor Who* in 1970/71. My family and I were living in England at the time and I was four years old. So, I have no idea which episode I saw first. But the show made an impression. Jon Pertwee remains my favorite Doctor to this day.

TELL US HOW YOU THEN BECAME A FAN OF THE SHOW.

I rediscovered the show in the late 1980's when PBS was showing Tom Baker episodes and started watching it again. I eventually went and watched all of the Doctors. In 1989 I attended a traveling *Doctor Who* exhibition and met a man who was a member of the Time Meddlers of Los Angeles, a local *Doctor Who* fan club. He told me that he and some of his friends were about to start a new *Doctor Who* convention called Gallifrey One. We kept in touch after that convention and I attended the very first Gallifrey One in 1990. I joined the Time Meddlers and made a lot of friends who I still know to this day. Ever since then I have been on the staff of Gallifrey One. I was a Guest Liaison and I am currently a member of the Daytime Programming staff.

TELL US YOUR FAVORITE MOMENT IN YOUR DOCTOR WHO FANDOM EXPERIENCE.

This is another hard question to answer. There have been so many wonderful experiences I have had as a result of being connected to *Doctor Who* fandom. I could say it was getting to meet Jon Pertwee at the very first Gallifrey One. I could also point to numerous conversations I have had through the years with actors, writers, directors, and so on, involved in the show. But I have to say that it's the friendships I have made with other fans of the show. There is nothing like spending a weekend with other people who get it. All fandoms have their issues, but I find that the majority of *Doctor Who* fans are respectful and kind.

IF YOU WERE TO INTRODUCE SOMEONE ELSE TO THE DOCTOR WHO SERIES, WHAT EPISODE/STORY WOULD YOU TELL THEM TO START WITH AND WHY?

"Blink" is a great episode to introduce people to the Doctor. It's so well written and the audience doesn't need to understand a lot about the Doctor to understand the story.

MIKE OLSON

WHAT WAS THE FIRST EPISODE/STORY OF DOCTOR WHO THAT YOU SAW?

First memory is the end of "The Deadly Assassin," as I recall how clever it would be to travel through time in a grandfather clock. (I tried to, but could not confirm the date when I tried at BroaDWcast.org.) My first formal introduction to *Doctor Who* was a Beta tape video recording of "Keeper of Traken" on 27 December 1981 before watching the WTTW broadcast of "Logopolis" later that night.

TELL US HOW YOU THEN BECAME A FAN OF THE SHOW.

It started after watching "Keeper of Traken" and "Logopolis." I continued watching on channel WTTW going forward, recording the episodes on VHS. I found Pinnacle books to read and sought out the latest stories in Target books before they aired on PBS. I wrote a short story loosely referencing *Doctor Who* that won the Illinois Young Authors Contest for my middle school. That allowed me to attend the Young Authors conference in Springfield, Illinois in 1983. I still have my Season 18 inspired scarf my grandmother crocheted.

TELL US YOUR FAVORITE MOMENT IN YOUR DOCTOR WHO FANDOM EXPERIENCE.

I have two favorite moments. First was while waiting in line at the Visions '90 convention for an autograph and Sylvester McCoy was having lunch at the cafe one floor above us. He threw sugar packets at us. Second is having the opportunity to direct Sophie Aldred in a small independent movie I directed and helped write titled *Thriller Theater!*.

IF YOU WERE TO INTRODUCE SOMEONE ELSE TO THE DOCTOR WHO SERIES, WHAT EPISODE/STORY WOULD

YOU TELL THEM TO START WITH AND WHY?

For the classic series, "Keeper of Traken" and "Logopolis," because the stories are connected. They reintroduce the Master; they explain how the TARDIS works; viewers get to see how Time Lords work; and lots of references/connections to previous stories. For the new series, "Rose" or "The Eleventh Hour." Both stories are designed as starting points for a new viewer, and they are written and directed for a modern audience.

JOSHUA ONG

WHAT WAS THE FIRST EPISODE/STORY OF DOCTOR WHO THAT YOU SAW?

My first episode was "Rose!"

TELL US HOW YOU THEN BECAME A FAN OF THE SHOW.

I've been a fan of the show for the past 12 years now, and I first discovered *Doctor Who* when I was in high school as many of my friends had referenced the show very frequently. At the time when I started watching, I followed the story of the Ninth Doctor and Rose, and while the show had been around for a while. I felt a sense of adventure that I never realized existed until I saw the adventures through time and space that came with endless possibilities! It's brilliant to see how much the show has evolved and how the themes bring a refreshing candor to both the characters and the stories. At times when I venture away, I find myself returning to the show quite often, which I believe is a testament to how timeless the stories are!

TELL US YOUR FAVORITE MOMENT IN YOUR DOCTOR WHO FANDOM EXPERIENCE.

My favorite moment lands within "The Day of the Doctor," where the three Doctors work past the differences of their past involvement in the Time War to work together to save Gallifrey in a fashion that was surreal and fulfilling to everyone! It was like a celebration of the past, present, and future with hope on the horizon. That is what solidified my love for the show, and the inspiration that it gives rise to, for everyone all around, that one must never give up and never give in, and to never be cruel or cowardly.

IF YOU WERE TO INTRODUCE SOMEONE ELSE TO THE DOCTOR WHO SERIES, WHAT EPISODE/STORY WOULD

YOU TELL THEM TO START WITH AND WHY?

    There's many to choose from that serve as a great start! I would begin their journey with "Vincent and the Doctor." This is one of my favorite episodes as it goes back to how *Doctor Who* has historical elements in their stories that conclude with meaning behind it. I will never forget the emotions I had seeing Vincent witness how he and his art had influenced the future, and I hope for someone to have that experience in engaging in a tale as heartwarming as that.

JENA PANTANO

WHAT WAS THE FIRST EPISODE/STORY OF DOCTOR WHO THAT YOU SAW?

I started with the Christopher Eccleston season on Netflix. So the Ninth Doctor, and modern Series 1.

TELL US HOW YOU THEN BECAME A FAN OF THE SHOW.

I had always heard about *Doctor Who* from others, as my social circle is large on fandoms and other correlating interests. When I saw it was on Netflix, and I didn't have to worry about BBC programming hoops, I jumped right in. I love Eccleston, so it was an easy way to get into it. The campy aspects took some getting into, especially the low budget costumes and graphics. I was hooked by the goofy aspects, the banana weapon, and "shouldn't have let me hit all those buttons." But let's be real, it was the banana.

The same day I was heartbroken in losing Eccleston, I was won over again with everyone's favorite human being, Tennant. They cast that change over brilliantly. Immediately I was immersed into Reddit, meme references, and looking into the history.

TELL US YOUR FAVORITE MOMENT IN YOUR DOCTOR WHO FANDOM EXPERIENCE.

My favorite moment is, hands down, watching my partner watch *Doctor Who* for the first time: The stress in his eyes when the angels move, the confusion of the silence, and him sneaking in episodes when I'm not home. There is nothing better than sharing one of your favorite things with someone you love and seeing them fall for it just as much.

I also volunteered at my first *Doctor Who* themed convention this past Thanksgiving weekend in 2024, Chicago TARDIS. Getting to see so many people bond over it was great.

The costumes, art, everything.

IF YOU WERE TO INTRODUCE SOMEONE ELSE TO THE DOCTOR WHO SERIES, WHAT EPISODE/STORY WOULD YOU TELL THEM TO START WITH AND WHY?

    I would, as much as I hate to be that person, recommend the revamped series. Netflix made access easy and its not-TOO-outdated feeling to get into it. Old British programming isn't for everyone. Especially with how long it took them to get onto equality, racism, and sexism in the media. In modern times, you have to go back to the older series with a pre-existing love to see past a lot of that.

ANDREW PEREGRINE

WHAT WAS THE FIRST EPISODE/STORY OF DOCTOR WHO THAT YOU SAW?

I'm not entirely sure I really remember. Thankfully my parents (especially my Dad) watched *Doctor Who,* so I may have seen some episodes I was not consciously aware of! But recently, I rewatched Tom Baker's first episode "Robot" and found that I remembered it in a way I'd not remembered the previous "Planet of the Spiders." Given I was four-years-old in 1974, all I'd remembered were snippets. But watching it again years later, those images and scenes were still ingrained, and I knew with certainty I'd seen them before, even if I couldn't remember much about the plot or the story. What had stayed with me was the wonder of it all, and that has never left.

As a side note, many DVD extras involve interviews from the TV shows *The Multi Coloured Swap Shop* or *Saturday Superstore* which I remember getting up early on a Saturday to watch, never knowing quite when Doctor Who would be interviewed during the show. I have the same feeling of remembering having seen them (still in my pyjamas) as I did with "Robot."

TELL US HOW YOU THEN BECAME A FAN OF THE SHOW.

I think I was a fan from the first episode I watched. It instantly resonated with me, I'm sure about that. For me, the Doctor has always felt like a hero I could try to live up to. He didn't shoot or fight people (well, often) and he certainly wasn't cool (at least in a conventional sense). He also didn't care about fitting in, he wasn't scared to be all he was, and help people no matter what. There are still few male leads like this. I knew I'd never be a cool spacepilot like Han Solo, or a dashing action hero like Tony Verdeschi, or a coldly efficient and organised officer like Spock. But this chaotic and often underestimated space bumpkin, doing what he could to help, and never in the way anyone expected, was always someone I felt I could aspire to be like.

TELL US YOUR FAVORITE MOMENT IN YOUR DOCTOR WHO FANDOM EXPERIENCE.

This is sort of retroactive, as I didn't know at the time what was ahead. Many years ago I used to date (and game with) the lovely Jac Rayner, who was even more of a Who fan than I was. We were both young writers trying to figure out how to get our work out there. Although she was a lot closer than I was for sure! When I look back at that time, I wish we could go back and tell our younger selves that in a few years I'd be one of the main writers of the role-playing game and she would have a stack of Big Finish credits and several novels published. Neither of us would have believed it was possible. While neither of us has been able to write an actual episode (although she absolutely should) to have anything a part of the show is a joy and a privilege. Even now, every piece of work I do on anything Who related has my inner teenager doing cartwheels.

I should also add that I was recently told the most depressing and complementary thing I've ever heard. When a colleague discovered I was the same person who wrote some of the RPG books she (an adult young woman) explained "Oh my god, I grew up on your books!" She used to play the game with her brother in the car on long journeys to family holidays. Wonderful compliment, but god I feel old (I'm still pretty spry for 748 though).

IF YOU WERE TO INTRODUCE SOMEONE ELSE TO THE DOCTOR WHO SERIES, WHAT EPISODE/STORY WOULD YOU TELL THEM TO START WITH AND WHY.

That is a very tough question, and would depend on who that person was. Do they like action, character, mystery, comedy? There is a good episode for each of those. It is unlikely to be my favourite episode ("Warriors' Gate," since you ask) as what I love is based on years of watching the show. I'd also probably avoid Classic Who, not because it wasn't as good, but these days, too many people get hung up on special effects and production design (although personally, that's just budget, so it's never bothered me).

"Blink" comes to mind first as it's such a self-contained episode and so a good starter. But it doesn't have a lot of the Doctor in it. So I'd probably pick "The End of the World." It is the first episode that gets into the Doctor and Rose's characters but has all the best elements of Who: mystery, strangeness, action, comedy and a serious underlying theme. It's also Rose's first experience away from Earth, making her the one being 'introduced to Doctor Who' herself. It's one of Russell T Davies' best, where his absolute joy at doing his dream job shines through.

BRANDON PETERS

WHAT WAS THE FIRST EPISODE/STORY OF DOCTOR WHO THAT YOU SAW?

"Mawdryn Undead."

TELL US HOW YOU THEN BECAME A FAN OF THE SHOW.

Doctor Who happened upon me as a kid late one Saturday evening in the early 1990s. *Saturday Night Live* that night was either a rerun or I was seeking something to watch after it concluded. My parents had moved us to a new home where they decided to forgo cable, limiting our household to 5 channels. PBS was where I stopped clicking the dial (my room had an older tube) as I became amused with some kind of spacey control station where a dashing young blonde British fellow in an irregular beige suit with red trim was in the middle of some kind of distressing situation with two (quite striking I must have thought then) female assistants. But what captivated me most was this eerie and unsettling feeling I had when they left their "ship" and went outside to some courtyard-like area. The switch from soap opera-looking scenes to the shot-on-film location scenes put me at a sense of unease. The show wasn't actively trying to be scary though it consistently gave off an eerie vibe when the film segments were playing (similar to the Diana Rigg-led *The Avengers* which I had watched regularly prior on A&E when we had cable).

As a burgeoning horror enthusiast, the strange British show I stumbled upon was right up my alley. I decided to stay tuned to the station to finish it out. I'd find it was called *Doctor Who* and I would turn to PBS on Saturday nights if I could remember or was home. (The only episodes I would see had Peter Davison or Tom Baker in the role of the Doctor). I wouldn't say I was a regular viewer or super knowledgeable during that time, but I caught it when I was able or remembered. It wasn't until last year (2023), as I was going back through the Season

20 Blu-ray Collection set that my mind jostled a memory and I realized the episode I'd seen that night of discovery came from the story "Mawdryn Undead" (I think it was the first episode of the serial, but I can't be sure)! When 1996 rolled around, I did clear my calendar and evening and told my friends at school they had to watch the TV Movie airing on Fox. At the time I remember thinking it was ok, but once it didn't lead to a series, I completely fell off paying attention to *Doctor Who*.

Fast forward to 2006, now living in Los Angeles, late one night I was flipping through channels and landed on the Sci-Fi Channel (pre "Syfy"). This time because I recognized things that looked like *Doctor Who*. Low and behold, it was BACK and this time in a cool leather jacket. During that initial first four series, I tried to convert everyone in Los Angeles I could to watch what I thought was the best show on TV at the time. Since that night, I haven't missed a beat. It led to my greater fandom, making the pilgrimage through the entire classic series (lost audios and recons included!), collecting, owning more shirts than I should, meeting other fans (and now collaborating with them) and professionals on multiple *Doctor Who* endeavors.

TELL US YOUR FAVORITE MOMENT IN YOUR DOCTOR WHO FANDOM EXPERIENCE.

While I've been a fan for most of my life, I feel my journey is always still just beginning due to the many new turns, twists, and opportunities that can arise. That's the fun with the program as it's ever so evolving, growing, and introducing you to wonderful new people, as well as new thoughts and aspects of the program. My most recent moment I'll always cherish and never forget was Doctoberfest 2023 (a *Doctor Who* festival in Indiana), where I met and interviewed Sophie Aldred. But that's not the coolest part! The day after the festival, I was invited to dinner at the festival owner's home. This evening consisted only of my friend Russell, the owners, and Sophie. We learned how to make Vietnamese spring rolls and spent an evening just hanging out as everyday equals chatting about all sorts of things like her everyday life and our thoughts on current events. As I found out, Sophie is exactly as everyone has described her:incredibly kind and incredibly generous. Which is completely the *Doctor Who* way of life, both on the screen and off (or "behind the sofa").

IF YOU WERE TO INTRODUCE SOMEONE ELSE TO THE DOCTOR WHO SERIES, WHAT EPISODE/STORY WOULD YOU TELL THEM TO START WITH AND WHY?

Typically, I say that when a new actor/Doctor begins, hop into the show right there. Currently that would mean "The Church On Ruby Road" is your best starting point. Most of the Doctor's beginnings work (the single episode "An Unearthly Child" still holds up over 60 years later in my opinion). However, if we are to go by my personal favorite Doctor launch story, that would be "The Eleventh Hour." It's a terrific little science fiction tale that also really introduces us to the new Doctor and companion in a fulfilling and unique way. Steven Moffat paints this one with a fairy tale atmosphere that is so very hard not to resist adoring it. For the younger person who may care about aesthetics, it's in HD and not the low-resolution standard definition Series 1 through 4 had, or the soap opera look of the classic series. I'm a big classic series person, so I must suggest an entry point to one of those stories as well. Seeing as Tom Baker's Fourth Doctor is my favorite, I will recommend "City of Death" as it is a quality serial that manages to hit on everything *Doctor Who* is and can be in one story; science fiction, history, time travel, sonic screwdriver, spaceships, lore, techno-babble, monsters/aliens, special effects, other planets, courage, a "romp" as they call it, and featuring non-violent solutions to major conflicts. All of which with some good silliness and cheeky wit to it.

JOEL PIERSEN

WHAT WAS THE FIRST EPISODE/STORY OF DOCTOR WHO THAT YOU SAW?

My first episode was "Logopolis," and it was strange starting on a regeneration episode, but it gave me a good sense of the wonder and creativity of the show. I kept watching after that, and like David Tennant, Peter Davison became "my Doctor" (but not my father-in-law). I've been watching ever since.

TELL US HOW YOU THEN BECAME A FAN OF THE SHOW.

I was in high school when I started watching in 1982, on Chicago's PBS station. As much as I wanted to watch with friends, it aired at 10:00PM on a Sunday. So, it became the last hurrah of my weekend, after which I could talk about the episode with my friends at school. I may or may not have come to school wearing a stalk of celery on some days. I'll never admit if it's true. If that blue box ever showed up at my door, I'd climb aboard without hesitation.

TELL US YOUR FAVORITE MOMENT IN YOUR DOCTOR WHO FANDOM EXPERIENCE.

One favorite moment is hard to isolate, since it's brought joy for decades. But the announcement of the 2004 reboot is high on the list. Knowing that the series was coming back was a thrill, after spending all those years thinking it was gone for good. I got to see an advance copy of two of the episodes, and I knew the show's future was in very good hands.

I can also tell you about my weirdest moment of fandom. It was 1987, and I was in college. I had a new girlfriend, and I brought her home to meet my family – and introduce her to *Doctor Who*. Unfortunately, it was 22 November 1987, the night a still-unknown hijacker interrupted "The Talons of Weng-Chiang" on WTTW, dressed in a Max Headroom mask and being spanked. We watched in confusion for the minute and a half of the piracy, and when the episode resumed, Piper turned to me and asked, "Was that... part of the show?"

IF YOU WERE TO INTRODUCE SOMEONE ELSE TO THE DOCTOR WHO SERIES, WHAT EPISODE/STORY WOULD YOU TELL THEM TO START WITH AND WHY?

I did introduce my older sister to the series, back in 2017, and I did so with "Vincent and the Doctor." It's such a wonderful episode, lovely and sad, and yet happy in its own way. Tony Curran's performance alone makes it a great choice. I would also invite them to watch "City of Death" from Tom Baker's era. In addition to the art theme, it is a lovely piece of the classic series' history and lets my new viewer know that things weren't always CGI and big budgets. It starts with a talented actor, and that's what's kept the series vibrant to this day. It's why I have "Allons-y" tattooed on my forearm.

GARETH PRESTON

WHAT WAS THE FIRST EPISODE/STORY OF DOCTOR WHO THAT YOU SAW?

"The Carnival of Monsters," Episode One. I remember being frightened by the Orderly being killed early on in the story. I might have been watching already though, since my dad had bought me the 10th Anniversary *Radio Times* magazine.

TELL US HOW YOU THEN BECAME A FAN OF THE SHOW.

Doctor Who is something I've grown up with ever since I was a small boy. I think my parents were watching it already and I became a fan because I loved anything science fiction since I can remember. Even so, *Doctor Who* was my favourite of all those shows I was watching, like *Star Trek*, *The Six Million Dollar Man*, and so on. I'd been collecting the annuals and the Target Books but it was the 1982 Five Faces of Doctor Who season on BBC2 and the accompanying *Doctor Who Monthly* issue that really turned me into a FAN, joining the Appreciation Society, buying and writing for fanzines, even making my own fan videos with my new friends.

TELL US YOUR FAVORITE MOMENT IN YOUR DOCTOR WHO FANDOM EXPERIENCE.

Very hard to choose one so I'll go for two. An Afternoon with Louise Jameson in 1995. This was a small fan event organised by a local comic shop called Galaxy Four. It was an excellent event in itself but Lousie Jameson was so open and down to earth with the audience. I really felt I'd met the woman rather than her professional front. Zip forward to 2013 and the cinema screening of "The Day of the Doctor." I attended with my girlfriend Tina, who's also a fan. The atmosphere was electric, the audience were so reactive and appreciative, and the story itself remains one of my favourites. The gasp when Tom

Baker's voice came from off-screen was magical. It's the only time I've worn my long scarf in public. It was the right decision.

IF YOU WERE TO INTRODUCE SOMEONE ELSE TO THE DOCTOR WHO SERIES, WHAT EPISODE/STORY WOULD YOU TELL THEM TO START WITH AND WHY?

It is such a difficult question because it depends so much on the someone and what they already enjoy. But some likely candidates would include "City of Death," for its fantastic script by Douglas Adams and Graham Williams, matched by a set of perfectly pitched performances and a glossier than normal look. "The Time Warrior" is an excellent story, again with a witty script, this time Robert Holmes, a great alien design and characterisation, plus you have an ideal entry point with Sarah Jane Smith meeting the Doctor for the first time. "Rose" remains an almost perfect pilot episode and one of Russell T Davis' smartest scripts for the way it balances the information, the reinvention, its love of the programme with some gentle mocking. Finally, "The Well" by Sharma Angel-Walfall and Russell T Davis has been the highlight of the last few years and a great example of how scary and clever the series can be.

AMBER RADEN

WHAT WAS THE FIRST EPISODE/STORY OF DOCTOR WHO THAT YOU SAW?

I started at the beginning of New Who so my first episode was "Rose" with the Ninth Doctor!

TELL US HOW YOU THEN BECAME A FAN OF THE SHOW.

Doctor Who was a show I'd had friends telling me for years to try and I just hadn't gotten around to it. I finally started watching while doing prep for my wedding in the spring of 2013. It took me a little while to warm up to it – for me, at the time, many of the aliens were silly and campy and not at all my kind of thing. I mean, weird, possessed mannequins? Skin-suit-wearing aliens making prolonged fart jokes? I really didn't understand why so many people thought I'd like this show.
 Then I watched "Dalek." Watching Rose almost die and then actually save this tortured creature who tried to kill her, at odds with the Doctor immediately moving to destroy it… I think this was the first time I realized I cared for these characters and this show had so much more depth and heart than just silly fart jokes and goofy aliens.
 After that I was hooked. Hard. I binged through the rest of New Who in time to catch the 50th Anniversary special when it aired. I loved it so much that my husband learned that there was actually a new *Doctor Who* convention called CONsole Room in our home state and it happened to be the same weekend as our first wedding anniversary. It was such a fun way to celebrate our anniversary and the only reason it wasn't our first ever pop culture/comic con-type event was because I hadn't previously known that cons like this were a thing, and the first Wizard World in our state was held just two weeks prior.
 I have now spent the past decade volunteering for CONsole Room, first as a part of the publications team, then as Co-Chair for seven years. (Did I mention how quickly and

deeply I was hooked on this universe?) I stepped down from the convention committee in 2024 – running cons is hard, time-consuming work, HUGE shout out to all the volunteers at all the cons for everything you do – so that I could make space for connecting with fandom in a different way. Right now, that's taking the form of a tour of all US-based *Doctor Who* conventions this year. It's been so wonderful to meet more fans from all over the country!

(And, for the record, those Slitheen that I found so silly early on have now become some of my favorite aliens in the show.)

TELL US YOUR FAVORITE MOMENT IN YOUR DOCTOR WHO FANDOM EXPERIENCE.

I think a lot of answers I hear for this question from others connect to unique experiences hanging out with actors from the show or visiting a set, that kind of thing. And those things are definitely cool, I love those and have so many stories like this of my own that I cherish!

But hands down, unironically and completely honestly, my favorite moments in this fandom are the quiet ones when I look back at the last decade, what I've accomplished and the people I've met, and realize how fundamentally changed my life and the lives of so many others in this community are because of this show. I have grown, personally and professionally, in immeasurable ways since diving into this fandom. I have friends I play *Dungeons & Dragons* and travel with and run races with now that I may have never met if we hadn't all met through this fandom. Even more, I've had the immense privilege to play a small part in connecting others in this community together through the convention and beyond.

This show is beautiful and wild and wonderful in all the best ways, but the community that has gathered around it? The way they connect with each other, support each other, celebrate this world with each other? That's something truly magical.

It's the people. It's always, *always* the people.

IF YOU WERE TO INTRODUCE SOMEONE ELSE TO THE DOCTOR WHO SERIES, WHAT EPISODE/STORY WOULD YOU TELL THEM TO START WITH AND WHY?

    I usually say to start with "Rose" and stick it out, even if it's a little goofy. Best to start at the beginning and go from there. However, knowing that that can be a tough ask for some, if someone is looking for a single story my next best suggestion is "Vincent and the Doctor" or "Human Nature"/"The Family of Blood." They are some of my favorite episodes, but I think they also do a good job capturing the essence of the show, the silliness, and the heart and the breadth of possibilities that the show presents.

FAIZ REHMAN

WHAT WAS THE FIRST EPISODE/STORY OF DOCTOR WHO THAT YOU SAW?

"Revenge of the Cybermen."

TELL US HOW YOU THEN BECAME A FAN OF THE SHOW.

I was about three and a half when I first stumbled upon the *Doctor Who* cards tucked inside boxes of Weetabix. Strange creatures, fantastical designs – and the realisation that it all came from a television show. I begged my mum to let me watch it. That was it: I was hooked. My first day of school at age four wasn't exactly smooth sailing. I clung to my parents, refusing to let go – until the teacher mentioned they'd be listening to a *Doctor Who* record one of the kids had brought in. That did the trick.

Fast forward to Season 17, and my enthusiasm had begun to fade. The show felt a bit silly to me then. I cancelled my newsagent order for *Doctor Who Weekly* and switched to other Marvel UK titles. But one day, browsing the shelves, I spotted the magazine again – transformed into a weightier monthly edition. On the cover was Tom Baker, in his new Season 18 costume. Inside? News of an impending regeneration. That was seismic. I had to see it. I convinced my dad that the time had come to invest in a VHS recorder. The show felt revitalised. I was sad to see Tom go, but I adored Davison. From that moment on I never missed an episode (or an issue of DWM) again.

TELL US YOUR FAVORITE MOMENT IN YOUR DOCTOR WHO FANDOM EXPERIENCE.

So many cherished moments spring to mind – but one of the earliest was meeting my dear friend Richard back in Form 1 (Year 7, for those keeping track in modern continuity). We bonded over a shared passion for *Star Wars* and *Doctor Who*, and that friendship became the gateway to countless fandom adventures. Together, we attended signings, conventions, and even had the thrill of meeting Doctors Three through Eight multiple times. We even found ourselves taking part in fan films alongside some of the stars – unreal experiences for a couple of devoted fans.

But the pinnacle has to be the 30th Anniversary celebration at the Novotel in Hammersmith, London. The energy, the lineup – it was nothing short of legendary. So many icons of the Whoniverse under one roof. It was a time when conventions felt magical and community-driven, rather than today's conveyor belt of photo ops and pricey encounters. No disrespect to modern con-goers, of course, but for me, those older gatherings had an unbeatable charm.

IF YOU WERE TO INTRODUCE SOMEONE ELSE TO THE DOCTOR WHO SERIES, WHAT EPISODE/STORY WOULD YOU TELL THEM TO START WITH AND WHY?

If I were introducing someone to *Doctor Who*, I'd probably start with "The Eleventh Hour." It's the perfect jumping-on point: a fresh Doctor, a gripping mystery, and a tone that balances modern style with classic charm. Matt Smith's debut is energetic, witty, and accessible – ideal for newcomers who want to get a sense of what the show's all about without needing a crash course in decades of lore. That said, if they lean more toward classic sci-fi and don't mind a slower pace, "Genesis of the Daleks" is hard to beat. Tom Baker is at his brilliant best, and the moral questions at the heart of the story give it real weight. It's iconic for a reason.

But I have to say – back in 1996, I gave a work friend a VHS recording with "The Robots of Death" and "Mark of the Rani." To my surprise, she preferred the Rani story! So really, who are we to say what works best? Sometimes the perfect episode is the one that resonates unexpectedly.

Ultimately, I'd tailor my recommendation to the person—whether they're drawn to drama, mystery, camp, or complexity.

The beauty of *Doctor Who* is that there's always a corner of the Whoniverse waiting to speak directly to you.

CHRIS RETTERATH

WHAT WAS THE FIRST EPISODE/STORY OF DOCTOR WHO THAT YOU SAW?

"Gridlock" - New Who Series 3, Episode 3, originally aired 20 July 2007. I'm pretty sure I first watched this as an airing on Sci-Fi/Syfy in 2007.

TELL US HOW YOU THEN BECAME A FAN OF THE SHOW.

Watching "Gridlock" with a cat man, married to a human woman, and they had a litter of kittens in this car driving in circles around the planet was so weird, and then you add in the Macra at the end and I was thoroughly confused but intrigued. Since we didn't have PBS growing up, I had never seen any of the classic series. So, when I went back to the "beginning" to watch Series 1, Episode 1 "Rose" and saw Christopher Eccleston as the Doctor, I became even more confused. I had to search what was going on and make sure I was watching the same show! Once I figured that out, I continued watching and have loved it ever since!

TELL US YOUR FAVORITE MOMENT IN YOUR DOCTOR WHO FANDOM EXPERIENCE.

I think my favorite fandom experience is actually recent! In February 2024 at the Gallifrey One convention, a few friends and I all purchased the "family" photo with Billie Piper, Camille Coduri, and Shaun Dingwall. We decided to do all of our photos together and make it into an awkward family photo series. One photo with us not paying attention, one with everyone looking in different directions, and one where we were fighting. At first everyone was confused, but they quickly got on board and we all absolutely loved the experience!

IF YOU WERE TO INTRODUCE SOMEONE ELSE TO THE

DOCTOR WHO SERIES, WHAT EPISODE/STORY WOULD YOU TELL THEM TO START WITH AND WHY?

    I truly believe that this changes based on the person. Each person will be grabbed by a different story which intrigues them enough to watch more. I'm partial to recommending the start of New Who with "Rose." Another good jumping on point is with Matt Smith in "The Eleventh Hour." I also feel like the double "Silence in the Library"/"Forest of the Dead" are great onboarding episodes to get people intrigued to watch more.

ALEXANDRA ROSENBAUM

WHAT WAS THE FIRST EPISODE/STORY OF DOCTOR WHO THAT YOU SAW?

"The Girl In The Fireplace."

TELL US HOW YOU THEN BECAME A FAN OF THE SHOW.

I am a lifelong Francophile. If it's to do with French or France, it's got my attention. In 2015 I knew I would not watch *Doctor Who* with my husband and kids; it had nothing to do with me.

A glimpse of a Clockwork Repair Droid in period appropriate costume. Versailles, both palace and gardens. The King, Mme De Pompadour. And I sat down. I watched, I was absolutely engrossed.

From that evening, I began watching from Christopher Eccleston all the way through Matt Smith. Cried when he regenerated and immediately fell for Doctor Twelve, grumpy Peter Capaldi.

My husband, who had grown up watching Classic Who Sunday nights on PBS, began feeding me knowledge. I learned I had a *Doctor Who* connection with my grandmother who had passed away eight years earlier. I read about the Doctor on the internet and read books and magazines. I eventually began streaming Classic Who on BritBox, in black and white, with my husband. My knowledge grew, my attachment grew. I marveled at the original ingenuity and tenacity used to create with limited resources that have now morphed into CGI.

And now, I see *Doctor Who* in my everyday. When there is a lesson to be learned in our current world, the Doctor has long since had an idea or solution to fix it.

TELL US YOUR FAVORITE MOMENT IN YOUR DOCTOR WHO FANDOM EXPERIENCE.

My favorite fandom experiences are:

- Getting my TARDIS tattoo
- Going to Chicago TARDIS. I was absolutely immersed in my joy for the series. Surrounded by complete acceptance and camaraderie, I walked amongst my peers, at ease in cosplay.
- Finding fellow *Doctor Who* fans in the wild. "Who is "your" Doctor"?

IF YOU WERE TO INTRODUCE SOMEONE ELSE TO THE DOCTOR WHO SERIES, WHAT EPISODE/STORY WOULD YOU TELL THEM TO START WITH AND WHY?

If I know someone well enough, I can pair them to an episode:

- Art teacher: "Vincent and the Doctor."
- History: "Demons of Punjab."
- You like an escapade: "Time Heist."
- Soccer fan: "The Lodger."
- Love: 'The Lone Centurion' arc.
- This horrible presidency and the hate in my country: "The Zygon Inversion," or "73 Yards."
- Horror: "The Empty Child"/"The Doctor Dances."
- When all else fails: "Blink;" I fail to see how anyone would not be intrigued.

ROSS RUEDIGER

WHAT WAS THE FIRST EPISODE/STORY OF DOCTOR WHO THAT YOU SAW?

"Planet of Evil" was my first story. It was a hot summer night, I recall, in 1984. The show played on my local PBS station – KETC out of St. Louis – on Sunday nights at 10:30PM. I'd read about the show in *Starlog* magazine and thought that Tom Baker's face was utterly captivating; you couldn't not want to watch a show with a lead who looked like that. The psychedelic trip to Zeta Minor did not disappoint and I was instantly smitten by not just Baker as an actor, but also by Elisabeth Sladen, who quickly became a major TV crush. I can still, to this day, watch "Planet of Evil" and be transported back to that balmy Missouri evening in the countryside and into the house where I spent a nice chunk of my teenage years, dreaming of the big city of St. Louis, from where the TV signal originated. That's a night that will forever be etched into my memory.

TELL US HOW YOU THEN BECAME A FAN OF THE SHOW.

My love for *Doctor Who* developed quickly. I tuned in every Sunday night that summer, and, by the time the summer was over, I was so addicted that my mother allowed me to stay up late on Sundays even though it was a school night. Target novelizations soon followed and anything else I could get my hands on (of course, in the American Midwest, there wasn't a whole lot). The show became more important to me than almost anything else, and I got my first job (dishwasher and busboy at a greasy spoon) so that I could buy a VCR to record *Doctor Who* and not be tired on Monday mornings.

TELL US YOUR FAVORITE MOMENT IN YOUR DOCTOR WHO FANDOM EXPERIENCE.

My first Doctor Who convention was in St. Louis in

1986. I can't necessarily say it was my favorite fan experience, but it was certainly an important one. I realized that day these were people I wanted to spend more time with; I had found my tribe. I have since attended many more Who cons, and generally speaking I must say that my numerous experiences interviewing series cast members on stage at Chicago TARDIS rank as definite high points.

My general love of and fascination with *Doctor Who* fans also led to the creation of *inDoctornated*, a documentary chronicling three American fans, that I wrote, co-produced, and co-directed. It's been an enormous undertaking and, at the time of writing, has screened at Chicago TARDIS and Gallifrey One, and is now playing the film festival circuit. While I consider it to be a professional rather than a fan endeavor, there's no question that without my own fandom, it never would have happened. Heck, we even got *Doctor Who* composer Dominic Glynn to do our score for us! So, yes, being a *Doctor Who* fan can take you to some pretty great places; hanging around with fellow fans, even more so. Highly recommended.

If I could travel back through time and tell 13-year-old me what the future had in store, his mind would be appropriately blown.

IF YOU WERE TO INTRODUCE SOMEONE ELSE TO THE DOCTOR WHO SERIES, WHAT EPISODE/STORY WOULD YOU TELL THEM TO START WITH AND WHY?

Introducing someone to *Doctor Who* can be a tricky endeavor. Think of the many potential fans we have lost over the years because they tuned in to "Underworld" or "The Long Game" and never bothered to return for another helping. Many people will say "Blink," which, while being an exceptional hour, isn't really what the show is like week to week. I would definitely pull an episode from the new series. The last time I was asked this question on record I said "Rose," but I think the show has grown and changed so much since then, that there are probably better choices. "The Eleventh Hour" is very good, but possibly too steeped in lore to be a guaranteed conversion tool.

How about "Mummy on the Orient Express?" Peter Capaldi is sinister and dashing. (He remains my favorite new series Doctor.) Jenna Coleman is a knockout in her sliver PJs and flapper girl attire. (And Clara, my favorite new series companion.) Their friendship – already clearly rocky – is put to the test. There's a complexity between them that begs for a new viewer to wonder how they got here. The story itself engages and has a sense of urgency from start to finish. It's gorgeous to look at and rooted in classic literature and film, with tropes that most people will recognize. Who among us does not love a hulking, terrifying mummy? Stalking passengers on a train? In space!?! Yes, I think that would be a fabulous place to start.

Or perhaps, since it worked its magic on me, "Planet of Evil" would get the job done.

JAMES RYAN

WHAT WAS THE FIRST EPISODE/STORY OF DOCTOR WHO THAT YOU SAW?

The first one I saw was "Planet of Evil."

TELL US HOW YOU THEN BECAME A FAN OF THE SHOW.

I became enamored of the show and would watch it regularly (which for me was on WOR-TV). It was when I got to college a few years later and found other fans of the show who introduced me to much of the lore and history. I hadn't been able to get it before then.

TELL US YOUR FAVORITE MOMENT IN YOUR DOCTOR WHO FANDOM EXPERIENCE.

In 1988, NJN (the Public Broadcasting System's New Jersey Network) produced *The Making of Doctor Who* and offered fans of the show a chance to contribute to produce the program; in exchange for $35, contributors would get end screen credit and attend a meet and greet with Sylvester McCoy and Sophie Aldred. It was the first "crowdsourcing" I participated in, years before that had a name.

IF YOU WERE TO INTRODUCE SOMEONE ELSE TO THE DOCTOR WHO SERIES, WHAT EPISODE/STORY WOULD YOU TELL THEM TO START WITH AND WHY?

For younger fans, I would have to start them off with "Rose," which is closer to their time than the episodes I grew up with. Once they had gotten acclimated to the show, I would push on them "An Unearthly Child."

BRIAN SAA

WHAT WAS THE FIRST EPISODE/STORY OF DOCTOR WHO THAT YOU SAW?

The first story I saw was "The Eleventh Hour." I was coming off a bad breakup and my friend Ben DeLoose said, "I'm coming over, we're watching *Doctor Who*." I had never seen it, but I could use the company. He had a whole roadmap of episodes to start me on, we drank Guinness, ate frozen fish fingers, and watched. Within minutes, I was blown away, ready to go on a journey wherever Matt Smith's Doctor was taking me. I had to know more about this show, who this gorgeous, talented Karen Gillan was and is she single. I shipped Amy and The Doctor, rooting for them to get together (a thought that my friend Ben despised) and upon watching more of the show, realized that would have been awful. That's not what this show is. Moffat did a brilliant job with the Ponds and made you so invested in the Amy-Rory relationship.

TELL US HOW YOU THEN BECAME A FAN OF THE SHOW.

Shortly after becoming a fan of the show, I went to my cousin's wedding in Washington D.C. A childhood friend who was currently living there, Jaclyn, said "I heard you like *Doctor Who*. I'm taking you to this bar." We went to The Black Cat and I was shocked to learn they did a *Doctor Who* screening on Fridays! I watched with Jaclyn and about ten other Whovians, amazed at the feeling of community and acceptance. It made me think about moving to D.C. Then I went back to LA, saw the sun again, and was like "never mind." But then I started thinking, could I start something like that out here?

I had a friend, Sarah, working at District Pub in North Hollywood and knew they had a big screen. She set me up with the owner, and thus GALLIDAYS was born! I marketed the event, a monthly *Doctor Who* happy hour with episode screenings, and was shocked at the first event that over 40 people showed up – most of whom I'd never met before! It took off from there, moving after a year to The Fox and Hounds British pub in Studio City, where we stayed for many happy years, and are now at Lawless Brewing in North Hollywood, where we have a huge room, big screen, and loads of fun.

People in the group have met and become best friends, gotten married, everything. It's wild what *Doctor Who* can do for people! GALLIDAYS is now in our eleventh year, never missing a month, even organizing virtual screenings during the pandemic. I can't believe we've lasted eleven years, but it's because *Doctor Who* is a community, a passionate group of kind nerds who just want to go on adventures through space and time together.

I even found love thanks to *Doctor Who*. Online dating for me was awful for years, no bites, no connections. I was ready to give up when the service said I had three free months left. I thought "screw it" and put into the search "hot girls into *Doctor Who*." That's how I met my wife Marilyn, and now we have a baby girl whose middle name is Amelia! Marilyn and I have gone to Gallifrey One every year, making new friends and having the best time partying and meeting talent from the show. It's a tradition that is an integral part of our relationship, as is the show. We even brought our baby girl last year to Gallifrey One and dressed her as an Adipose! I got to thank Steven Moffat in person – without his brilliant writing for the Matt Smith years, my wife and I might have never met!

TELL US YOUR FAVORITE MOMENT IN YOUR DOCTOR WHO FANDOM EXPERIENCE.

My favorite moment was honestly the first-time watching *Doctor Who*. It felt like everything in my world was about to change. This show was something special, written with such whimsy and heart – two hearts, in fact.

IF YOU WERE TO INTRODUCE SOMEONE ELSE TO THE DOCTOR WHO SERIES, WHAT EPISODE/STORY WOULD

YOU TELL THEM TO START WITH AND WHY?

    I would introduce someone to the show starting with "The Eleventh Hour," especially if they're a Disney fan. There's a magic and fantasy to that first Matt Smith story that really clicks with that crowd, myself included. I know if my friend had started me with the first episode of New Who, I would have stopped once I got to "Aliens of London." Farting aliens? OUT!

NICHOLAS SEIDLER

WHAT WAS THE FIRST EPISODE/STORY OF DOCTOR WHO THAT YOU SAW?

The first *Doctor Who* story I ever saw was the omnibus version of "Genesis of the Daleks," which was broadcast on Saturday, 16 April 1983 on my local Public Television station, WMVS Milwaukee (Channel 10). I tuned in just as the Kaled scientists were confronting Davros and I was absolutely hooked. My mother's friend, Theresa Mueller, was visiting and watched the show regularly in Chicago, and let me know what show we were watching. I really owe her a debt of gratitude, as from then on I knew what to look for.

TELL US HOW YOU THEN BECAME A FAN OF THE SHOW.

I immediately tuned in the next week and caught the next story ("Revenge of the Cybermen") and the next ("Terror of the Zygons") and I was absolutely surprised about the creativity and quality of writing in the show. Each one was different. The hero was a quirky and smart oddball. This was the end of my freshman year of high school and I had found a thing that was intellectual and inspiring to me. As I neared my birthday, my very wonderful and loving parents went to the local comic book store, The Turning Page, and bought me photos of the Fourth Doctor and a Target novelization ("The Power of Kroll") which became my first ever collectables once my birthday arrived. I started to read the novelizations, and buy them regularly with my pocket money. A purchase of Jean-Marc Lofficier's *Doctor Who - The Programme Guide - Volume 1: The Programmes* became a critical book for me to learn the history of the show, though it only covered up to the end of the Tom Baker era.

I recall a pivotal moment in my life in mid-1983, when the film "Return of the Jedi" came out. Until then, I had been a big *Star Wars* fan and collected books and action figures from that franchise. Having heard that George Lucas was going to close that series when the trilogy ended, I made the conscious decision from that point on to collect *Doctor Who* items rather than *Star Wars* related items. The adult 'me' is particularly happy about that decision as I now have money for food as well as a great *Doctor Who* collection. *Star Wars* collecting would have put me in the poor house.

As *Doctor Who*'s 20th Anniversary neared, I learned about special events that were happening. On 23 November 1983, WMVS was going to air the special broadcast of the special "The Five Doctors". I also saw that the TV station was actually hosting a special screening of that same anniversary story a day early on the Tuesday before (22 November 1983) at a local dance club named Park Avenue (located in Milwaukee at the Northeast corner of Water and Clybourne streets). That special event was co-sponsored by a local club known as The Renegade Time Lords from the local university (UW-Milwaukee), but I could not attend as I was not old enough to go to a bar that served alcohol yet. I have since learned that this private screening at Park Avenue is actually the first ever public screening of "The Five Doctors" held anywhere in the world. That month, I also bought the seminal Peter Haining book, *Doctor Who: A Celebration* as well as *Starlog*'s American reprinting of the *Radio Times*' "Doctor Who 20th Anniversary Special" magazine. Once I saw the story "The Five Doctors" for myself, broadcast in the USA on PBS on Wednesday, 23 November 1983, I had seen at least one appearance of all of the existing Doctors.

My interest in the show exploded as the desire to see more of the series took hold. Even with only 20 years of the show, being a *Doctor Who* fan was a huge undertaking as finding access to old stories was very difficult. The following year, my mom knitted me a Fourth Doctor scarf for Christmas (thanks Mom and Dad, it's still the best holiday present I ever got!). In 1985, I co-founded a *Doctor Who* club at Marquette University High School called the Earthbound TimeLords. I began writing and editing the club's fanzine, which got distributed for free around town. I started going to other clubs' meetings to see episodes

I had not seen yet and to meet other fans. I began trading rare episodes with others to get copies of unseen stories. I attended my first dedicated *Doctor Who* convention, TARDIS 22, where I met actors from the show and got my first autographs. Late in my college career, the show went into hiatus, but I continued to support it by buying the official magazine and the New Adventure books, and by creating my own content for other fans to enjoy.

I started running adventures and playing the FASA *Doctor Who* Role-Playing Game in 1985 and began a long-running gaming campaign. This now over 40-year-long RPG campaign continues to this day and is one of the longest continuous running games within the whole of role-playing game hobby. It is thought to be the longest continuing non-*Dungeons & Dragons* RPG campaign in the world. Role-playing games allow participants to engage in their own shared storytelling adventures. This campaign, comprising over 5000 game play sessions, has included over 400 players who participated in it. It has allowed me to tell literally thousands of my own *Doctor Who* adventure stories. All that practice has made me a solid storyteller. I have also had the honor to also play with other top notch Game Masters with other amazing ideas. If you are craving more *Doctor Who* in any way, or want to engage with even more Whovian content, I encourage you to get involved in a *Doctor Who* RPG game, for you will never run out of stories, enjoyment, and laughs.

As I went to graduate school and the internet became a thing, in 1997 my friend John Curtis and I pivoted the Earthbound TimeLords fan club to an online entity, and soon it became the first academic website and fanclub focused on *Doctor Who*. The site featured peer reviewed papers and articles about the series. I continued attending conventions and volunteering at them, and soon found myself on the staffs and volunteer teams of various cons to include Chicago TARDIS, Gallifrey One, and CONsole Room. With the students at the university where I work, we even began our own convention, Concinnity, which, while broadly open to many fandoms, still features *Doctor Who* connected guests every year. In 2017, some of my closest friends and I wrote a book named "Red, White, and Who: The Story of Doctor Who in America". This non-fiction book proudly remains the definitive book about the *Doctor Who* experience in the United States. My fandom and connection to the series has never waned and continues to this day as I remain very involved in the show's fandom.

While this book asks us to tell our stories connected to the series, I pass these moments on not to celebrate moments that I was a part of, but rather to celebrate my closest friends who are often fans of the series. I celebrate the fans that write fanzine articles, the actors and directors who make fan films, Game Masters and players in *Doctor Who* role-playing games, and my friends who have composed original music inspired by the show. I celebrate my extended family that I see each year at conventions, the convention runners who I consider close friends, the actors and actresses that I have gotten to know connected to the series, those who worked behind-the-scenes to make this joyful program a reality. I especially value my friends that sit in the room with me as we watch a new story, whether they consider themselves fans or not.

All of the adventures that I mentioned above were not alone. I always had others at my side, just like the Doctor. Those people made my life a joy and continue to do so. Those friends, those fans, are what have made my life so amazing. If you are reading this, that includes you.

TELL US YOUR FAVORITE MOMENT IN YOUR DOCTOR WHO FANDOM EXPERIENCE.

The people connected to this awesome show. Honestly, there is nothing better than meeting other fans and seeing how intelligent and brilliant they are. They care about the world and being kind, and I know the future is in good hands as I see the amazing people I have gotten to know because of the series. They all inspire me. The contributors to this book. The fans at cons. My creative friends. You are my favorite part of my *Doctor Who* experience without equal.

IF YOU WERE TO INTRODUCE SOMEONE ELSE TO THE DOCTOR WHO SERIES, WHAT EPISODE/STORY WOULD YOU TELL THEM TO START WITH AND WHY?

In my opinion, there is no wrong place to start watching *Doctor Who*. Because the show is so unique, I tell people that they should watch at least three successive stories in a row to really understand the series. This is because the show has such an original concept and can tell stories set in the future, in the past, in present day, or even in a parallel universe sideways in time where World War II never happened. The show is limitless in the stories it can tell, which is what makes *Doctor Who* the greatest storytelling idea ever.

That said, given a choice to introduce others to the series, I often recommend new viewers begin at "Rose," the first story from 2005 of the continuing series (it's not a reboot, or a new show)! This usually makes the series accessible to new viewers with a pace that modern viewers are more used to, as well as a color widescreen stereo presentation and special effects that modern viewers expect. This way they also discover the most important ideas and tropes of the show within the first new series. Then watch the series through the modern current run. Afterwards, I recommend going back to "Robot" and watching forward to where you started, and then back to "An Unearthly Child" and watching forward to see all of this amazing program.

LIBBY SHEA

WHAT WAS THE FIRST EPISODE/STORY OF DOCTOR WHO THAT YOU SAW?

The first Ninth Doctor episode: "Rose."

TELL US HOW YOU THEN BECAME A FAN OF THE SHOW.

After watching "Rose," I continued watching with my boyfriend (now husband) and our friend. Shortly after, that same friend invited us to play in his *Doctor Who* tabletop role-paying game campaign. I continued watching and playing and got involved as part of the convention staff at Chicago TARDIS. Now: I still keep up with current *Doctor Who* as it airs. I still play in that friend's RPG campaign. I run my own home *Doctor Who* RPG campaign. I run *Doctor Who* games at cons like Chicago TARDIS, CONsole Room, and Gen Con. And it is a Thanksgiving tradition to work Chicago TARDIS!

TELL US YOUR FAVORITE MOMENT IN YOUR DOCTOR WHO FANDOM EXPERIENCE.

I have two favorite moments to share. The first is when we watched the premier of "The Star Beast" at Chicago TARDIS with everyone at the convention. The excitement and energy of the reactions to that episode filled my heart. It was made even better that Rachel Talalay (the episode's director) was in the room, watching alongside us. At the end of the episode, all 700+ people gave a very long and loud standing ovation for her and the episode.

My second favorite memory was getting to run one of my custom written *Doctor Who* RPG adventures for Greg Austin, the actor who played Charlie Smith in the *Doctor Who* spin-off series *Class,* and a small group of friends.

IF YOU WERE TO INTRODUCE SOMEONE ELSE TO THE

DOCTOR WHO SERIES, WHAT EPISODE/STORY WOULD YOU TELL THEM TO START WITH AND WHY?

If you want an episode that gives you the general concept of Doctor Who while being a great story and leads into a big plot that builds over the next multiple series, I would recommend starting with "Rose" (featuring the Ninth Doctor with Rose Tyler). If you want an episode with, in my opinion, one of the best Doctor/companion duos in the whole series, a lot of comedy, and a very interesting creature, I would recommend "Partners in Crime" (the Tenth Doctor with Donna Noble). If you want a true work of art (pun intended) and you don't mind starting mid-season, I would recommend watching "Vincent and the Doctor" (featuring the Eleventh Doctor with Amy Pond).

GRAEME SHERIDAN

WHAT WAS THE FIRST EPISODE/STORY OF DOCTOR WHO THAT YOU SAW?

The episode I remember first was "Genesis of the Daleks," at three years old, because I remember Sarah Jane looking over the wall at the weapons testing of the Dalek.

TELL US HOW YOU THEN BECAME A FAN OF THE SHOW.

I grew up with *Doctor Who* on TV in the UK, and as a massive sci-fi fan from a young age I was drawn to it. *Space: 1999* and other Gerry Anderson shows were on repeat, or as with *Space: 1999* on first showing. I was probably in the minority at that time, as ,until *Star Wars* was shown in cinemas, sci-fi such as *Doctor Who* was a niche fandom along with other sci-fi shows and films.

TELL US YOUR FAVORITE MOMENT IN YOUR DOCTOR WHO FANDOM EXPERIENCE.

As the internet finally made it possible to connect up with other fans, finding fanclubs even in Germany.

IF YOU WERE TO INTRODUCE SOMEONE ELSE TO THE DOCTOR WHO SERIES, WHAT EPISODE/STORY WOULD YOU TELL THEM TO START WITH AND WHY?

I'd split it into two parts. Even though it's far away from my favorite New Who, "Blink." It just seems that specific episode draws people in. Though, personally, "The Eleventh Hour" would be the one I'd recommend. As to Classic Who, "Tomb of the Cybermen," "Genesis of the Daleks," and "Earthshock" are the episodes I'd recommend. Though I find other stories better, these serve a good purpose as they show all aspects of *Doctor Who*.

NICKY SMALLEY

WHAT WAS THE FIRST EPISODE/STORY OF DOCTOR WHO THAT YOU SAW?

I believe my first memory is of "Remembrance of the Daleks"; however, given I was three years old when it aired, I could be mixing this up with a memory of watching it on UK Gold, as I watched most of the episodes on there. Though, I also remember watching "The Green Death" at my Nan's, which would have been in 1994.

TELL US HOW YOU THEN BECAME A FAN OF THE SHOW.

Doctor Who became my weekend viewing. I also remember being so excited for "Dimensions in Time"; I made my parents drive to Meadowhall so we could buy the 3D specs from Sainsburys. I also used to seek out all those colourful New Adventures novels in bookshops.

TELL US YOUR FAVORITE MOMENT IN YOUR DOCTOR WHO FANDOM EXPERIENCE.

I have so many I could share: from being spotted in Matthew Sweet's documentary during the 50th Anniversary night, publishing an article in the *Celestial Toystore*, or, more recently, performing Shakespeare with Louise Jameson. But I think it's meeting my friends from the Sheffield Who group, who are now as close to me as family.

IF YOU WERE TO INTRODUCE SOMEONE ELSE TO THE DOCTOR WHO SERIES, WHAT EPISODE/STORY WOULD YOU TELL THEM TO START WITH AND WHY?

It would depend on their age. For a younger person I would always recommend "Blink," as it's about as perfect as an episode could get. As someone who is used to slower drama,

I'd choose something like "The Seeds of Doom" or "The Green Death."

GENE SMITH

WHAT WAS THE FIRST EPISODE/STORY OF DOCTOR WHO THAT YOU SAW?

Can't recall but it was a Pertwee episode in the mid-late 1970s on WTTW Public Television. I do not remember much from what I saw in the UK as a child.

TELL US HOW YOU THEN BECAME A FAN OF THE SHOW.

It was a fun series to watch every week as I like sci-fi and mystery stories. I kept up with the series till the end, read all of the Target books (which was a great way to get the stories that were lost/missing) plus some of the Virgin and BBC novels.

TELL US YOUR FAVORITE MOMENT IN YOUR DOCTOR WHO FANDOM EXPERIENCE.

The coolest thing for *Doctor Who* (in the US, as that is where I live) was the Spirit of Light convention in 1983 for the 20th Anniversary. There were so many people there plus a ton of guests. A bit disorganized as the promoters did not know what to expect nor how to handle it, but I think most people had a good time with lots of good energy. Gallifrey One and Visions (followed by Chicago TARDIS) carried on the live events throughout the "Wilderness Years" with strong support from the fans (live events are the best place to enjoy your fandom experiences and meet other people with similar interests).

We did not see that euphoria again until 2012-13 with all the 50th Anniversary hype and excitement (Gallifrey One and Chicago TARDIS were packed) plus everyone was getting in on the bandwagon to sell *Doctor Who* or bring *Doctor Who* guests to a Comic-Con or convention (even companies and stores that knew nothing about it nor did they care - the money was too good for them to resist).

IF YOU WERE TO INTRODUCE SOMEONE ELSE TO THE DOCTOR WHO SERIES, WHAT EPISODE/STORY WOULD YOU TELL THEM TO START WITH AND WHY?

It's hard to just pick one story but any of the following would be a great place to show someone a good story, whether they knew anything about the series or not. I am choosing four each from the classic and modern series stories. Any of these are a good place to start as they hold up due to a great story.

CLASSIC SERIES: "Genesis of the Daleks," "The Caves of Androzani," "City of Death," or "Horror of Fang Rock."

NEW SERIES: "Blink," "Vincent and the Doctor," "Empty Child"/"Doctor Dances," or "Dalek."

NICK SMITH

WHAT WAS THE FIRST EPISODE/STORY OF DOCTOR WHO THAT YOU SAW?

The first story that I glimpsed was "The Planet of the Spiders," Jon Pertwee's final adventure, stuck in my mind when I was very young, specifically the eeriness of Metebelis III, the evolved spiders and their human subjects, and the Doctor confronting the Queen. It was not until years after, when I watched the full adventure on VHS, that the image resonated again and I understood the context of my memories.

TELL US HOW YOU THEN BECAME A FAN OF THE SHOW.

I was nine years old when my babysitter, a jolly middle-aged lady, gushed about the *Doctor Who* cliffhanger she'd seen on Saturday night. "The Doctor got his arms and legs pulled off," she told me gleefully. I was intrigued, not just by her gruesome description of the scene, but also by her excitement. I had to watch the next episode of "The Leisure Hive," and from then on I was an avid viewer. 1980-81 were exciting times for *Doctor Who*, with glossy production values, Tom Baker's regeneration into Peter Davison, a repeat season showing all five Doctors, and a regular magazine that took the show seriously and explored the program's past. It was *Doctor Who Monthly* that gave a real sense of community – the articles and letters page indicated that there were many readers who cared about the show as much as, or more, than I did. Between seasons, there was plenty for a young fan to enjoy. I read the magazine, the annuals, and the Target novelizations. *Doctor Who* was an unfolding text that my parents had grown up with, and I was content to do the same.

TELL US YOUR FAVORITE MOMENT IN YOUR DOCTOR WHO FANDOM EXPERIENCE.

Sharing *Doctor Who* with my son, Sam. I was a die-hard fan when he was a baby and I did not know whether he would be interested or not. He did not care for *Star Wars* – it just did not hold his attention. For some inexplicable reason, 1960s *Doctor Who* captivated him. Perhaps the short episodes helped, or the fact that I watched it with him from infancy onward. The poor kid didn't stand a chance, hooked on Who along with his dad. While we've had our ups and downs through the years (he's 25 now), Doctor Who is a constant. We have journeyed the stars via this show, and it has broached themes and ideas that open discussions for us. We read spin-off books and comics, and share opinions with each other. We don't go to *Doctor Who* conventions together, and he does not participate in the podcasts I'm on, as a guest or a viewer. As a family, our fandom experience is humble and homebound, a shared memory of adventures and social media posts. As far as I am concerned, that is enough. *Doctor Who* is comfort viewing for me, and I hope it gives Sam a source of relaxation and escape as well.

IF YOU WERE TO INTRODUCE SOMEONE ELSE TO THE DOCTOR WHO SERIES, WHAT EPISODE/STORY WOULD YOU TELL THEM TO START WITH AND WHY?

"The Christmas Invasion," David Tennant's introductory story as the Tenth Doctor. The plot is a simple story – aliens lurk over London, while the Doctor recovers from his regeneration. Supporting characters Rose and Jackie are thoroughly down-to-earth, helping viewers to relate to the science fiction craziness. All the performances are rock solid and entertaining, and there are plenty of British quirks that make this feel like a traditional *Doctor Who* adventure. The main reason why this is a great kick-off story is because of Tennant's total commitment to the role and his palpable joy as he plays the part.

STACEY SMITH?

WHAT WAS THE FIRST EPISODE/STORY OF DOCTOR WHO THAT YOU SAW?

"The Green Death," Episode Six (in June 1978).

TELL US HOW YOU THEN BECAME A FAN OF THE SHOW.

My father had been a fan of William Hartnell and was watching the episode for old time's sake. I was immediately hooked and tuned in to "The Time Warrior," Part One the next day. I watched it religiously thereafter and joined Australian fandom, then Canadian fandom when I moved across the world. Later still, I became a writer of non-fiction books about the show.

TELL US YOUR FAVORITE MOMENT IN YOUR DOCTOR WHO FANDOM EXPERIENCE.

As a kid: meeting Peter Davison when he came to Australia and touching his finger while he was signing someone else's book (before running away).
As an adult: Getting to write populist books about the show and being feted for our contributions was amazing.

IF YOU WERE TO INTRODUCE SOMEONE ELSE TO THE DOCTOR WHO SERIES, WHAT EPISODE/STORY WOULD YOU TELL THEM TO START WITH AND WHY?

"The Face of Evil" is the perfect jumping-on point, with Tom Baker's insouciance utterly transfixing.

BOB STAHLEY

WHAT WAS THE FIRST EPISODE/STORY OF DOCTOR WHO THAT YOU SAW?

I don't recall the episode/story, but it was some time in the early eighties – I recall it was a Tom Baker episode. Being a comic book fan with knowledge of nerdy stuff, I was aware of *Doctor Who,* but since they were running it in the afternoon, I knew I couldn't follow it.

TELL US HOW YOU THEN BECAME A FAN OF THE SHOW.

I saw an ad for "Twice Upon a Time" at a local cinema. I was impressed with how much the actor playing the first Doctor looked like Hartnell. I figured it was something worth watching. Then I started watching the new series and simultaneously watching the classic program from their beginnings. I'd retired by then.

TELL US YOUR FAVORITE MOMENT IN YOUR DOCTOR WHO FANDOM EXPERIENCE.

Cosplaying the First Doctor at conventions and having people stop me in the hallways for photographs.

IF YOU WERE TO INTRODUCE SOMEONE ELSE TO THE DOCTOR WHO SERIES, WHAT EPISODE/STORY WOULD YOU TELL THEM TO START WITH AND WHY?

"Blink" because one doesn't need a lot of backstory to appreciate it. And it's a great story.

ATHENA STAMOS

WHAT WAS THE FIRST EPISODE/STORY OF DOCTOR WHO THAT YOU SAW?

When I was four years old, my mom and I were flipping through the TV channels. She stopped on PBS as she recognized Tom Baker from watching *Doctor Who* in the 1970s. I was so young that I don't remember what episode it was. It likely was a Leela story, but I definitely recall... Tom: teeth, curls, big eyes, and that fantastic scarf!

TELL US HOW YOU THEN BECAME A FAN OF THE SHOW.

I was drawn to the whole concept for very personal reasons. My parents divorced when I was very young, and I would soon not have a relationship with my dad. My mother was strict and overbearing, so I had a desire to fly away. The idea that a father figure could show up, believe in me, and whisk me away into a universe of unlimited adventures pulled me in.

I hated waking up early for school, but it was easy to get up on Saturday morning for *Doctor Who* when it aired. We lived in a one-bedroom apartment, with my mom in the living room... so usually, it would be quietly playing as she slept in. One memory that sticks out is how much the spiders in "Full Circle" freaked me out! Specifically, the idea that spiders can just pop out of anything... including the seeds in your produce! I still can't look at the inside of a papaya. I blame "Full Circle" and "Planet of the Spiders" for my fear of spiders. I eventually saw all of Jon Pertwee, Tom Baker, and Peter Davison's stories. And though no one compares to Tom, Pertwee became my favorite Doctor. Pertwee's spy-like persona won me over, and I love his charming relationship with Jo Grant.

After graduating high school in 2000, I discovered the Doctor Who community on IRC Chat and Outpost Gallifrey. This led me to Los Angeles' Doctor Who convention, Gallifrey One, in 2003. Despite being introverted and nervous about walking into the convention alone, I attended dressed as one of my favorite companions, Leela. To my relief, it wasn't weird! Everyone was quite welcoming and accepting. How refreshing! I have gone through a lot over the years, and Gallifrey One has been my constant. I've grown because of this fantastic community.

When *Doctor Who* came back to us in 2005, I was pumped! My favorite character, whom I had grown up watching, was returning! The show brought me so much joy and also touched an emotional nerve. I really identified with Rose Tyler. During most of her episodes, I cried for one reason or another. And although Pertwee is my favorite, Christopher Eccleston became my Doctor.

TELL US YOUR FAVORITE MOMENT IN YOUR DOCTOR WHO FANDOM EXPERIENCE.

Doctor Who has been intertwined into so much of my life that I've been fortunate to have several unforgettable moments…

Meeting Eccleston (Gallifrey One) and Tom Baker (Cygnus Alpha Events). Conducting press interviews with Matt Smith and Karen Gillan (San Diego Comic-Con). Producing "The Doctor Games," a Doctor Who/Hunger Games viral video that was nominated for a Geekie Award in 2014. Producing and performing in The Idiot's Lantern sketch comedy group at Gallifrey One for 10 years. I even appeared on the cover of a Thirteenth Doctor comic book. It helped that I'm a doppelganger for Jodie Whittaker; same age and height, too.

But if I were to choose one moment… the moment Author George Mann chose me to be the character model for Cinder in the *Doctor Who: Legacy* video game. Cinder is the War Doctor's companion in his novel *Engines of War*. To be the face of an official companion, a strong woman with a sense of morality, after a lifetime of looking up to the Doctor… what a gift.

IF YOU WERE TO INTRODUCE SOMEONE ELSE TO THE

DOCTOR WHO SERIES, WHAT EPISODE/STORY WOULD YOU TELL THEM TO START WITH AND WHY?

I did this! In 2010, I introduced my boyfriend (now husband) to *Doctor Who*. He agreed to watch only three episodes to see if he liked it. I decided to start with New Who as it's easier for modern audiences to appreciate than slower-paced Classic Who.

I showed him: "Blink," "Dalek," and "Girl in the Fireplace." I believe all three episodes leave the viewer wanting to know more about The Doctor and his universe. I started with "Blink" because it gives an outsider's perspective on who the Doctor is. Then, "Dalek" provides a glimpse into the destructive power of his enemies. And finally, "Girl in the Fireplace" draws you into the Doctor's soul.

My boyfriend enjoyed them immensely, then immediately watched New Who in its entirety. And subsequently, most of the classic series. Success!

KATHY SULLIVAN

WHAT WAS THE FIRST EPISODE/STORY OF DOCTOR WHO THAT YOU SAW?

I had seen the theatrical films *Doctor Who and the Daleks* and *Invasion Earth: 2150 AD* on the then new UHF channel in Chicago when I was in eighth grade, but that didn't make me join fandom.

I saw "The Brain of Morbius" in 1981 when a fanzine editor sat me down and showed it to me to convince me to write stories in that fandom. This was on our way to MediaWest*Con, a convention of fanzines of various fandoms.

That story hooked me because it had psi powers (which I enjoyed reading and writing about), a matriarchal society that was as powerful as the Doctor's, and Sarah Jane Smith rescuing the Doctor.

TELL US HOW YOU THEN BECAME A FAN OF THE SHOW.

At MediaWest*Con that year I hunted down any zine that contained a *Doctor Who* story (most of the *Doctor Who* fanzines, unfortunately, didn't start to appear until a few months after the convention). Independent stations around the U.S. were airing the Tom Baker stories in half hour episodes and several fan writers already had exposure to the show. The stories and poetry those writers produced touched on the friendship between the characters as well as the Doctor's adventures in time and space.

I had a panel on *Doctor Who* as well as one on British science fiction shows. There were also a few video showings at room parties, so I was able to learn about more than one episode. It wasn't enough for me to spark any ideas about a story to write, so I kept trying to find out more. I found those Target novelizations that had reached the U.S. and got more details from those about the various Doctors.

My editor made dubs of the episodes that aired in her area, and I started having viewing parties in my living room of those stories for friends who were interested in the show. I had already started writing both local PBS stations to carry the show and convinced my friends to do the same. Eventually the viewing parties moved to the nearby university and I became faculty advisor of a *Doctor Who* club.

TELL US YOUR FAVORITE MOMENT IN YOUR DOCTOR WHO FANDOM EXPERIENCE.

Representing my club at Panopticon West 1985 in New Orleans in a wonderful ceremony with all the chapter heads (Cardinals) dressed in Time Lord robes. Colin Baker, John Nathan-Turner, Nicholas Courtney, and Gary Downie, guests at that convention, were presented with Time Lord robes and collars for the ceremony. Colin's robes and collar were polka-dotted, while JNT's had a Hawaiian shirt pattern. Nicholas Courtney (as befitting the Brigadier) had olive green robes with gold trim on the collar.

IF YOU WERE TO INTRODUCE SOMEONE ELSE TO THE DOCTOR WHO SERIES, WHAT EPISODE/STORY WOULD YOU TELL THEM TO START WITH AND WHY?

It depends on what they are interested in. There are so many genres represented in the show. Nowadays for a possible NuWho fan, I'd tell them to start with the first episode of a new Doctor, as those tend to give enough backstory while focusing on what type of person the new Doctor will be.

LEE THOMPSON

WHAT WAS THE FIRST EPISODE/STORY OF DOCTOR WHO THAT YOU SAW?

I was eleven years old when WTTW Channel 11 in Chicago aired Episode One of "The Mutants" in 1975.

TELL US HOW YOU THEN BECAME A FAN OF THE SHOW.

Doctor Who was something different compared to the sci-fi shows at that time. I was an avid watcher but really did not become a true Whovian until Tom Baker took over as the Doctor. He was and is still amazing. Tom Baker will always be my doctor.

TELL US YOUR FAVORITE MOMENT IN YOUR DOCTOR WHO FANDOM EXPERIENCE.

I have to say becoming the Guinness World Record holder for the largest *Doctor Who* memorabilia collection was memorable. Especially since I accomplished this with my son. However, my most favorite/memorable moment was when I took my son and daughter to see the airing of the 50th Anniversary *Doctor Who* special at our local theater. I can still remember hearing Tom Baker speak on camera and the whole audience went crazy. When he walked onto the screen as the Curator everyone started clapping and even jumped up out of their chairs. Eleven years ago, and I can still see and hear it if I close my eyes. What a fantastic experience to have with my children.

IF YOU WERE TO INTRODUCE SOMEONE ELSE TO THE DOCTOR WHO SERIES, WHAT EPISODE/STORY WOULD YOU TELL THEM TO START WITH AND WHY?

I think this question really has two parts. Do you want to be introduced to the classics or the revival? A classic is

"Genesis of the Daleks" with Tom Baker as the Doctor. This has a fantastic script and Tom Baker with Elisabeth Sladen as his companion Sarah Jane Smith make it memorable.

I know this will be controversial but Christopher Eccleston as the Ninth Doctor brought Doctor Who back to modern TV with his first episode "Rose". His companion Billie Piper as Rose Tyler also helped revive the series. A great first episode to be introduced to the revival doctors.

WILLIAM THOMPSON

WHAT WAS THE FIRST EPISODE/STORY OF DOCTOR WHO THAT YOU SAW?

My father showed my sister and I "Rose" as it aired live in the states. Up until that point at age seven, I had never heard of *Doctor Who*.

TELL US HOW YOU THEN BECAME A FAN OF THE SHOW.

From that first episode I was hooked. My father also shared that this "brand new show" had a rich history behind it. So, with my Netflix DVD loaded into my Wii, I started watching all the Classic Who episodes I could. That is where I truly found my love for *Doctor Who*, allowing me to enjoy the revival even more knowing the rich history behind it.

TELL US YOUR FAVORITE MOMENT IN YOUR DOCTOR WHO FANDOM EXPERIENCE.

I will be honest, I have so many to choose from! The Who community is so welcoming that I've been able to be part of once-in-a-lifetime experiences almost every month! However, I believe I'm "legally contracted" to state that my favorite moment was securing the title of the largest *Doctor Who* memorabilia collection by Guinness World Records with my father Lee Thompson (also in this book). Our collection and shared experiences have only made us closer and love this fandom even more. Though it was an extremely challenging and stressful experience. We made it through all the hurdles together, we were even able to drag our third member of our little collecting group into the process too. That would be Mr. Randy Holndoner, who was the individual that changed our love of *Doctor Who* from just watching the show, to now owning the largest collection of *Doctor Who* collectibles. Who knows where or when we can go from here, who knows!

IF YOU WERE TO INTRODUCE SOMEONE ELSE TO THE DOCTOR WHO SERIES, WHAT EPISODE/STORY WOULD YOU TELL THEM TO START WITH AND WHY?

As weird as it may be, I would suggest the 50th Anniversary "The Day of the Doctor." Unlike a normal episode, this was filmed to be closer to a movie experience. Thus, allowing new viewers a chance to experience the show while also explaining its history to the audience in a more condensed fashion. In my opinion, this episode sets the standard for the show moving forward and allows new fans to know what the show is capable of. However, I would recommend watching the "extended edition" which shows the mini episodes before the main episode, as it helps to build suspense and additional context. This allows the viewer to experience their first regeneration concept (Eighth Doctor to the War Doctor), the brutality of this Time War narrative, and introduces you to the Eleventh Doctor, Clara, and UNIT. So far, I've used this method on so many of my friends, Amazon states I've bought the Blu-ray thirteen times!

BRAD TRECHAK

WHAT WAS THE FIRST EPISODE/STORY OF DOCTOR WHO THAT YOU SAW?

The first story I started *Doctor Who* with was Colin Baker's first full story as the main character, "The Twin Dilemma." I watched it on public access in New Jersey. They showed entire stories about once a month (back then they were broken up into 30 or 45 minute episodes in England). I recall fans really didn't take to the new Doctor due to his ostentatious costume and arrogant attitude. I had no preconceptions. My joke is I started liking *Doctor Who* when the fans didn't.

TELL US HOW YOU THEN BECAME A FAN OF THE SHOW.

When I was a freshman in high school, an upperclassman widescribed the show to me during a bus trip with the marching band, and I thought the concept sounded cool and interesting. I watched the previously mentioned "Twin Dilemma" episode and, as an intelligent person that could come off as loud and obnoxious sometimes, I felt kinship with the main character. I didn't even mind the multicolored coat. At the time, "The Twin Dilemma" was the latest episode of the show and the following month, public access restarted the show from the beginning, so the second full story I watched was "An Unearthly Child" and while it took many months of watching, I did the full circuit of the historical shows while keeping up with the new ones. At the time, I really didn't know anybody else that watched the show other than the aforementioned upperclassman. The Internet did not exist yet. My interactions with fandom came many years later.

TELL US YOUR FAVORITE MOMENT IN YOUR DOCTOR WHO FANDOM EXPERIENCE.

When *Doctor Who* became mainstream in 2005, I found

a new community to socialize with. Suddenly, there were *Doctor Who* social clubs and even a *Doctor Who* themed bar in Brooklyn. I met my wife at a *Doctor Who* meet-up in a bar in Manhattan. We dated for about nine months and then she moved into my condo. We pretty quickly knew that we would marry each other. The perfect opportunity for a proposal fell into my lap when David Tennant and Matt Smith were participating in a meet-and-greet arranged by Wizard World conventions in New York City. I bought us tickets and brought a ring. The tickets included a photo and an autograph with the former Doctors. When it was time for our photo with both actors, I got down on my knee and proposed. Nobody was aware this was going to happen except me so there was a legitimate look of shock on my wife, David Tennant, and Matt Smith. Thankfully, she said "Yes." Wizard World was kind enough to take multiple photos of this proposal and give them to us. We had the final one signed by both actors. The photos of my proposal lit up the internet for about a week. In that time, to paraphrase the movie *To Be Or Not To Be*, we were world-famous in England.

We actually had two weddings. The first was in my parents' backyard and had a *Doctor Who* theme. The second was in Disneyworld. That's another story.

IF YOU WERE TO INTRODUCE SOMEONE ELSE TO THE DOCTOR WHO SERIES, WHAT EPISODE/STORY WOULD YOU TELL THEM TO START WITH AND WHY?

The best place to start the series is the first episode of any Doctor. Whenever a new Doctor begins, the show sheds a lot of its baggage and does a soft reboot. I also sometimes tell modern newbies to start with the first episode "Rose" of the series relaunch in 2005. The episodes before that tend to have slow-moving plots and laughable special effects.

RUDY TRIZNA

WHAT WAS THE FIRST EPISODE/STORY OF DOCTOR WHO THAT YOU SAW?

"Destiny of the Daleks," Season 17 with Tom Baker.

TELL US HOW YOU THEN BECAME A FAN OF THE SHOW.

I had a friend who was a big fan who showed me the Doctor on PBS Channel 11, the only way to see it in 1981, as a rerun. My friend bought a *Doctor Who* boardgame in the early 1980s. It was fantastic and four of us were fans and played it endlessly through junior high school.

TELL US YOUR FAVORITE MOMENT IN YOUR DOCTOR WHO FANDOM EXPERIENCE.

The end of "Day of the Doctor" in the museum when Matt Smith talks to Tom Baker.

IF YOU WERE TO INTRODUCE SOMEONE ELSE TO THE DOCTOR WHO SERIES, WHAT EPISODE/STORY WOULD YOU TELL THEM TO START WITH AND WHY?

The new revival 2005 episode "Rose." The return of the Doctor with Christopher Eccleston did introduce him to modern audiences.

LISA TRUANT-TAN

WHAT WAS THE FIRST EPISODE/STORY OF DOCTOR WHO THAT YOU SAW?

I'm not sure of the exact episode/story of *Doctor Who* that I first saw. I do know that it was in the very early stories of Tom Baker (Fourth Doctor) with Elisabeth Sladen (Sarah Jane Smith). She's still my favorite companion. I think it might have been "Genesis of the Daleks" or "Revenge of the Cybermen." I watched these stories in repeats when they were shown on WNED TV out of Buffalo, New York.

TELL US HOW YOU THEN BECAME A FAN OF THE SHOW.

After I watched these first episodes I was hooked and intrigued. I tried to watch as much *Doctor Who* as I could (this was before our family had a VCR, it was the mid 1980s after all). I discovered that TVOntario also broadcast *Doctor Who* but they were repeating Tom Baker's later stories. I didn't know anybody else who watched the show. I visited a downtown Toronto book store that sold the Target novelizations and was able to buy books of episodes that I had not even seen on TV! Also purchased was a *Starlog* magazine that had an ad in it about a documentary book called *Doctor Who: A Celebration* by Peter Haining. I sent away for it and it came in the mail. It was a beautiful day and filled in so many questions that I had! In the back of this book there was a section about fan clubs around the world including the Doctor Who Information Network (DWIN) club, I wrote them and quickly joined.

I made a lot of new friends who answered other questions that I had. It made me happy and these lifelong friends were integral to meeting other people. I joined one of DWIN's "chapters" (area groups) the "Dark Tower of Toronto", in later years there was the "Not the BBC Props Dept." and then started our own chapter the "Eye of Harmony." I attended *Doctor Who* conventions including numerous "Who Parties," "Visions,"

"Who Con," and "Chicago TARDIS," and we ran about six small *Doctor Who* conventions called the "Eye of Orion." I found it so amazing that the actor guests would actually talk to you! We also played the *Doctor Who* Role-Playing Game with characters that we had created. I also was the Fan Art Director for DWIN's newsletter/fan magazine *Enlightenment* for many years and was the fan editor for a while. With these *Doctor Who* friends, there was a strong sense of belonging.

TELL US YOUR FAVORITE MOMENT IN YOUR DOCTOR WHO FANDOM EXPERIENCE.

My favorite moment in my *Doctor Who* experience is not one moment but a string of interrelated moments. It started during my first month of classes at the University of Toronto, waiting in a small classroom for the Anthropology TA to show up. Two ladies who I had never met before were talking about some everyday things including the weather. I uncharacteristically spoke up and said to one "It's amazing how humans always state the obvious like it's a nice day, you're very tall, or this is it, we're going to die!" which is from the book *The Hitchhikers Guide To the Galaxy*. She turned to me and said "I know where that's from... don't tell me, don't tell me..." After about a minute or so she gave up and asked me where it was from. I told her and she said "Oh yes!" We started talking about other interests and hobbies. I mentioned *Doctor Who* and she said that she had to introduce me to her Math TA as he liked *Doctor Who* too. She did. He did love the show. He joined our *Doctor Who* chapter. A few years later he invited us to a party that he was having where I met his friend Irwin. He wasn't able to get my contact information, but he heard from our mutual friend that I was going to be running the *Doctor Who* Room (mini-get together) at the Toronto Trek VII convention. Irwin showed up there, made himself very helpful with helping out with whatever I needed and we hit it off very well. And it also didn't hurt that his favorite Doctor was Jon Pertwee! Irwin also has a quick typing speed so he typed a lot of things for the *Enlightenment* fanzine for me. And the rest as they say is history. Irwin and I have been married for over 27 years now and we have a twenty-four-year-old son. That lady who I met at U of T, well she was one of our bridesmaids at our wedding. Our mutual friend who likes *Doctor Who,* well we see him at one of the Eye of Harmony's annual get-togethers every year.

IF YOU WERE TO INTRODUCE SOMEONE ELSE TO THE DOCTOR WHO SERIES, WHAT EPISODE/STORY WOULD YOU TELL THEM TO START WITH AND WHY?

If I was to introduce someone else to the *Doctor Who* series, what episode/story would you tell them to start with is a difficult one to answer. I'm not much of an official of the newer episodes as most of them I've only seen once. There are so many really good stories from the classic series that I remember fairly well. "Genesis of the Daleks" is a good one for many reasons but since it's six episodes long and mirrors happenings in the WWII, it might not be good for some people. I really liked "Destiny of the Daleks" too and has Lalla Ward (as the Second Romana who's one of my favorites too). Her cliffhanger at the end of one of the episodes where the Daleks show up suddenly, I found surprisingly chilling and well done.

Thinking about all these stories though, maybe the best story to introduce new viewers to *Doctor Who* might be "Logopolis." As you know it's a regeneration story that I thought was done well. It would be a good one to introduce new people to this concept as long as a fan is nearby. This story also holds a special place in my heart(s) as it was the first regeneration story that I ever saw. This was before I discovered *Doctor Who* fandom. So at the time I didn't know, hadn't heard ANYTHING about regenerations! I thought that they'd killed off my favorite character of all time! I had to wait six weeks for TVOntario to finish showing *The Hitchhikers Guide to the Galaxy* TV series before they ran "Castrovalva" showing that the Doctor had not actually died but regenerated!

Our twenty-four-year-old son would answer this

question with one of the episodes of the Christopher Eccleston era. Eccleston is his favorite. When our son was about five years old, he said something like "I know that there were many actors to play the Doctor before the new series, but Christopher Eccleston is MY Doctor because he's the one I watched first, Mummy." You always remember your first Doctor!

JASON TUCKER

WHAT WAS THE FIRST EPISODE/STORY OF DOCTOR WHO THAT YOU SAW?

I'm reasonably sure that it was "The Robots of Death," on a public television station in Alamogordo, New Mexico in 1983. I was probably watching *3-2-1 Contact*, and the station showed a promo with a blue box spinning in space, and some crazy-looking guy with curly hair and a long multi-coloured scarf. That little pop was the sound of my brain exploding inside my head. I made sure that I was able to watch the show this ad was promoting, the omnibus-version of, as I said, most likely "The Robots of Death," and I was immediately hooked.

TELL US HOW YOU THEN BECAME A FAN OF THE SHOW.

I discovered *Doctor Who* shortly before the PBS airing of "The Five Doctors," and seeing that episode, with new and different actors playing the Doctor, along with companions and locations I'd never heard of, not to mention Time Lords, the Master, Daleks, Cybermen, Yeti, and even the Raston Warrior Robot made me even more of a fan. I discovered that my friends also watched *Doctor Who*, that there were also novelisations of the stories, and original comics coming out from Marvel, and I knew I had stepped into a larger universe.

A few years later in 1986, I attended my first convention, in St Paul, Minnesota, featuring Peter Davison, followed a few months later by an even bigger event with Colin Baker and Patrick Troughton. This eventually led to me attending more general sci-fi conventions, and a lifelong love of sci-fi and fantasy of all sorts, culminating in my helping to found CONsole Room, the annual Twin Cities *Doctor Who* convention, in 2014.

TELL US YOUR FAVORITE MOMENT IN YOUR DOCTOR WHO FANDOM EXPERIENCE.

It sounds trite, but in the case of *Doctor Who* fandom, it really is about the friends we've made along the way. It wouldn't really be a stretch to say that the people who I've made some of the deepest connections with are people I met through *Doctor Who* fandom. I've traveled with them, I've shared joy and grief with them, and I really do consider them to be a chosen family. Much like the TARDIS, my heart is bigger on the inside, thanks to all of the people I've met in this community, sharing our love of *Doctor Who* together.

IF YOU WERE TO INTRODUCE SOMEONE ELSE TO THE DOCTOR WHO SERIES, WHAT EPISODE/STORY WOULD YOU TELL THEM TO START WITH AND WHY?

I have to admit that this is my least favorite question when it comes to *Doctor Who*. I started watching because I came across a promo for a random Tom Baker episode, very similar to how I became an avid comic book fan because of picking up a random *Captain Carrot* comic book on a spinner rack in a convenience store (Issue #5, now that I remember distinctly). I think that as adults, something happens in our brains that makes it difficult to jump into a story without knowing everything that came before. We've lost our ability to just relax and let the story unfold. As a kid, I never saw things from the beginning or even read a book series starting with the first book, and it never bothered me. Why can't we do this as adults? So basically, I'd say the best place to start is anywhere, as long as you can give it a chance on its own, and not worry about what's happening in the story, knowing that you'll figure it out as it goes along.

LARRY VANMERSBERGEN

WHAT WAS THE FIRST EPISODE/STORY OF DOCTOR WHO THAT YOU SAW?

"The Mutants" on Saturday, 27 September 1975 on WTTW Chicago (Channel 11).

TELL US HOW YOU THEN BECAME A FAN OF THE SHOW.

I never missed an episode after that moment. I was excited in 1981 when I visited a comic book store in Morton Grove, Illinois that had *Doctor Who* books and magazines. I bought *Doctor Who Monthly* Issue number 70 and a copy of *Doctor Who and The Day of the Daleks* Target novelization. In 1983, I went to my first convention where I met Peter Davison and John Nathan-Turner. I was so inspired to continue collecting *Doctor Who* that I established several pen-pals in the UK who would send *Doctor Who* merchandise back to me without extra cost. I had so much that I had enough to open a small store. In November 1984, I launched Bundles From Britain and took my traveling store to every *Doctor Who* Fan club in the Chicago area. I joined the Many Companions of Dr. Who in December 1984. My second customer was Gene Smith. We became partners and built this enterprise up to be the largest *Doctor Who* store in the country. Much later, I continued to collect until I had one of the largest collections in the USA. I started speaking and interviewing guests at the Chicago TARDIS convention. I travel to conventions like Doctoberfest, Concinnity, Ego-con, and Twin Cities' CONsole Room, and I am the host of a podcast on Doctor Who Collecting. I have appeared in documentaries, fan films, and even a PBS interview.

TELL US YOUR FAVORITE MOMENT IN YOUR DOCTOR WHO FANDOM EXPERIENCE.

In 1984, I met Katy Manning, the actress who played the

role of Jo Grant in the series. We have kept up our correspondence to this very day and have been good friends for 40 years.

IF YOU WERE TO INTRODUCE SOMEONE ELSE TO THE DOCTOR WHO SERIES, WHAT EPISODE/STORY WOULD YOU TELL THEM TO START WITH AND WHY?

I would say start with "Spearhead from Space", the first Third Doctor story, and work forwards, then backwards. This story has no regeneration and a little hint of the past but needs no foreknowledge of the first two Doctors. Some of this is filled in later, but it is a good starting point.

VAL VERSE

WHAT WAS THE FIRST EPISODE/STORY OF DOCTOR WHO THAT YOU SAW?

"Doctor Who and the Silurians" in 1971 on PBS.

TELL US HOW YOU THEN BECAME A FAN OF THE SHOW.

I kept watching, ordered *Doctor Who* merchandise including the weekly magazines from the UK, had my grandmother crochet me a Tom Baker scarf, and finally went to the *Doctor Who* convention in the early 1980s in Chicago.

TELL US YOUR FAVORITE MOMENT IN YOUR DOCTOR WHO FANDOM EXPERIENCE.

When Tony Ainley and I became best friends and soulmates.

IF YOU WERE TO INTRODUCE SOMEONE ELSE TO THE DOCTOR WHO SERIES, WHAT EPISODE/STORY WOULD YOU TELL THEM TO START WITH AND WHY?

I would tell them to start with Tom Baker's "Robot." Other people are doctors, but he is The Doctor – the definitive article! Tom is just endearing.

DAVID WALKER

WHAT WAS THE FIRST EPISODE/STORY OF DOCTOR WHO THAT YOU SAW?

I grew up knowing about *Doctor Who* because my dad was a big fan of the show. He was born in the 1950s in Scotland and watched the classic series growing up. But I never got into it myself until I was in my mid-20s.

My partner and I had started hanging out with a new group of friends who were into it, and since enough people around us were fans, we figured we should finally give it a shot. This was right at the tail end of the Matt Smith era, so while we were waiting for new episodes, we started from the beginning of the reboot. So, my first Doctor was Christopher Eccleston, and my first companion was Rose.

The first new episode we watched "live" as it came out was the 50th Anniversary special in the cinema. The first episodes we started watching with friends each week were from the start of Peter Capaldi's era.

Ironically, over ten years later, we're the only ones in the group that are still watching. Though I did recruit some of them back into the fold for Ncuti's run

TELL US HOW YOU THEN BECAME A FAN OF THE SHOW.

Watching the first few seasons, I really loved the creativity and the chaos of the show. It was zany when it wanted to be and serious when it needed to be. Christopher Eccleston was a great introduction to the show's lore. My partner and I dove headfirst into the *Doctor Who* universe.

TELL US YOUR FAVORITE MOMENT IN YOUR DOCTOR WHO FANDOM EXPERIENCE.

Since we were so behind when we started, we kind of lived the show in reverse, catching up while everyone else was already talking about it. One of the best parts was how that led to unexpected conversations with friends.

I remember posting something like "Noooo!!! Please David Tennant, don't go" on Facebook when we got to the end of his run, and my partner joked that maybe we should stop there and make Tennant the final Doctor. That post kicked off a whole thread of comments from friends, some of whom I didn't even know were fans. I'd keep posting little updates as we watched more episodes, and I'd get DMs and replies from people who wanted to talk about what was coming up or relive their favourite moments with us.

We also visited Cardiff in 2013 and made a whole *Doctor Who* day out of it. We hit the Doctor Who Experience, had lunch at the American Diner from "The Impossible Astronaut," and did a filming locations tour. That was a real fandom highlight.

Over the years, *Doctor Who* has become an easy litmus test for new people I meet. Regardless of where I am, if I spot a TARDIS pin or an Adipose tattoo, I know that we'd at least have something to talk about.

IF YOU WERE TO INTRODUCE SOMEONE ELSE TO THE DOCTOR WHO SERIES, WHAT EPISODE/STORY WOULD YOU TELL THEM TO START WITH AND WHY?

I'd generally recommend new viewers to start from the 2005 reboot like I did, as it's a great entry point. That being said, I'd say just start wherever you find it. One of the best things about *Doctor Who* is that it's so flexible; aside from a few big arc finales, you can drop in almost anywhere and get the gist. If someone wants to go deeper, they can always loop back to the start of the 2005 reboot and catch up. And if they're really curious, the classic stuff is sitting there too.

PHILIP WARD

WHAT WAS THE FIRST EPISODE/STORY OF DOCTOR WHO THAT YOU SAW?

"An Unearthly Child" – BBC TV, Saturday, 23 November 1963.

TELL US HOW YOU THEN BECAME A FAN OF THE SHOW.

At the time, there were only two television channels in the UK and on Saturday afternoon, a lot of Sports coverage was shown live followed by the day's racing and football results, which parents would be watching. At about 5pm, *Doctor Who*, an educational children's drama series was shown on the BBC channel followed by an evening of light entertainment programmes. It was common practice for family meals to be taken late afternoon and then for the family to watch the evenings programmes together. I was nine years old when *Doctor Who* started broadcasting and I became a regular viewer of the show, watching with my two younger brothers. It was drama for children, exciting adventures in time and space but with historical and educational content. Shown in 25-minute episodes with multi-episode stories shown weekly, the programmes were interesting and gripping as well as sometimes scary. When the Daleks were involved in a story, my siblings and I would be hiding behind the sofa and peeking out to watch what was happening. So I was a fan of the show from the very beginning and have followed through childhood and into adulthood as the show has evolved over the past sixty years

TELL US YOUR FAVORITE MOMENT IN YOUR DOCTOR WHO FANDOM EXPERIENCE.

I thoroughly enjoyed attending the Doctor Who 50th Anniversary Exhibition at the ExCeL Exhibition Centre, London in 2013. A display of scenery, monsters, and costumes, as well as the chance to meet production staff, cast, and crew from the show. I also enjoyed the Doctor Who Experience static exhibition, which was at the London Olympia Exhibition Centre in 2011, before it transferred to a purpose-built building in Cardiff, where the BBC Production Studios are based.

IF YOU WERE TO INTRODUCE SOMEONE ELSE TO THE DOCTOR WHO SERIES, WHAT EPISODE/STORY WOULD YOU TELL THEM TO START WITH AND WHY?

Personally, I think that any newcomer to the Whoniverse should watch "An Unearthly Child," the first *Doctor Who* episode from 1963 to see historically how the show started, and then pick a selection of stories from the seven Doctors in Classic Who until the show was dropped by the BBC in 1989. If we look at the three times that the show has been reinvented since, I recommend watching the TV movie, "The Night of the Doctor" transmitted in 1996 starring Paul McGann as the Eighth Doctor. This US made version was made as a pilot for a new series and had a good story/cast, but the ratings were poor resulting in the show being dropped again. After another long gap, in 2005 the BBC brought the show back on air in the UK with a new showrunner, production team, and format. In this more woke/enlightened era of *Doctor Who* there are several interesting stories which I think would give an overview of numerous incarnations of the Doctor and his adventures in time and space. Three particularly interesting stories from the 2005 revival are "Blink," "Silence in the Library"/"Forest of the Dead," and "The Girl in the Fireplace." "Blink" is notable for its unique narrative structure and introduction of the chilling Weeping Angels. "Silence in the Library"/"Forest of the Dead" offers a compelling mystery and introduces River Song, a complex character with a significant impact on the Doctor's life. "The Girl in the Fireplace" explores the Doctor's relationship with Madame de Pompadour in a poignant and thought-provoking story. The current incarnation of *Doctor Who* since 2023 has been a joint BBC/Disney co-production and there has been an interesting storyline over the past two years, but sadly the series has allegedly now been curtailed abruptly due to Disney withdrawing funding and fans will be waiting to see what happens next!

ROBERT WARNOCK

WHAT WAS THE FIRST EPISODE/STORY OF DOCTOR WHO THAT YOU SAW?

I first watched "Planet of Evil" on 29 March 1981. It was the beginning of spring break, so I was able to stay up late and watch as it aired at 11:00PM in Chicago at the time. I had previously seen part of what I think may have been "The Sontaran Experiment," but for whatever reason, it didn't grab my attention initially.

TELL US HOW YOU THEN BECAME A FAN OF THE SHOW.

Because I was in high school when I first saw it, and it was on fairly late at night, I didn't really become a regular viewer until the summer of 1981. I attended my first convention in July of 1982, so it didn't take me too long to become a fan.

TELL US YOUR FAVORITE MOMENT IN YOUR DOCTOR WHO FANDOM EXPERIENCE.

I've been involved with *Doctor Who* for so long now, that it's hard to pick one. Being involved in conventions has allowed me to meet a lot of *Doctor Who* guests. I've also been fortunate enough to be able to compose *Doctor Who*-related music for the Chicago TARDIS convention since 2010. Both of these things are very important to me. However, I think my favorite memory would be visiting the UK and the Doctor Who Experience exhibition in 2010. I went with my sisters Sue, and Kathleen, and Sue passed away from cancer a few months later, so I'm glad we were able to experience it together.

IF YOU WERE TO INTRODUCE SOMEONE ELSE TO THE DOCTOR WHO SERIES, WHAT EPISODE/STORY WOULD YOU TELL THEM TO START WITH AND WHY?

I don't think there's a definitive answer to this question. If you're trying to introduce the how to a specific person, you could pick a story that might be suitable to that person's interests, but I don't think there's one story that would work in every situation.

IAN WHEELER

WHAT WAS THE FIRST EPISODE/STORY OF DOCTOR WHO THAT YOU SAW?

I've vague memories of watching the Fourth Doctor and Leela when I was very young, but I think I found the show too scary and avoided watching it for a while, so the first story I remember with clarity was "Destiny of the Daleks." I was intrigued by the eccentric Doctor with his floppy hat, long scarf, and bulging eyes, and I loved K9, as any child would. Davros and the Daleks fascinated me, as did the other-worldly theme music. I was hooked as a regular viewer from then on. To this day, I remain a staunch defender of the Graham William years – despite its faults, it was an era of the programme which appealed to a large section of the general public, as its viewing figures testify.

TELL US HOW YOU THEN BECAME A FAN OF THE SHOW.

I had a school friend who loved *Doctor Who* and he made me aware of some of the many items of merchandise that were available. I started with the usual things – buying the Target books and *Doctor Who Magazine*, and the VHS videos when they started coming out. In 1987, I joined the UK-based Doctor Who Appreciation Society (DWAS), which remains the longest running *Doctor Who* fan club to this day. I got more involved when I became Coordinator of the Society from 2001 to 2007. I also edited a few issues of its long-running *Celestial Toyroom* fanzine, as well as other publications such as *TARDIS* and *Cosmic Masque*. I've also helped out at many of the Society's conventions over the years. Most importantly, I've made some very good friends out of my involvement with the Society.

TELL US YOUR FAVORITE MOMENT IN YOUR DOCTOR WHO FANDOM EXPERIENCE.

I have many, many happy moments to look back on. I was in the studio audience when the *Doctor Who* episode of *Mastermind* was recorded and saw Christopher Eccleston present the trophy to my friend Karen Davies. I attended a special event at BBC Television Centre in 2002, where three plaques (dedicated to William Hartnell, Patrick Troughton and Jon Pertwee) were unveiled in the presence of a galaxy of *Doctor Who* stars. I've also been privileged to interview a number of actors from the series including three Doctors – Tom Baker, Colin Baker and Sylvester McCoy (four if you count the Valeyard, Michael Jayston!). I also interviewed Louise Jameson in a cafe in Darlington – if you've never had lunch with Louise, I can heartily recommend it! She is lovely company as I'm sure you can imagine.

IF YOU WERE TO INTRODUCE SOMEONE ELSE TO THE DOCTOR WHO SERIES, WHAT EPISODE/STORY WOULD YOU TELL THEM TO START WITH AND WHY.

I'd go for "The Unquiet Dead" by Mark Gatiss. It demonstrates to a new viewer that the show is about time travel and that the Doctor has the ability to go back to any time and meet any famous historical figure. It's a good, atmospheric, scary story, borrowing heavily from old-fashioned horror movies as *Doctor Who* so often does. It has high production values, with the costumes, locations, and special effects all working together to create a sense of place and time. Most importantly, it has a great Doctor/companion dynamic. The Ninth Doctor and Rose, played so ably by Christopher Eccleston and Billie Piper, clearly love travelling in time and love being together. It's hard not to get wrapped up in their joy and enthusiasm.

FANTASTIC FINAL THOUGHTS

Each of these stories and experiences is important and worth recording. They are moments of joy and happiness (or at the very least history and recollection) for those who shared them with us. Some answers were more straightforward, others a bit more philosophical. In each answer, the contributors celebrated their connection to the series and what it means to them. Hearing their favorite moments cannot help but put a smile on the face of someone with the same interest.

What surprised us when we embarked on this project was twofold. First, we learned fans were enthusiastic to tell us about their *Doctor Who* story. They wanted to share their journey of discovery with others. They acknowledged that this specific science fiction program had captured their imagination and influenced them (often from a very young age). There is something special when a piece of media motivates people. It elevates that media to a level of influence and importance that is worth both noting and studying.

Second, we discovered how many people wanted to be included and connected. To have a meaningful connection to something that brings one joy is a truly human condition. These fans yearn to be a part of *Doctor Who* in a meaningful way in which they can contribute to it. Some have extensive memorabilia collections, some have had encounters with the actors or production team, some have even worked on the program and its related properties, and all shared the experience of watching the show. In contributing here, many of them have become concretely connected to something that they hold so dear.

This book celebrates *Doctor Who* and its fans (whether casual viewers or involved in organized fandom). It is about the effect that a creative piece of artwork (in this case a series of television programs) can have on a person's mindset and journey. It demonstrates how media engages the imagination and motivates people to become involved and do amazing things with their lives. Each story is unique because we all navigate life in our own way. In this case, there is one common connection in each of these journeys. That is the power of art. That is the power of hope. That is the power of looking to the future but not forgetting the past.

As we close this book we are reminded of a quote from the *Doctor Who* series:

"For some people, small, beautiful events is what life is all about!"
- The Fifth Doctor in "Earthshock"

We realize that this is not only an end but a new beginning. A chance for us to learn from others and consider our future choices. A chance for us to decide how moving forward we will celebrate ourselves and celebrate what makes us happy. To each of the contributors, thank you for sharing your lives with us. To each of our readers we hope you are willing to do the same so we can learn from you as well. Our journey has been, and will continue to be, Fantastic!

Until we meet again, safe travels in the TARDIS.

THE PURPOSE OF THIS BOOK

Many of the people that have worked on making this book a reality are academics (as well as a few contributors). These are people, most usually a teacher or scholar at a college or institute of higher education, devoted to the study of a subject to add to the greater knowledge for the benefit of humanity. This is not unique to *Doctor Who* fandom, but few other science fiction television series celebrate learning, knowledge, and exploration as much as this show does. The main character is even known by their academic credentials rather than their given name.

With the publication of John Tulloch and Manuel Alvarado's book *Doctor Who: The Unfolding Text* in 1983, the fandom got its first serious academic work. By the 1980s, fan clubs such as the Doctor Who Appreciation Society (DWAS) and some of its most devoted members began doing extensive research into the series, uncovering yet-unknown facts about the show's production. Their work laid a foundation into researching the series. While many of the researchers may not have been professional academics employed by a college or a university, the work they did (while meticulously documenting what they had learned and citing their sources) counts as academic work of the highest order. Accurate and exacting research, even by devotees of a subject without academic credentials, are no less valuable and important. Quite often, those who designate themselves as fans – deep followers of a subject matter – have a better and more holistic understanding of a subject than those who only engage a subject for professional or entertainment reasons. Experts are born out of a love for the subject matter, not necessarily because they have a certain pedagogical approach.

As the *Doctor Who* series matured in the 1980s and 1990s, more attention was paid to the series as a source of evidence in various academic fields. Driven by student's interest in the show, the series became a focus for various academic projects. In 1995, the Bristol University Doctor Who society began a project collecting and transcribing the Doctor Who scripts of missing episodes in the UK. Students and fans transcribed the scripts so the lost episodes of the show could be shared and experienced when no episodes were available. Around the same time, fans in Australia, the UK, and the USA began assembling telesnap videos that combined recently discovered photographs taken off the final television recordings with recently discovered full audio recordings of the missing episodes. These fans from different continents started to work together thanks to the internet making these international projects. These projects further blurred the lines of academic and restoration work as international and cross-discipline collaboration became necessary to move the projects forward and increase their quality.

By the mid-1990s, the Earthbound TimeLords fan club became the first fan club dedicated to the academic study of *Doctor Who*. By 1997, the club moved online and its website began hosting academic projects such as the Doctor Who Missing Episodes Scripts Project (moved from Bristol in 1999 when they would lose their webspace), The Doctor Who Fanzine Preservation Project (which continues to this day), The Diary of Doctor Who Role-Playing Games gaming fanzine (documenting various games), as well as hosting academic articles connected to the series' fiction and production. Academics who were fans of the series finally had a place where they could exercise their style of writing and presentation.

In the United States, beginning in the year 2000, the Milwaukee School of Engineering, a university in Milwaukee, Wisconsin, USA hosted a display at the university library and brought in a speaker from Baldwin-Wallace College (now Baldwin Wallace University) to talk about the series. The show's basis in science and engineering was connected to the fields that the students at the university were studying. The display was so popular it was held over for over a year. From there, colleges around the world began offering symposiums and papers. By the mid- 2000s, academic journals and universities began to host conferences and accept papers connected to the series. Universities began seeing that a long-running television program was a great way to engage students and teach important concepts about popular culture, sociology, and media. In 2006

Manchester University held a symposium on *Doctor Who* and papers that were submitted were collected into the book *Time and Relative Dissertations in Space; Critical Perspectives on Doctor Who*.

By the show's 50th Anniversary, *Doctor Who* had become a legitimate subject for colleges to teach about. Media Studies classes were held devoted to the show such as at DePaul University. DePaul's College of Communication held an all-day colloquium for the show's 50th Anniversary in 2013. The students in the club at that university have regularly given panels and presentations on the series at conventions now for over a decade. Syracuse University professor Anthony Rotolo began teaching a commercial class called a "Doctor Who (Un)Class" in 2014. Aquinas College in Stockport, Greater Manchester, offered a class in 2015. Kennesaw State University held a Fall Symposium of Student Scholars in 2021 which featured "Oh the Whomanity: An Analysis of the Theme of Humanity in Doctor Who" by Sarah Williams. In 2023, The University of Queensland in Australia held a Doctor Who 60th Anniversary Symposium. This is but a small sample of the academic engagement that the series has seen. Museums began to host displays connected to the series as well. And astride all of this, devoted fans and fan clubs continue to add to the experience, research, and opinions connected to the series.

And that leads us here, to this book. The opening of this book points out that while the questions posed in this project are questions that fans almost always discuss with one another, the answers that are shared are rarely documented and have not been compiled anywhere in book format. This project was born out of the academic desire to document first-hand accounts of these answers to aid researchers in their understanding of the fandom and the field of study. We hope that this book becomes a useful resource for those who hope to understand the fandom, especially in the academic realm.

Zepo Publishing encourages the use of this book to further academic research and as an avenue to amplify the fans' memories and voices.

SOME FUN STATISTICS

With the assistance of television researchers Steven Warren Hill and John Lavalie who crunched the numbers, we thought we would share just a few statistics about the fans that replied and their responses.

Respondents live in the countries of Australia, Canada, Germany, Turkiye, the United Kingdom, and the United States. 73.6% of respondents were from the USA.

75.5% of respondents had names that presented as male.

Of the respondents who could remember the first *Doctor Who* story that they saw, here were the top answers (the list was limited to the top five vote-getters because of the broad range of answers):

10 Respondents - "Rose" (Ninth Doctor)
 8 Respondents - "Robot" (Fourth Doctor)
 6 Respondents - "The Planet of Evil" (Fourth Doctor)
 4 Respondents - "Genesis of the Daleks" (Fourth Doctor)
 3 Respondents [tie] - "The Sontaran Experiment" (Fourth Doctor)
 3 Respondents [tie] - "The Mutants" (Third Doctor)
 3 Respondents [tie] - "The Hand of Fear" (Fourth Doctor)
 3 Respondents [tie] - "The Brain of Morbius" (Fourth Doctor)
 3 Respondents [tie] - "Destiny of the Daleks" (Fourth Doctor)

Respondents most recommended the following stories as the *Doctor Who* story they would choose to introduce another person to the series (again, the list was limited to the top five vote-getters because of the broad range of answers):

33 Respondents - "Rose" (Ninth Doctor)
22 Respondents - "The Eleventh Hour" (Eleventh Doctor)
16 Respondents - "Blink" (Tenth Doctor)

12 Respondents - "An Unearthly Child" (First Doctor)
8 Respondents [tie] - "Vincent and the Doctor" (Eleventh Doctor)
8 Respondents [tie] - "Genesis of the Daleks" (Fourth Doctor)

Analyzing the results, the majority of respondents replied that the first story that they saw was from either the start of the recent revival run, or a Fourth Doctor story likely reflecting the many airings on PBS and cable as the show popularized in the USA.

Most respondents wanted to introduce new viewers to *Doctor Who* stories that were produced more recently. Many comments weighed the details of television production, quality of special effects to the modern eye, the pacing of modern television storytelling, and current viewer expectations.

Respondents were positive, excited, and willing to share their fandom with others who were interested.

THE QUESTIONS
(ANSWER THEM YOURSELF)

WHAT WAS THE FIRST EPISODE/STORY OF DOCTOR WHO THAT YOU SAW?

TELL US HOW YOU THEN BECAME A FAN OF THE SHOW.

TELL US YOUR FAVORITE MOMENT IN YOUR DOCTOR WHO FANDOM EXPERIENCE.

IF YOU WERE TO INTRODUCE SOMEONE ELSE TO THE DOCTOR WHO SERIES, WHAT EPISODE/STORY WOULD YOU TELL THEM TO START WITH AND WHY?

HOW TO CELEBRATE YOUR *DOCTOR WHO* FANDOM

Here are fun things to do to enjoy your interest in the *Doctor Who* TV series and get more involved in the fandom and celebrate your enjoyment of it.

O - Ask your friends or co-workers if they like *Doctor Who* or have watched the series. Let them know that you enjoy it. They may be interested or know others who enjoy it as well. Having even passing discussions about a common interest brings us joy.

O - Have a *Doctor Who* episode watch party with friends. If your group is mostly familiar with the modern series, watch an original series episode, so you learn more about the series as a whole.

O - Decorate some cookies with frosting in a style of the *Doctor Who* series, maybe putting the TARDIS, a Cyberman, a Dalek, or another related design on it. Sharing the cookies is a great way to meet others or find other fans.

O - Make a button, badge, or pin related to *Doctor Who* that you can wear on a jacket or backpack to let others know that you love the show. You can use a sticker and decorate that and put it over an existing badge if you need to.

O - Put together a *Doctor Who* cosplay costume that you can wear for Halloween or a special event. Costumes are how you can use fashion to display your fandom. Some people like doing really subtle cosplays that are in the style of a character, or wear an accessory that only those who know the fandom well might spot.

O - Write and illustrate your own comic book about a *Doctor Who* adventure that we never saw on television, and share it with some other fans.

O - Knit yourself a multi-colored scarf, like the Fourth Doctor and some of the other Doctors sometime wear, or make one as a gift for a friend. Don't know how to knit? Learn a cool new and useful skill. A multi-colored scarf is the perfect way to practice!

O - Check the internet to see if there is a *Doctor Who* meetup or fan club in your area and go attend one of their get-togethers.

O - Write up some *Doctor Who* trivia questions and hold a trivia contest with some friends you know. You can reward them with a piece of candy for each question they get correct, or give a prize to the winner of a whole contest.

O - Write your own *Doctor Who* adventure story. We recommend starting with a short story that is 3 to 10 pages long. You can share this story with friends or online.

O - Attend a *Doctor Who* convention, where you can meet other fans, listen to panels and interviews, shop the dealers hall, get autographs or photographs with the actors or writers, and make some new friends.

O - Try playing a *Doctor Who* role-playing game, and experience an adventure first hand as if you are the Doctor, companions, or your own original characters.

O - Check a book out of the library about *Doctor Who*. Choose a book about an aspect of the series that you do not know about. There are some very good books about the history or the series and its production.

O - Suggest to a friend that they should start watching the series, and watch it with them when they start.

O - Live your life like the Doctor. Be kind, help those in need, always keep learning, and travel the world merrily with your friends sharing moments of laughter and philosophy.

DOCTOR WHO EPISODE GUIDE

This episode guide presents all of the stories that a viewer would need to watch to get the full narrative storyline of the canonically televised and streamed *Doctor Who*. While there can be endless debate over what should or should not be included in this list, the following would provide the fullest experience of the live-action series.

This guide is presented in chronological order of presentation and identifies which season of the series the shows were presented (with single broadcast in a year without a full season being identified as a stand alone series). The actor playing the Doctor is identified with their introduction. A code representing the Doctor and which story precedes the title of each story in **bold**. Any alternate titles are given in {braces}. Story production codes are given in [brackets], and the number of episodes in a story are in (parenthesis). The individual name of a part of a story is given unless it was presented as either "Episode", "Part", or "Chapter". Special TARDISodes, video release extras, online specials, Children in Need specials, Red Nose Day Specials, online in-character clips, Tales of the TARDIS intros and outros, and so on are included where they were released to create the most complete list of live-action fiction *Doctor Who*.

Seasons are organized by the season or series the show was broadcast a part of. If there was a special story broadcast in a given year, or a series of specials, these might be put into a category as a "season" to simply show that it was a year or separate one-off time in which the show was broadcast.

Episodes or Parts that ended with a "to be continued" are grouped with other episodes into a title for their single storyline. Often this is the title of the first episode.

We understand that some details of this list and their canonicity may be debated by fans.

The exact listing of episodes/parts under one story title may be one example of debatable content, but we feel that this is the most complete and logically assembled list for the show. Our intent is to simply provide a useful resource for those who want to see as much live-action *Doctor Who* content that seems to fit the show's established fictional (non-parody) canon as possible.

FIRST SEASON *(William Hartnell as the Doctor)*
H-1. **An Unearthly Child** {*aka 100,000 BC*} [A](4)
  1. An Unearthly Child
  2. The Cave of Skulls
  3. The Forest of Fear
  4. The Firemaker

H-2. **The Daleks** {*aka The Mutants*} [B](7)
  1. The Dead Planet
  2. The Survivors
  3. The Escape
  4. The Ambush
  5. The Expedition
  6. The Ordeal
  7. The Rescue

H-3. **Edge of Destruction** {*aka Inside the Spaceship*} [C](2)
  1. The Edge of Destruction
  2. The Brink of Disaster

H-4. **Marco Polo** [D](7)
  1. The Roof of the World
  2. The Singing Sands
  3. Five Hundred Eyes
  4. The Wall of Lies
  5. Rider From Shang-Tu
  6. Mighty Kublai Khan
  7. Assassin at Peking

H-5. **The Keys of Marinus** [E](6)
  1. The Sea of Death
  2. The Velvet Web
  3. The Screaming Jungle
  4. The Snows of Terror
  5. Sentence of Death
  6. The Keys of Marinus

H-6. **The Aztecs** [F](4)
- 1. The Temple of Evil
- 2. The Warriors of Death
- 3. The Bride of Sacrifice
- 4. The Day of Darkness

H-7. **The Sensorites** [G](6)
- 1. Strangers in Space
- 2. The Unwilling Warriors
- 3. Hidden Danger
- 4. A Race Against Death
- 5. Kidnap
- 6. A Desperate Venture

H-8. **The Reign of Terror** [H](6)
- 1. Land of Fear
- 2. Guests of Madame Guillotine
- 3. A Change of Identity
- 4. The Tyrant of France
- 5. A Bargain of Necessity
- 6. Prisoners of Conciergerie

SECOND SEASON

H-9. **Planet of Giants** [J](3)
- 1. Planet of Giants
- 2. Dangerous Journey
- 3. Crisis

H-10. **The Dalek Invasion of Earth** [K](6)
- 1. The World's End
- 2. The Daleks
- 3. Day of Reckoning
- 4. The End of Tomorrow
- 5. The Waking Ally
- 6. Flashpoint

H-11. **The Rescue** [L](2)
- 1. The Powerful Enemy
- 2. Desperate Measures

H-12. **The Romans** [M](4)
- 1. The Slave Traders

    2. All Roads Lead to Rome
    3. Conspiracy
    4. Inferno
H-13. **The Web Planet** [N](6)
    1. The Web Planet
    2. The Zarbi
    3. Escape From Danger
    4. Crater of Needles
    5. Invasion
    6. The Centre
H-14. **The Crusade** [P](4)
    1. The Lion
    2. The Knights of Jaffa
    3. The Wheel of Fortune
    4. The Warlords
H-15. **The Space Museum** [Q](4)
    1. The Space Museum
    2. The Dimensions of Time
    3. The Search
    4. The Final Phase
H-16. **The Chase** [R](6)
    1. The Executioners
    2. The Death of Time
    3. Flight Through Eternity
    4. Journey Into Fear
    5. The Death of Doctor Who
    6. The Planet of Decision
H-17. **The Time Meddler** [S](4)
    1. The Watcher
    2. The Meddling Monk
    3. A Battle of Wits
    4. Checkmate

THIRD SEASON
H-18. **Galaxy 4** [T](4)
    1. Four Hundred Dawns
    2. Trap of Steel

3. Air Lock
   4. The Exploding Planet
H-19. **Mission to the Unknown** {*aka Dalek Cutaway*} [T/A](1)
H-20. **The Myth Makers** [U](4)
   1. Temple of Secrets
   2. Small Prophet, Quick Return
   3. Death of a Spy
   4. Horse of Destruction
H-21. **The Daleks' Master Plan** [V](12)
   1. The Nightmare Begins
   2. Day of Armageddon
   3. Devil's Planet
   4. The Traitors
   5. Counter-Plot
   6. Coronas of the Sun
   7. The Feast of Steven
   8. Volcano
   9. Golden Death
   10. Escape Switch
   11. The Abandoned Planet
   12. Destruction of Time
H-22. **The Massacre** {*aka The Massacre of St. Bartholomew's Eve*} [W](4)
   1. War of God
   2. The Sea Beggar
   3. Priest of Death
   4. Bells of Doom
H-23. **The Ark** [X](4)
   1. The Steel Sky
   2. The Plague
   3. The Return
   4. The Bomb
H-24. **The Celestial Toymaker** [Y](4)
   1. The Celestial Toymaker
   2. The Hall of Dolls
   3. The Dancing Floor
   4. The Final Test

H-25. **The Gunfighters** [Z](4)
   1. A Holiday for the Doctor
   2. Don't Shoot the Pianist
   3. Johnny Ringo
   4. The OK Corral
H-26. **The Savages** [AA](4)
H-27. **The War Machines** [BB](4)

FOURTH SEASON
H-28. **The Smugglers** [CC](4)
H-29. **The Tenth Planet** [DD](4)

FOURTH SEASON (Continued) *(Patrick Troughton as the Doctor)*
T-1. **The Power of the Daleks** [EE](6)
T-2. **The Highlanders** [FF](4)
T-3. **The Underwater Menace** [GG](4)
T-4. **The Moonbase** [HH](4)
T-5. **The Macra Terror** [JJ](4)
T-6. **The Faceless Ones** [KK](6)
T-7. **The Evil of the Daleks** [LL](7)

FIFTH SEASON
T-8. **The Tomb of the Cybermen** [MM](4)
T-9. **The Abominable Snowmen** [NN](6)
T-10. **The Ice Warriors** [OO](6)
T-11. **The Enemy of the World** [PP](6)
T-12. **The Web of Fear** [QQ](6)
T-13. **Fury From the Deep** [RR](6)
T-14. **The Wheel in Space** [SS](6)

SIXTH SEASON
T-15. **The Dominators** [TT](5)
T-16. **The Mind Robber** [UU](5)
T-17. **The Invasion** [VV](8)
T-18. **The Krotons** [WW](4)
T-19. **The Seeds of Death** [XX](6)

T-20. **The Space Pirates** [YY](6)
T-21. **The War Games** [ZZ](10)

SEVENTH SEASON *(Jon Pertwee as the Doctor)*
P-1. **Spearhead From Space** [AAA](4)
P-2. **Doctor Who and the Silurians** [BBB](7)
P-3. **The Ambassadors of Death** [CCC](7)
P-4. **Inferno** [DDD](7)

EIGHTH SEASON
P-5. **Terror of the Autons** [EEE](4)
P-6. **The Mind of Evil** [FFF](6)
P-7. **The Claws of Axos** [GGG](4)
P-8. **Colony in Space** [HHH](6)
P-9. **The Daemons** [JJJ](5)

NINTH SEASON
P-10. **The Day of the Daleks** [KKK](4)
P-11. **The Curse of Peladon** [MMM](4)
P-12. **The Sea Devils** [LLL](6)
P-13. **The Mutants** [NNN](6)
P-14. **The Time Monster** [OOO](6)

TENTH SEASON
P-15. **The Three Doctors** [RRR](4)
P-16. **Carnival of Monsters** [PPP](4)
P-17. **Frontier in Space** [QQQ](6)
P-18. **Planet of the Daleks** [SSS](6)
P-19. **The Green Death** [TTT](6)

ELEVENTH SEASON
P-20. **The Time Warrior** [UUU](4)
P-21. **Invasion of the Dinosaurs** [WWW](6)
P-22. **Death to the Daleks** [XXX](4)
P-23. **The Monster of Peladon** [YYY](6)
P-24. **Planet of the Spiders** [ZZZ](6)

TWELFTH SEASON *(Tom Baker as the Doctor)*
B-1. **Robot** [4A](4)
B-2. **The Ark in Space** [4C](4)
B-3. **The Sontaran Experiment** [4B](2)
B-4. **Genesis of the Daleks** [4E](6)
B-5. **Revenge of the Cybermen** [4D](4)

THIRTEENTH SEASON
B-6. **Terror of the Zygons** [4F](4)
B-7. **Planet of Evil** [4H](4)
B-8. **Pyramids of Mars** [4G](4)
B-9. **The Android Invasion** [4J](4)
B-10. **The Brain of Morbius** [4K](4)
B-11. **The Seeds of Doom** [4L](6)

FOURTEENTH SEASON
B-12. **The Masque of Mandragora** [4M](4)
B-13. **The Hand of Fear** [4N](4)
B-14. **The Deadly Assassin** [4P](4)
B-15. **The Face of Evil** [4Q](4)
B-16. **The Robots of Death** [4R](4)
B-17. **The Talons of Weng-Chiang** [4S](6)

FIFTEENTH SEASON
B-18. **Horror of Fang Rock** [4V](4)
B-19. **The Invisible Enemy** [4T](4)
B-20. **Image of the Fendahl** [4X](4)
B-21. **The Sunmakers** [4W](4)
B-22. **Underworld** [4Y](4)
B-23. **The Invasion of Time** [4Z](6)

SIXTEENTH SEASON (The Key to Time)
B-24. **The Ribos Operation** [5A](4)
B-25. **The Pirate Planet** [5B](4)
B-26. **The Stones of Blood** [5C](4)
B-27. **The Androids of Tara** [5D](4)
B-28. **The Power of Kroll** [5E](4)

B-29. **The Armageddon Factor** [5F](6)

SEVENTEENTH SEASON
B-30. **Destiny of the Daleks** [5J](4)
B-31. **City of Death** [5H](4)
B-32. **The Creature From the Pit** [5G](4)
B-33. **Nightmare of Eden** [5K](4)
B-34. **The Horns of Nimon** [5L](4)

EIGHTEENTH SEASON
B-35. **The Leisure Hive** [5N](4)
B-36. **Meglos** [5Q](4)
B-37. **Full Circle** [5R](4)
B-38. **State of Decay** [5P](4)
B-39. **Warrior's Gate** [5S](4)
B-40. **The Keeper of Traken** [5T](4)
B-41. **Logopolis** [5V](4)

NINETEENTH SEASON *(Peter Davison as the Doctor)*
D-1. **Castrovalva** [5Z](4)
D-2. **Four to Doomsday** [5W](4)
D-3. **Kinda** [5Y](4)
D-4. **Visitation** [5X](4)
D-5. **Black Orchid** [6A](2)
D-6. **Earthshock** [6B](4)
D-7. **Time-Flight** [6C](4)

TWENTIETH SEASON
D-8. **Arc of Infinity** [6E](4)
D-9. **Snakedance** [6D](4)
D-10. **Mawdryn Undead** [6F](4)
D-11. **Terminus** [6G](4)
D-12. **Enlightenment** [6H](4)
D-13. **The King's Demons** [6J](2)
D-14. **The Five Doctors** [6K] (1 -90 min.)

TWENTY-FIRST SEASON

D-15. **Warriors of the Deep** [6L](4)
D-16. **The Awakening** [6M](2)
D-17. **Frontios** [6N](4)
D-18. **Resurrection of the Daleks** [D-18](2 –50 min.)
D-19. **Planet of Fire** [6Q](4)
D-20. **The Caves of Androzani** [6R](4)

TWENTY-FIRST SEASON (Continued)   *(Colin Baker as the Doctor)*
CB-1. **The Twin Dilemma** [6S](4)

TWENTY-SECOND SEASON
CB-2. **Attack of the Cybermen** [6T](2 –50 min.)
CB-3. **Vengeance on Varos** [6V](2 –50 min.)
CB-4. **The Mark of the Rani** [6X](2 –50 min.)
CB-5. **The Two Doctors** [6W](3 –50 min.)
CB-6. **Timelash** [6Y](2 –50 min.)
CB-7. **Revelation of the Daleks** [6Z](2 –50 min.)

TWENTY-THIRD SEASON
CB-8. **The Trial of a Timelord** [7A,7B,7C](14)

TWENTY-FOURTH SEASON   *(Sylvester McCoy as the Doctor)*
Mc-1. **Time and the Rani** [7D](4)
Mc-2. **Paradise Towers** [7E](4)
Mc-3. **Delta and the Bannermen** [7F](3)
Mc-4. **Dragonfire** [7G](3)

TWENTY-FIFTH SEASON
Mc-5. **Remembrance of the Daleks** [7H](4)
Mc-6. **The Happiness Patrol** [7L](3)
Mc-7. **Silver Nemesis** [7K](3)
Mc-8. **The Greatest Show in the Galaxy** [7J](4)

TWENTY-SIXTH SEASON
Mc-9. **Battlefield** [7N](4)

Mc-10. **Ghost Light** [7Q](3)
Mc-11. **Curse of Fenric** [7M](4)
Mc-12. **Survival** [7P](3)

TWENTY-SEVENTH SEASON
Mc-13. **Dimensions in Time** (2)

TWENTY-EIGHTH SEASON *(Paul McGann as the Doctor)*
MG-1. **Doctor Who** [TV Movie](1)

TWENTY-NINTH SEASON {aka SERIES ONE}
(Christopher Eccleston as the Doctor)
E-1. **Rose** [1.1](1)
E-2. **The End of the World** [1.2](1)
E-3. **The Unquiet Dead** [1.3](1)
E-4. **Aliens of London** [1.4/1.5](2)
   1. Aliens of London
   2. World War Three
E-5. **Dalek** [1.6](1)
E-6. **The Long Game** [1.7](1)
E-7. **Father's Day** [1.8](1)
E-8. **The Empty Child** [1.9/1.10](2)
   1. The Empty Child
   2. The Doctor Dances
E-9. **Boom Town** [1.11](1)
E-10. **Bad Wolf** [1.12/1.13](2)
   1. Bad Wolf
   2. The Parting of the Ways

THIRTIETH SEASON {aka SERIES TWO} *(David Tennant as the Doctor)*
DT-1. ***[Untitled Children In Need Special]*** *{aka Born Again, aka Pudsey Cutaway}* [CIN](1)
DT-2. **The Christmas Invasion** [2.X](1)
DT-3. **Attack of the Graske** (1)
DT-4. **New Earth** [2.1](2)
   1. *[untitled TARDISode]*

2. New Earth
DT-5. **Tooth and Claw** [2.2](2)
   1. *[untitled TARDISode]*
   2. Tooth and Claw
DT-6. **School Reunion** [2.3](2)
   1. *[untitled TARDISode]*
   2. School Reunion
DT-7. **The Girl in the Fireplace** [2.4](2)
   1. *[untitled TARDISode]*
   2. The Girl in the Fireplace
DT-8. **Rise of the Cybermen** [2.5/2.6](4)
   1. *[untitled TARDISode]*
   2. Rise of the Cybermen
   3. *[untitled TARDISode]*
   4. The Age of Steel
DT-9. **The Idiot's Lantern** [2.7](2)
   1. *[untitled TARDISode]*
   2. The Idiot's Lantern
DT-10. **The Impossible Planet** [2.8/2.9](4)
   1. *[untitled TARDISode]*
   2. The Impossible Planet
   3. *[untitled TARDISode]*
   4. The Satan Pit
DT-11. **Love & Monsters** [2.10](2)
   1. *[untitled TARDISode]*
   2. Love & Monsters
DT-12. **Fear Her** [2.11](2)
   1. *[untitled TARDISode]*
   2. Fear Her
DT-13. **Army of Ghosts** [2.12/2.13](4)
   1. *[untitled TARDISode]*
   2. Army of Ghosts
   3. *[untitled TARDISode]*
   4. Doomsday

THIRTY-FIRST SEASON {aka SERIES THREE}
DT-14. **The Runaway Bride** [3.X](1)

DT-15. **Smith and Jones** [3.1](1)
DT-16. **The Shakespeare Code** [3.2](1)
DT-17. **Gridlock** [3.3](1)
DT-18. **Daleks in Manhattan** [3.4/3.5](2)
   1. Daleks in Manhattan
   2. Evolution of the Daleks
DT-19. **The Lazarus Experiment** [3.6](1)
DT-20. **42** [3.7](1)
DT-21. **Human Nature** [3.8/3.9](2)
   1. Human Nature
   2. The Family of Blood
DT-22. **Blink** [3.10](1)
DT-23. **Utopia** [3.11/3.12/3.13](3)
   1. Utopia
   2. The Sound of Drums
   3. Last of the Time Lords
DT-24. **Time Crash** [CIN2](1)

THIRTY-SECOND SEASON {aka SERIES FOUR}
DT-25. **Voyage of the Damned** [4.X](1)
DT-26. **Partners in Crime** [4.1](1)
DT-27. **The Fires of Pompeii** [4.3](1)
DT-28. **Planet of the Ood** [4.2](1)
DT-29. **The Sontaran Stratagem** [4.4/4.5](2)
   1. The Sontaran Stratagem
   2. The Poison Sky
DT-30. **The Doctor's Daughter** [4.6](1)
DT-31. **The Unicorn and the Wasp** [4.7](1)
DT-32. **Silence in the Library** [4.9/4.10](2)
   1. Silence in the Library
   2. Forest of the Dead
DT-33. **Midnight** [4.8](1)
DT-34. **Turn Left** [4.11](1)
DT-35. **The Stolen Earth** [4.12/4.13](2)
   1. The Stolen Earth
   2. Journey's End

THIRTY-THIRD SEASON {aka THE SPECIALS}
DT-36. **The Next Doctor** [4.14](1)
DT-37. **Planet of the Dead** [4.15](1)
DT-38. **The Waters of Mars** [4.16](1)
DT-39. **The End of Time** [4.17/4.18](2)

THIRTY-FOURTH SEASON {aka SERIES FIVE} (Matt Smith as the Doctor)

S-1. **The Eleventh Hour** [1.1](1)
S-2. **The Beast Below** [1.2](1)
S-3. **Victory of the Daleks** [1.3](1)
S-4. **The Time of Angels** [1.4/1.5](2)
  1. The Time of Angels
  2. Flesh and Stone
S-5. **The Vampires of Menace** [1.6](1)
S-6. **Amy's Choice** [1.7](1)
S-7. **The Hungry Earth** [1.8/1.9](2)
  1. The Hungry Earth
  2. Cold Blood
S-8. **Vincent and the Doctor** [1.10](1)
S-9. **The Lodger** [1.11](1)
S-10. **The Pandorica Opens** [1.12/1.13](2)
  1. The Pandorica Opens
  2. The Big Bang
S-11. **A Christmas Carol** (1)

THIRTY-FIFTH SEASON {aka SERIES SIX}
S-12. **Space Time** (2)
  1. Space
  2. Time
S-13. **The Impossible Astronaut** [2.1/2.2](3)
  1. *[untitled prequel]*
  2. The Impossible Astronaut
  3. Day of the Moon
S-14. **The Curse of the Black Spot** [2.9](2)
  1. *[untitled prequel]*
  2. The Curse of the Black Spot

S-15. **The Doctor's Wife** [2.3](1)
S-16. **The Rebel Flesh** [2.5/2.6](2)
   1. The Rebel Flesh
   2. The Almost People
S-17. **A Good Man Goes to War** [2.7](2)
   1. *[untitled prequel]*
   2. A Good Man Goes to War
S-18. **Let's Kill Hitler** [2.8](2)
   1. *[untitled prequel]* {aka The Answerphone}
   2. Let's Kill Hitler
S-19. **Night Terrors** [2.4](1)
S-20. **The Girl Who Waited** [2.10](1)
S-21. **The God Complex** [2.11](1)
S-22. **Night and the Doctor** (5)
   1. Bad Night
   2. Good Night
   3. First Night
   4. Last Night
   5. Up All Night
S-23. **Closing Time** [2.12](1)
S-24. **The Wedding of River Song** [2.13](2)
   1. *[untitled prequel]*
   2. The Wedding of River Song
S-25. **Death is the Only Answer** (1)

THIRTY-SIXTH SEASON {aka SERIES SEVEN}
S-26. **The Doctor, the Widow, and the Wardrobe** (2)
   1. *[untitled prequel]*
   2. The Doctor, the Widow, and the Wardrobe
S-27. **Good as Gold** (1)
S-28. **Pond Life** (5)
   1. April
   2. May
   3. June
   4. July
   5. August
S-29. **Asylum of the Daleks** [3.1](2)

1. Asylum of the Daleks Prequel
  2. Asylum of the Daleks
S-30. **Dinosaurs on a Spaceship** [3.2](1)
S-31. **A Town Called Mercy** [3.3](2)
  1. The Making of the Gunslinger
  2. A Town Called Mercy
S-32. **The Power of Three** [3.4](1)
S-33. **The Angels Take Manhattan** [3.5](1)
S-34. **The Snowmen** [3.6](3)
  1. The Great Detective
  2. Vastra Investigates
  3. The Snowmen

THIRTY-SEVEN SEASON {aka SERIES SEVEN} Continued
 S-35. **The Bells of Saint John** [3.7](2)
  1. Prequel
  2. The Bells of Saint John
S-36. **The Rings of Akhaten** [3.8](1)
S-37. **Cold War** [3.9](1)
S-38. **Hide** [3.10](1)
S-39. **Journey to the Centre of the TARDIS** [3.11](1)
S-40. **The Crimson Horror** [3.12](1)
S-41. **Nightmare in Silver** [3.13](1)
S-42. **The Name of the Doctor** [3.14] (6)
  1. She Said, He Said - A Prequel
  2. Clarence and the Whispermen
  3. Strax Field Report - The Name of the Doctor
  4. Strax Field Report - A Glorious Day Is Almost Upon Us
  5. The Name of the Doctor
  6. Strax Field Report - The Doctor's Greatest Secret
S-43. **The Day of the Doctor** [3.15](6)
  1. Strax Field Report - Doctor at Trafalgar Square
  2. Strax Field Report - Zygons
  3. Night of the Doctor
  4. Strax Field Report - Queen Elizabeth
  5. The Last Day

   6. The Day of the Doctor
S-44. **The Time of the Doctor** [3.16](4)
   1. Strax Field Report - A Sontaran's View of Christmas
   2. Strax Field Report - The Doctors
   3. The Time of the Doctor
   4. Strax Field Report - The Doctor Has Regenerated

THIRTY-EIGHT SEASON {aka SERIES EIGHT} *(Peter Capaldi as the Doctor)*

C-1. **Deep Breath** [1.1](1)
C-2. **Into the Dalek** [1.2](1)
C-3. **Robot of Sherwood** [1.3](1)
C-4. **Listen** [1.4](1)
C-5. **Time Heist** [1.5](1)
C-6. **The Caretaker** [1.6](1)
C-7. **Kill the Moon** [1.7](1)
C-8. **Mummy on the Orient Express** [1.8](1)
C-9. **Flatline** [1.9](1)
C-10. **In the Forest of the Night** [1.10](1)
C-11. **Dark Water** [1.11/1.12](2)
   1. Dark Water
   2. Death in Heaven
C-12. **Last Christmas** [1.X](1)

THIRTY-NINTH SEASON {aka SERIES NINE}

C-13. **The Magician's Apprentice** [2.1/2.2](4)
   1. Prologue
   2. The Doctor's Meditation
   3. The Magician's Apprentice
   4. The Witch's Familiar
C-14. **Under the Lake** [2.3/2.4](2)
   1. Under the Lake
   2. Before the Flood
C-15. **The Girl Who Died** [2.5/2.6](2)
   1. The Girl Who Died
   2. The Woman Who Lived
C-16. **The Zygon Invasion** [2.7/2.8](2)

   1. The Zygon Invasion
   2. The Zygon Inversion
C-17. **Sleep No More** [2.9](1)
C-18. **Face the Raven** [2.10](1)
C-19. **Heaven Sent** [2.11/2.12](2)
   1. Heaven Sent
   2. Hell Bent
C-20. **The Husbands of River Song** [2.X](2)
   1. The Husbands of River Song
C-21. **Introducing the New Companion…** {aka Friend from the Future, aka Bill's Intro}

THIRTY-EIGHTH SEASON {aka SERIES TEN}
C-22. **The Return of Doctor Mysterio** [3.X] (1)
   1. Telephone Call With Newt Scamander (CIN)
   2. The Return of Doctor Mysterio
C-23. **The Pilot** [3.1](1)
C-24. **Smile** [3.2](1)
C-25. **Thin Ice** [3.3](1)
C-26. **Knock Knock** [3.4](1)
C-27. **Oxygen** [3.5](1)
C-28. **Extremis** [3.6/3.7/3.8](3)
   1. Extremis
   2. The Pyramid at the End of the World
   3. The Lie of the Land
C-29. **Empress of Mars** [3.9](1)
C-30. **The Eaters of Light** [3.10](1)
C-31. **World Enough and Time** [3.11/3.12](2)
   1. World Enough and Time
   2. The Doctor Falls
C-32. **Twice Upon a Time** [3.XX](1)

FORTY-FIRST SEASON {aka SERIES ELEVEN} *(Jodie Whitaker as the Doctor)*

W-1. **The Woman Who Fell to Earth** [11.1](1)
W-2. **The Ghost Monument** [11.2](1)

W-3. **Rosa** [11.3](1)
W-4. **Arachnids in the UK** [11.4](1)
W-5. **The Tsuranga Conundrum** [11.5](1)
W-6. **Demons of the Punjab** [11.6](1)
W-7. **Kerblam!** [11.7](1)
W-8. **The Witchfinders** [11.8](1)
W-9. **It Takes You Away** [11.9](1)
W-10. **The Battle of Ranskoor Av Kolos** [11.10](1)
W-11. **Resolution** [11.NY](1)

FORTY-SECOND SEASON {aka SERIES TWELVE}
W-12. **Spyfall** [12.1/12.2](2)
  1. Part One
  2. Part Two
W-13. **Orphan 55** [12.3](1)
W-14. **Nikola Tesla's Night of Terror** [12.4](1)
W-15. **Fugitive of the Judoon** [12.5](1)
W-16. **Praxeus** [12.6](1)
W-17. **Can You Hear Me?** [12.7](1)
W-18. **The Haunting of Villa Diodati** [12.8](1)
W-19. **Ascension of the Cybermen** [12.9](1)
W-20. **The Timeless Children** [12.10](1)
W-21. **Revolution of the Daleks** [12.NY](1)

FORTY-THIRD SEASON {aka SERIES THIRTEEN}
W-22. **Flux** [13.1/13.2/13.3/13.4/13.5/13.6](6)
  1. Chapter One - The Halloween Apocalypse
  2. Chapter Two - War of the Sontarans
  3. Chapter Three - Once, Upon Time
  4. Chapter Four - Village of the Angels
  5. Chapter Five - Survivors of the Flux
  6. Chapter Six - The Vanquishers

FORTY-THIRD SEASON continued {aka THE SPECIALS}
W-23. **Eve of the Daleks** [13.NY](1)
W-24. **Legend of the Sea Devils** [13.E](1)
W-25. **The Power of the Doctor** [13.BBCC](1)

FORTY-FOURTH SEASON {aka THE 60th ANNIVERSARY SPECIALS} *(David Tennant as the Doctor)*
DT2-1. **The Star Beast** [14.1](1)
  1. Tales of the TARDIS - Earthshock
  2. Tales of the TARDIS - The Mind Robber
  3. Tales of the TARDIS - Vengeance on Varos
  4. Tales of the TARDIS - The Three Doctors
  5. Tales of the TARDIS - The Time Meddler
  6. Tales of the TARDIS - The Curse of Fenric
  7. The Fourteenth Doctor is Here (CIN)
  8. The Star Beast
DT2-2. **Wild Blue Yonder** [14.2](1)
DT2-3. **The Giggle** [14.3](1)

FORTY-FOURTH SEASON {aka THE 60th ANNIVERSARY SPECIALS} (Continued) *(Ncuti Gatwa as the Doctor)*
G-1. **The Church on Ruby Road** [14.4](1)

FORTY-FIFTH SEASON {aka SEASON ONE}
G-2. **Space Babies** [1.1](1)
G-3. **The Devil's Chord** [1.2](1)
G-4. **Boom** [1.3](1)
G-5. **73 Yards** [1.4](1)
G-6. **Dot and Bubble** [1.5](1)
G-7. **Rogue** [1.6](1)
G-8. **The Legend of Ruby Sunday** [1.7/1.8](2)
  1. The Legend of Ruby Sunday
  2. Tales of the TARDIS - The Pyramids of Mars
  3. Empire of Death

FORTY-SIXTH SEASON {aka SEASON TWO}
G-9. **Joy to the World** [2.X](1)
G-10. **The Robot Revolution** [2.1](1)
G-11. **Lux** [2.2](1)
G-12. **The Well** [2.3](1)
G-13. **Lucky Day** [2.3](1)
G-14. **The Story & The Engine** [2.4](1)

G-15. **The Interstellar Song Contest** [2.5](1)
G-16. **Wish World** [2.6](2)
   1. Wish World
   2. The Reality War

EDITOR BIO

Nick Seidler is a multiple international award-winning book author and veteran who has worked in the field of higher education for over a quarter of a century. He co-authored the books *Red, White, and Who: The Story of Doctor Who in America*, *How to Celebrate Your Fandom*, and *Not Everyone Walks the Stage,* and has written and edited various other fiction, non-fiction, and gaming books. The academic study of *Doctor Who* is one of his lifelong passions. He appreciates his supporters and team who work with him at Zepo Publishing.

HOW TO BE A HELPER

We really hope that you have enjoyed reading this book and hope that it has made you think and brought you joy. **If you like this book please help us out by leaving a review of the book on Amazon, Goodreads, or any other story or book review website that you trust.** This really helps us more than most people know!

If you would like to join our mailing list to learn about our upcoming releases or other projects that maybe you too can be a part of (or to apply to be an Advance Reader and possible reviewer of our forthcoming books), please send an email to: zepopublishing@gmail.com .

HOW TO CITE THIS BOOK

APA (7th Edition)
Seidler, Nicholas (Ed.) (2025). *Fantastic!: A Celebration of Fans Discovering Doctor Who.* Zepo Publishing.

MLA (9th Edition)
Seidler, Nicholas, editor. *Fantastic!: A Celebration of Fans Discovering Doctor Who.* Zepo Publishing, 2025.

Chicago Style
Nicholas Seidler, ed., 2025. *Fantastic!: A Celebration of Fans Discovering Doctor Who.* Wauwatosa, Wisconsin: Zepo Publishing.

Turabian Style
Seidler, Nicholas, ed. *Fantastic!: A Celebration of Fans Discovering Doctor Who.* (Wauwatosa, Wisconsin: Zepo Publishing, 2025).

IEEE Style
N. Seidler, Ed. *Fantastic!: A Celebration of Fans Discovering Doctor Who.* Wauwatosa, Wisconsin: Zepo Publishing, 2025.

OTHER ZEPO PUBLISHING BOOKS

HOW TO CELEBRATE YOUR FANDOM
By Libby Shea, Nicholas Seidler, Robert Warnock, and Steven Warren Hill

HOW TO GROW AS A FAN!

Spark your creativity as you grow into your fandom! This book helps you develop as you embrace the passions and interests that give you joy.

Fandoms build friendships and communities through many engaging activities. With the help of this book, you can learn new ways to enjoy being a fan. Inside are numerous pathways that one can connect with others with similar pursuits! Whether it is through starting a collection, dressing in cosplay, writing a blog, or attending a convention, each of these brings happiness to those who participate.

This book also contains interviews with fans of all ages (5 to 101), who tell their stories and share how they participate in their hobbies.

Celebrate your fandom and the things that you enjoy the most! Fun Things to Do! New Things to Learn! Cool Things to Try!

Winner of the 2025 Firebird International Book Award for Children's How-To Book. Winner of the September 2025 Literary Titan Gold Award for Best Non-Fiction Book.

For All Ages (aimed at ages 8 to 15)

NOT EVERYONE WALKS THE STAGE
By Sierra Andrews and Nicholas Seidler
Illustrated by Alisa Tverdokhleb

A STORY ABOUT KNOWING THAT BEING DIFFERENT REALLY MEANS YOU ARE THE SAME AS EVERYONE ELSE!

Sophia is excited about kindergarten and just wants to fit in. She is worried that at graduation at the end of the year she won't walk the stage like everyone else. Join her as she learns about -- how things work at school, how to make friends, how sometimes we all struggle, how learning is fun, and how she is exactly like her friends!

Sophia has a mobility impairment that makes her think that she might not succeed in school. Her literal misunderstanding of "being able to walk the stage" at the end of the year worries her. We follow her journey through her first year in school, where we discover that her experiences are identical to all other students. Sophia's wheelchair is hidden in the book until the very end to emphasize her common experiences with other students. This wonderful book is perfect for all students to learn important broad lessons about how we are all the same, yet all different at the same time.

The book includes an interview with author Sierra Andrews who herself is in a wheelchair due to a car accident at 18-years old. She gives information about being wheelchair-bound to parents, educators, and students. She answers questions people want to ask but are often afraid to do so. It also includes special sections called Can You Find, Other Ways to Use This Book, Fun Things to Do, and Fun Facts that give readers additional activities that they can do to learn and enjoy themselves. An interview with illustrator Alisa Tverdokhleb gives advice to those who want to be artists.

Winner of the Summer 2025 1st Place "Super Champion" Outstanding Creator International Book Award for Best Children's Book. Winner of the August 2025 Literary Titan Gold Book Award. 2nd Place 2025 Booksshelf Writing Awards.

For All Ages (aimed at ages 4 to 8)